PSYCHOSYNTHESIS

THE ELEMENTS
AND BEYOND

Will Parfitt is a registered psychotherapist with thirty years experience of working with personal and spiritual development. He is the director of PS Avalon, and the author of several books which have been translated into more than ten languages.

Will lives in Glastonbury, England, from where he organises distance education programmes for both Psychosynthesis and Kabbalah, and travels internationally to run seminars and courses on a variety of subjects. He also offers psychotherapy, mentoring, coaching and professional supervision.

PSYCHOSYNTHESIS

THE ELEMENTS
AND BEYOND

*Psychosynthesis
in Theory and Practice*

WILL PARFITT

PS AVALON
Glastonbury, England

First published in the U.K. in 2003 by PS Avalon

PS Avalon
Box 1865, Glastonbury
Somerset, BA6 8YR, U.K.

*Will Parfitt asserts the moral right
to be identified as the author of this work*

ISBN 0-9544764-0-9

CONTENTS

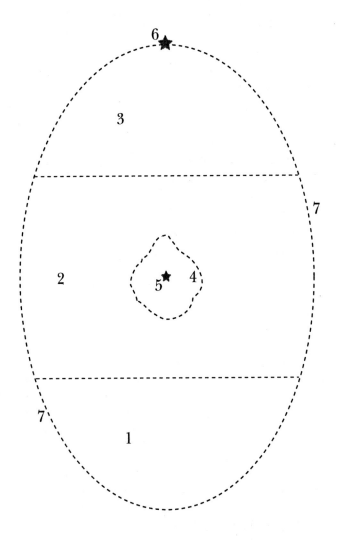

Diagram 1: The Psychosynthesis Egg Diagram

PREFACE

Part 1 of this book, *the Elements of Psychosynthesis*, was originally published in 1990. My brief from Element Books was to write a book on Psychosynthesis that could be easily understood by a casual reader purchasing the book at an airport bookstand. The reviews I received were by and large complimentary and suggested I had indeed made Psychosynthesis available to a wider audience. After several reprints of the English edition, and translations into Italian, German, Dutch, Portuguese, Spanish and Slovenian, the book only went out of print when the publisher went out of business.

Part 2, *Beyond the Elements*, is new material that takes Psychosynthesis into both deeper and wider realms. The emphasis is towards the psychospiritual and transpersonal aspects of Psychosynthesis, including a detailed description of its esoteric roots. The interface between Psychosynthesis and the Kabbalah, how Psychosynthesis can be used to increase our understanding of various areas, including sexuality, dreaming, connecting with and effectively using the inner witness are some of the topics covered in a direct and practical way.

Roberto Assagioli said that Psychosynthesis may take someone to the doorway of spiritual attainment but not beyond, thus aligning it with major esoteric teachings. To the existential truism that we both enter and leave life alone, esoteric teachings add that each of us has to step through the doorway of spirituality alone. Psychosynthesis offers many perspectives on how to reach that doorway and the potential of companionship along the way. Like the Western mystery schools, it also focuses on how to bring our visions and insights back into the everyday world in a grounded and meaningful way. The purpose of this book is to aid such process, and position Psychosynthesis as the psychology of choice not only as we transit difficult global times in the early stages of a new millennium, but also as we enter more fully into the exciting and challenging times ahead. The aim, to quote Assagioli, is to develop '...*the strength and the power to express compassion according to wisdom; the wisdom and compassion to use power for the greatest good.*'

PART 1

THE ELEMENTS OF

PSYCHOSYNTHESIS

1

WHAT IS PSYCHOSYNTHESIS?

Psychosynthesis is a method of psychological development and Self realization for those who refuse to remain the slaves of their own inner phantasms or of external influences, who refuse to submit passively to the play of psychological forces which is going on within them, and who are determined to become the master of their own lives. (Roberto Assagioli)

Psychosynthesis is a comprehensive approach to self-realization and the development of human potential. The essential aim of Psychosynthesis is to help people discover their true spiritual nature, then to effectively utilize this discovery in everyday life. Psychosynthesis helps us to realize our creative potential, increase our ability to function harmoniously in the modern world, and improve the quality of all our relationships.

Whilst its application in counselling and psychotherapy is perhaps its best-known use, Psychosynthesis is more than just a form of therapy. Designed to help us move away from what we don't want in our lives and towards what we do, Psychosynthesis is a practical, working method that integrates principles and techniques from many approaches to personal growth. Unlike some other approaches, however, it has no fixed idea of what someone 'should' be like - indeed, with Psychosynthesis, it is quite the contrary. It is only successful when we have become more what we want to be like. This is not in the sense of gratifying unbalanced or partial desires, but when we have become more able to be ourselves in whatever situation we find ourselves, and to do what we want to do when we tune into our innermost sense of self and purpose. So Psychosynthesis is a kind of therapy, and it is a method of self-improvement, but more than this, it is also a process that co-operates with the unfolding evolution of all nature. It aims to bring awareness, wholeness and connection to the process of evolution as this happens in each of us.

Psychosynthesis has been described as 'a psychology with a soul', and this is what distinguishes it from many other forms of psychotherapy. Emphasizing the value of intuition, inspiration and creative insight, it is a form of 'transpersonal psychology'. Whilst it concentrates on the personality, it also includes the realms usually ascribed to more mystical or esoteric doctrines. Yet, whilst it explores these areas that we could call spiritual, it in no way imposes any form of doctrine or belief system upon the person using it. Psychosynthesis is not a religion, nor would it ever want to be. Although once you start Psychosynthesis it becomes a way of life, one of its greatest qualities is that it allows you to be and do whatever you want, so is equally suitable for Christians, Buddhists, Pagans, Moslems, atheists, agnostics - indeed, anyone at all.

Psychosynthesis is a way of understanding our lives, of helping us to know ourselves and trust in our own processes of growth and unfoldment. But Psychosynthesis does not deal only with the individual, for each of us is part of many different groups of people, including our families, our friends, our work mates, and so on. We are also members of a society and of the one human family that covers the whole planet.

Psychosynthesis honours both the individual and the groups of which the individual is a part. Partly because of this inclusive attitude, and partly by the nature of its transpersonal connection, Psychosynthesis is not a way of putting ourselves above or over anyone else. We can honour and utilise our own wishes and power but not at the expense of other people. Psychosynthesis does not rigidly analyse or label people and it is expected that we will not do this either.

Psychosynthesis theory says that each of us is constantly growing. This viewpoint helps to put meaning and value back into life, and helps us make decisions about who we are and what we want. It can also help us realise our responsibility both to ourselves and the world as a whole. It can add a dynamic sense of self to the present moment, and a sense of meaning to ourselves and to our future. Psychosynthesis can help you to 'know yourself' in the fullest sense of these words. Anything that helps people know themselves better, both as individuals and in the context of living a life in accord with others, has to be useful.

To summarise, Psychosynthesis offers:
• a means whereby we can grow and learn more about ourselves;
• more ability to do our will, to take actions that improve our situation both from an inner and outer viewpoint;
• a connection to the transpersonal realms of soul and spirit;

- a clearer connection to our conscious life processes and to the unconscious realms behind these;
- more creativity;
- a way of grounding creative energies and manifesting our true life purpose;
- an improvement to our inner life;
- better interpersonal relations.

BACKGROUND

Psychosynthesis was founded by an Italian called Roberto Assagioli early in the 20th century. He had trained as a psychoanalyst but also had a deep interest in the esoteric. The more he worked with people in the analytical mode, the more he felt there was something missing, some vital aspect of the person that was not being honoured or addressed in any way. This was the transpersonal or spiritual realm that includes spiritual understanding, wisdom, love and inspiration. Assagioli once said that psychoanalysis was primarily concerned with the basement of the psyche whereas Psychosynthesis is concerned with the whole building. Once we learn to access the whole building, it is then possible to include all aspects of ourselves. We can live in a more holistic way, including not only ourselves but, through the connections that are inevitably made once the spiritual realms are accessed, also all other living beings.

The key to understanding the development of Psychosynthesis out of psychoanalysis can be found in the words themselves. Analysis is the separation of something into its component parts so that its nature and function can be understood. This, indeed, forms part of Psychosynthesis. Synthesis goes further, however, by putting everything back together again, in a new way that more harmoniously synthesizes these component parts. They create a new unity, placed around a centre at the core of the being, from where the individual can more effectively direct his or her life. Synthesis actually means putting together the parts of something so as to form an integrated whole. All our parts - mental, emotional, physical and spiritual - have to be included for the synthesis to be effective and complete.

Modern psychologists, particularly those working with people in a practical way, whatever their discipline, take the role that was once ascribed to the 'wise person' or 'shaman' in the society. They are expected to have an understanding of the inner world and to be able to use this understanding to heal people. If you want to heal someone you have to 'make them whole' (the word heal is connected to the word 'whole'). Psychosynthesis, by including the spirit and soul, allows a more thorough healing to take place. It also, incidentally, has a connection through this to esoteric traditions that are much older than modern psychology.

Since Assagioli's death in the early 1970s, Psychosynthesis has grown worldwide and there are now training centres in many countries in the world, and Psychosynthesis practitioners in all walks of life. Psychosynthesis does not only teach you how to work with and 'heal' other people. Many people who train in Psychosynthesis do just that, but the majority of people who undertake Psychosynthesis - either as a training, with an individual guide or simply through using the techniques they learn from books - then utilise Psychosynthesis in their own field of work. This includes education, medicine, social work, the arts, engineering - you name it and the principles of Psychosynthesis can be applied to it. All the signs suggest that Psychosynthesis is continuing to grow, for unlike some other similar methods for personal understanding, it is not a finished system but one that is willing to change and grow as the world changes and grows.

HARMONIOUS GROWTH

Psychosynthesis is not only a method for self-realisation, but is a continuous and organic process that is happening in the psyche of everyone at all times. This process happens naturally, but it tends to get blocked. The methods of Psychosynthesis include techniques for unblocking this process. These techniques are not used mechanically, but are applied with care and attention. They can then act as transforming agents in our lives, and put us in touch with the natural flow of growth and development.

To help understand the process of Psychosynthesis, it has been found useful to split it into two parts - 'personal' and 'transpersonal' (or 'spiritual') Psychosynthesis. Personal Psychosynthesis concentrates on building a personality that is effective and relatively free from blocks of any kind, is able to direct its energies constructively, and has a clear awareness of its own centre or 'I'. At the core of Psychosynthesis is the idea that each of us has a centre or 'self' which when contacted helps us organize, and ultimately synthesize, all the various parts of our make up. To reach this centre we have to use our will. This will is not at all like the old fashioned concept of will power - something that you have to struggle with in order to make things work - but is rather something fluid and easy, something which, as we approach our self or centre, we find becomes easier, and is even fun.

To really harmonize all the various parts of the individual. it is essential to have this centre, called the 'I' in Psychosynthesis, around which the synthesis can take place. The more the sense of this 'I' is realised, and the more contact is made with it, the more we can then realise our even deeper connection with the transpersonal or spiritual realms. In Psychosynthesis this deeper centre is called the Self (with a capital 'S' to distinguish it from the self with a small 's' which is another name for the 'I').

When we succeed in unifying the different parts of ourselves, we experience the release of positive energies such as Joy, Truth, Happiness, and Unity. Psychosynthesis facilitates this process and helps us to enjoy beauty, sharpen our minds, become more self determined, creatively utilize our vital energies, enrich our imagination, awaken our intuition, express our potential, and realize the power of undistorted love.

The first stage of Psychosynthesis is, therefore, analysis which helps the individual get a thorough knowledge of the personality. Next comes the work of personal Psychosynthesis, focussing on ways to control and integrate the various parts of the personality. This is based on the main principle of Psychosynthesis which states: 'We are dominated by everything with which we become identified or attached. We can dominate and control everything from which we disidentify or disattach ourselves.'

We can achieve this disidentification through contacting our unique and unattached centre. When we feel the surge of an overwhelming wave of anger, for example, we no longer either need to suppress it or let it take us over and explode out in whatever form it chooses - both ways in which it has us rather than us having it. Instead, we can have the anger and find ways to express it appropriately, or to discharge the energy in other ways (for example in creative acts) if the anger is inappropriate.

When you have it rather than it having you, the 'you' that has it can say 'I have anger (or whatever it is.)' Who is this

'I' that has it? The 'I' that is your centre or self, the you that is pure self awareness, unattached to anything but willing to identify with the contents of your consciousness as appropriate. Once you have made good strong connections with this 'I', the next step of Psychosynthesis is the reconstruction of your personality around this centre.

Transpersonal Psychosynthesis explores the spiritual regions, areas beyond our ordinary awareness. It is in such areas that we find the source of all intuition and our sense of value and meaning in life. For many people personal Psychosynthesis is enough, as it helps them become harmonious individuals, well adjusted within themselves and within the communities or groups to which they belong. However worthy an achievement this may be, however, for some people it is not enough and they touch on a real need inside to develop spiritually as well - this is when transpersonal Psychosynthesis comes into its own.

Psychosynthesis includes the whole person, which is composed of the personality plus the spiritual realms, including the Self that is, in this sense, our connection to the divine (whether that is seen as some outside energy or ultimately within us). Using Psychosynthesis we can learn to grow on all these levels - so we can develop as a personality and find more effective ways to experience life and to express ourselves. We can also grow in our connection to the transpersonal realms, thus unleashing more positive, beneficial qualities into our lives. We find more effective ways of utilising our creative energies. Creativity, in the Psychosynthesis sense, is not just about drawing, painting, making music, sculpting or whatever (although it is these things as well), but acknowledges the fact that we are all creative in our own ways. With the right attitude we can be as equally creative doing housework as in painting a masterpiece, in changing a baby's nappy as in encouraging it to walk and talk.

Everything in nature appears to be evolving towards increased wholeness. This could even be considered to be the definition of evolution. Psychosynthesis co-operates with this process. An atom comes together with other atoms to form a molecule, and these form cells, which then group into tissues that become organs that make up a whole body. A similar process of synthesis can be seen in our psychological world, too, as all the parts of us come together to make us into one, whole person. We can use Psychosynthesis to help us explore all these parts so we become more centred and able to function more effectively. If one molecule was at war with another, and your heart didn't agree with your lungs, you'd have problems. So it is with the psychological functions too - when our sensations, feelings, thoughts, emotions, imagination, intuition, everything that makes us up, are harmoniously synthesized, then we work well and without conflict.

For a true synthesis, the individuality of each part must be respected. No bit of us is 'better' or 'worse' than another bit. On the contrary, each part has to be whole before it can truly be synthesized and integrated. The conflicts we experience can be seen in this light - as the source of the energy which allows us to know more about ourselves. When we work on our inner conflicts, we can utilise the released energy to bring ourselves through into more effective functioning. In other words, apparent obstacles can be seen as gifts which we can value as much as the more obvious gifts when things are going well.

We can know what we want, and have an idea of where we are going in life, but once we start moving in that direction we find there are all kinds of blocks that stop us. If we see these blocks as our helpers, then through looking at them and dealing with them, we can more effectively move in the direction in which we desire to go. The blocks are, indeed, the very energy of our being, so the more we deal with the blocks the more we are moving towards our true being, rather than cutting off from ourselves and not allowing our potential to grow and blossom.

Once we start making choices about where we are going or what we want in life, one of the first major obstacles we meet is all the conditioning we have received as children (and often are still receiving through advertising and political control). This conditioning is most clearly seen in the things we believe we 'should' do - should go to bed early, should wash your teeth, should be a good girl and so on. We have to move towards a freedom of choice and not allow these 'shoulds' to control our actions. This is not always so easy. We know we 'should' do something even though it is not what we really want to do, so how do we do what we want to do without being in conflict with the part of us that says 'you should...'? One of the aims of Psychosynthesis is to help us understand that we are always bigger than the dynamic of any such conflict - if we move out of the conflict and connect with the self, from this better vantage point we can make clearer decisions.

When we have peak experiences, times when we feel really connected and 'right', when everything around us feels harmonious, and our lives are filled with qualities such as Love, Joy, and Truth, we can make positive affirmations that will expand us and help us to include more of these qualities. But we also have to find ways of manifesting or grounding these energies or they will dissipate into illusion. Psychosynthesis deals both with the connection to these qualities and the ways we can ground them. In Psychosynthesis the work is never a process of 'getting rid of' something but is rather aimed at transformation through inclusion. Nothing that exists in the transpersonal realms of the spirit is in conflict, so all qualities can easily co-exist. Yet when they come through to the realm of the actual (that is, the personality) then we find that conflicts do exist. Through honouring the transpersonal qualities and getting more in touch with them, then expressing them clearly, we can bring more harmony to our personality. In other words, we are able to manifest more of our potential.

Although you can go to a Psychosynthesis therapist (sometimes called a guide) for individual sessions, or to a Psychosynthesis group either for training or group therapy, Psychosynthesis is basically a system of self help. This is not to say that seeing a guide or going to a group does not enrich and often speed up the movement towards wholeness, but the ultimate aim of Psychosynthesis, whether we learn about it through a book or go to a guide, is to enable us to do it for ourselves. Psychosynthesis does not promise any kind of standard result; how any individual's Psychosynthesis unfolds depends upon that person alone. With practice, experience, intelligence and intuition, however, real and satisfactory results can be achieved.

EXERCISE: THE SYNTHESIS OF PARTS

The exercises in this book are placed at the end of each chapter so that you have a greater choice when to practice them. You might like to do so immediately after reading the chapter, or you may prefer to leave them until later, for instance if you are reading this book whilst travelling,

Before starting any exercise, spend a few moments relaxing and centring yourself, ensuring you have enough time to complete the activity without being disturbed. Take as long as you need to go through the instructions, as it is always better to err on the side of slowness rather than rushing through it. At the end of any exercise it is good practice to find a way of expressing what you've learned in your everyday life. Mostly, however, have fun with the exercises as taking a light approach can help you connect with and keep a perspective on the work.

If you are the sort of person who doesn't do exercises in books, then at least read them so you know what they are suggesting. For many people, simply reading through an exercise has a powerful effect.

Make yourself comfortable, take a few deep breaths and allow yourself to become as calm as possible. Imagine a single atom. See the nucleus and the electrons spinning around it. Take some time to really imagine this atom in your mind's eye.

Now imagine this atom combines with another atom, then several more atoms until they form a molecule. Clearly imagine a molecule composed of several atoms.

Molecules can come together to form cells. Imagine you see this happen, your molecule merging with other molecules and cells forming. Take time to really imagine this process.

Every living thing on our planet is composed of such cells. Your body is made up from an innumerable number of cells that have formed themselves into tissues, organs, blood, bones - everything which makes you what you physically are.

Realise that you are made up from cells. Your unity is dependant upon the harmonious interaction between countless cells that are, in turn, dependant upon the synthesis of equally countless numbers of molecules and atoms.

On a physical level, all these parts come together to make up 'the whole you'. Allow yourself to really connect with how wonderful this is.

Realize the same is true for your inner world, too. All the parts of you - your thoughts, feelings, emotions, sensations - everything that makes you up, is part of this one, whole being you call 'myself'. Allow yourself to really connect with how wonderful this is, too.

In your own time, bring your awareness back into your room and spend some time simply being with any thoughts, feeling and sensations you may be experiencing.

2

THE INNER JOURNEY

Spiritual development is a long and arduous journey, an adventure through strange lands full of surprises, difficulties and even dangers. It involves a drastic transmutation of the 'normal' elements of the personality, an awakening of potentialities hitherto dormant, a raising of consciousness to new realms, and a functioning along a new inner dimension.
(Roberto Assagioli)

When we are exploring ourselves and our relationship with other people and the world around us, it is very helpful if we have a map. There are lots of different maps of consciousness, some better than others. One of the best maps is that used in Psychosynthesis which is sometimes called 'the egg of being' or quite simple 'the egg diagram' (see diagram 1.)

One way of testing a map of consciousness is to see whether it becomes dated as new information about our human consciousness and how we operate comes to light. Just as if we were travelling in, say, Spain, we would fare much better if our map was up to date, and showed Spain as it is now, not as it was a hundred or a thousand years ago. It is also important, of course, that we choose a relevant map - a map of Italy would be of little use to us on our trip to Spain. Similarly, an out-of-date map of human consciousness will also be of little use to a modern day traveller.

A good map helps us to see where we are, and our relationship to both where we have come from (the past) and to where we are travelling (the future). It will help us to see who we are, particularly as it focuses us onto our present moment in both time and space. And a good map should help us understand ourselves, both intrinsically and in relation to other people and things.

A map shouldn't really need too much data to be read properly, but all maps need some explanation. At the very least we need a guide to the symbols on the map. Without it how would we know that a little black circle with a cross above it is a church with a spire? A good guidebook will help us to read the map in the most effective way. It might tell us, for example, that the brown lines with numbers are contour lines, and that when they are close together the ground is steep, or when they are far apart it is flat. A good guidebook will also give us some information to help us really appreciate where we are, the 'local colour' of the place, so to speak. It is the primary purpose of this chapter to act as a guidebook to the Psychosynthesis map, 'the egg of being'.

It is of vital importance, wherever we travel inside or outside of our own consciousness, to be ourselves. But when we travel in unknown or new places, it is well worth remembering to proceed with caution, checking with our map and guidebook more frequently than we might once we are familiar with the territory. And, finally, it is of most important to remember that if any particular map doesn't work for us, we are probably better off finding a different one that does. Psychosynthesis will work for us even if we don't really like or wish to use 'the egg of being' map. Indeed, Psychosynthesis will work equally well with other maps such as, for example, 'the tree of life'. Whether we choose to use another map or this one, it is always worth remembering and reminding ourselves that the map is most definitely not the territory. All maps are static versions of a dynamic reality. They are not the truth, but representations of it. They are, however, useful tools for facilitating our inner exploration.

When we get right down to it, and are 'out there' exploring ourselves, we have to really experience the territory, to become fully involved in the experiences we are having. Thus it is well worth spending some time studying the map so that when we are actively travelling - climbing a psychological mountain, bridging an emotional river, descending into a well of spiritual understanding, whatever we are doing, we are helped through our familiarity with the territory.

THE EGG OF BEING

The main Psychosynthesis map (diagram 1) called 'the egg diagram', represents the whole psyche. The three horizontal divisions of the egg stand for our past (1), present (2) and future (3). All three are constantly active within us, although in different ways. This is obvious when we consider the present moment - after all, we are here and now not then and there! Within this present moment, this 'here and now', we carry the past with us in the form of all our memories and experiences whether we remember them or not. It is everything from the past, in one sense, that makes us what we are in the present moment. In another sense, perhaps more 'esoteric' but no less real, we also carry the future within us. It has not happened yet, but all of us have right now the potential to become something else, to have new experiences, to find new ways to express ourselves. Or perhaps someone's potential might be to always remain the same, to experience or express nothing new - but that, too, is something they carry within themselves.

If we look at the egg of being in this way, we can see it is a complete map of the continuum of time. Whilst its primary focus is on the present moment, because that is, after all, the moment in which we want to use the map, like all good maps it will help us tune into where we have been (the past) and where we are going (the future). By reference to the past, we can get a clearer understanding of where we are in the present moment. This then helps us decide where we want to go and how to get there.

The egg of being is chiefly concerned, however, with our inner journey and so its 'divisions' represent the different aspects of ourselves as individual beings, and our connection to other beings too. Study the map as you read the following descriptions so that, as your familiarity with the map increases, so does your familiarity with the different aspects of yourself.

(1) represents the lower unconscious, our personal psychological past which includes repressed complexes, long-forgotten memories, instincts and physical functions over which we (ordinarily) have no conscious control. All our fundamental drives and 'primitive urges' are part of this realm as are the activities of basic bodily functions. It is primarily the repressed material, often experienced in the form of unconscious controls upon us, phobias, obsessions, compulsive urges and so on, with which we are primarily concerned in Psychosynthesis.

If you had recently travelled through, say, Turkey, all the experiences you would have had would have changed you, and would 'colour' your experience right now. Some things might have happened to you that you have pushed out of your consciousness because they are too unpleasant to remember (equivalent to repressed material). Although you might have chosen to 'consciously forget' these incidents, they would nevertheless have an effect on you. If you had been chased by a pack of growing dogs, for example, and you only escaped by the skin of your teeth, you might not want to remember their glaring eyes and dripping fangs. Their effect would still be there, however, as shown by your reaction right now to that friendly little poodle!

You might have had it instilled in you as a child that you must wash your hands every time after using the toilet. This in itself is sound advice, but you were conditioned into believing you have to do this or you are naughty. But here in 'Turkey' you cannot always do this and after every time you use the toilet you keep feeling a little sick. Of course it may be that you are being affected by some bacterium. It could equally be that, although you have forgotten it, you are really being affected by the parental voice that somewhere in your unconscious still tells you off when you don't do what you are told.

These are just two examples of items within us that may affect us at any moment. See if you can think of other such examples but don't be surprised if you find this difficult - after all, part of the power of such items from the past is that they are no longer remembered and thus exert a much stronger hold on us.

When we explore our lower unconscious it helps our growth because as we learn to integrate more of these 'older' or repressed aspects of ourselves, the more whole we become. When we release previously repressed energies, we feel healthier, have more energy available to us, and feel more freedom in our lives.

(2) represents the middle unconscious, the place where all states of mind reside which can easily be brought into our field of awareness (4). For example, in our readily accessible 'middle unconscious', we carry all sorts of information and knowledge that is not always relevant. We know how to do simple arithmetic, but do we really want to choose to have that in our consciousness when we are making love? We know how to bake a cake but do we want to be thinking about that when we are reading these pages?

You might know that later tonight you have an important meeting with a friend, but you can safely let that knowledge reside in your middle unconscious until later. Of course, if it is a very exciting meeting, then all through the day it will keep popping into your mind, perhaps distracting you from whatever else you are doing.

The middle unconscious also holds suppressed material. This differs from repressed material that has been 'pushed down' into the lower unconscious. With repressed things we no longer 'remember' or own them as part of us. Suppressed material, on the other hand, we know is there, it is just that we are choosing, for one reason or another, not to bring it out at this moment. For example, you really want to eat something, but you have to suppress the desire until lunchtime when you are free to go to a cafe. Or you know something about a friend of yours but you are choosing to suppress this knowledge for fear of upsetting or hurting them.

There is nothing wrong with suppression, but we have to be careful that things that we suppress in our consciousness do not get completely forgotten, and then become part of the contents of our lower unconscious from where they will start controlling us rather than us controlling them.

The field of awareness (or consciousness) (4) is shaped like an amoeba to emphasize how it is constantly changing as our field of awareness changes. Often it is simple shown as a circle, but I prefer to shape it like an amoeba to emphasize how it constantly changes. The field of awareness is constantly alive with sensations, images, thoughts, emotions, feelings, desires and impulses all of which we can observe and act upon or not as we see fit. One moment you are relaxing with your lover, say, and have a 'pseudopod' stretched out to your feelings. Then the phone rings, it is a call from your work and now you retract the pseudopod that was into feelings, and 'stretch yourself', as it were, into a mental place, where you can connect with the conversation about work.

Our field of awareness is constantly fluid, changing as our feelings or thoughts or sensations send us information about our environment. If we become really cut off from our experiences it can be as if the amoeba of awareness 'encysts', it hardens its semi-permeable skin and stops letting through clear messages, either from inside to outside or vice versa. Part of the work of Psychosynthesis is to bring freedom of movement to our amoeba, and to increase our awareness of its function and abilities.

(3) represents the superconscious, our evolutionary future, the region from where we receive all inspiration and illumination, however we experience it. Indeed, true inspiration can come to

us in artistic or scientific, very grand or very simple ways. It is the source of our 'inner genius' and is thus perhaps the major area of exploration for us when we wish to more clearly and successfully move into our future. We will be looking at the realm of the superconscious later in this book.

Perhaps the most obvious way that most people connect with their superconscious is through insights and 'inspirational flashes' that just seem to appear in their consciousness. For instance, you might suddenly realize the solution to a problem that has been bugging you for days or even longer. Or you might suddenly know more about what you want to do with your life after months of feeling uncertain and directionless. Usually such insights, and other similar experiences, show that the superconscious has been contacted.

The exploration of these three realms, the lower, middle and higher unconscious, is one of the main tasks of Psychosynthesis. Any distinction between higher (or super) unconscious and lower unconscious is developmental, not moralistic. The lower unconscious is not bad, or in some sense not as good or as important, it is simply earlier in our evolution. It is described as 'lower' simply because it is behind us, and forms the 'foundation' of our present awareness. The superconscious is not merely an abstract possibility but a living reality with an existence of its own. Calling it superconscious (or 'higher' unconscious) does not mean it is above us or better than us in some way, but is merely meant to describe the sense that as we evolve and move towards it is as if we are raising our consciousness into new experiences. Alternatively, when insights come from this realm of the unconscious, we often get a sense of things 'dropping into place'.

(7) represents the collective unconscious that is common to all living beings. We are not isolated pieces of individuality, we are not islands, so although at times we may feel isolated and alone, in reality we are part of a collective field in which all other beings play a part. There is a constant and active interchange between us and all other sentient beings, whether we are aware of it or not.

Note how in the egg diagram the lines are dotted to show there are no rigid compartments impeding free interplay between all these "levels". If we become too rigid it is as if the egg 'hardens' and our work might be to crack it a little to let more fluidity into our lives. On the other hand, if we are too sloppy, too 'nice' for our own good, if we find it difficult to separate ourselves from other people, then it is as if the spaces in the egg have become too large, letting in (or out) too much. Our work is then to strengthen the eggshell, and create more of an individual identity.

(5) is the personal self, our individual 'I' who experiences all these different states of consciousness. It is the 'I' that experiences itself as having thoughts, emotions and sensations. It is not these changing contents of consciousness (thoughts, emotions, sensations, and so on) but is the inner you that experiences these contents. Generally during life we do not experience this 'I' in a very clearly defined way. The more we work on ourselves through Psychosynthesis, the more we can start contacting the 'I' and making it a living, experienced reality in our consciousness. In one sense we could say on both a psychological but also a physiological level, that the more we get in touch with our 'I' the healthier or more whole we become.

This personal self is a reflection or spark of the spiritual or transpersonal Self (6) that is both universal and individual. The realization of this 'transpersonal' Self is a sign of spiritual success and achievement. Awareness of the personal self is the primary goal of Psychosynthesis, being the place from where we can effectively direct the personality. This leads to a clearer and fuller contact with, and understanding of the Spiritual Self.

THE INNER WORLD

Although it may seem obvious that the map is not the territory, often in our lives we confuse the two, and think that what we know about something is what it actually is. If we look into our inner world, using the egg diagram as a map, we find that all the divisions and so forth are very static representations of what is really an ever-changing, dynamic reality. But the map can help us to find our way round.

Similarly, when we start investigating our inner world, we find that certain images and symbols seem to easily represent various aspects of ourselves. In Psychosynthesis exercises, use is often made of the image of a meadow. This 'meadow', which you can visualize quite easily, corresponds roughly to the 'field of awareness'. Anything we then find in the meadow, or imagine to be there, is something within the contents of our middle unconscious.

We can imagine a track leading from the meadow down through some thick undergrowth into a mysterious, dark valley. This 'valley' can then represent our lower unconscious. We can also imagine a track leading up to a mountain on top of which we might imagine a Temple of the Self. This 'mountain' would then correspond to the superconscious. Of course, the mountain, the meadow, and the valley are not 'real' places, but how you imagine them, and what you imagine within them, are real representations of your inner world. In the following exercise, use is made of such imagery.

EXERCISE: VISITING THE MEADOW

Either lie down or sit in a comfortable position. Loosen any tight clothing you might be wearing, take a few deep breaths, then close your eyes.

Imagine you are in a meadow. Let your imagination really take you to a meadow on a summer's day...Feel your feet on the grass. How long is it?...Look around you - what can you see? Are there birds, insects, trees? Really fill in as much detail as possible, and remember it is your meadow, there is no right or wrong way to imagine it.

Let your other senses come into play. What can you hear - perhaps the humming of insects, bird song, the sound of wind gently swaying distant trees... What can you smell in your meadow on this warm summer's day?...If you breathe in deeply, what can you taste?...Really take your time now to build the image of your meadow so that you feel really present in this place. Perhaps you might like to walk around a little, exploring the field. What are you wearing? What does it feel like to be in this meadow?

Be aware that at one edge of your meadow the ground gets rougher, and starts to slope away into what looks like a deep, dark valley. You can decide that perhaps one day you will explore that valley, but for now just be aware of its presence. How do you feel when you look towards that valley? What can you see in that direction?

Now turn around in your meadow and see that in another direction there is a path that leads up to a mountain. Really picture this mountain in all its splendour. Again decide that one day you will explore that mountain, but for now just be aware of its presence. How do you feel when you look towards the mountain? What can you see in that direction?

As you look towards the mountain, you see a bird flying towards you. See the bird getting bigger and bigger as it gets closer to you. In its beak in has a jewel and as it flies over you it drops this jewel and you catch it in your hands. Thank the bird for this gift, and sense the power and strength of this object as you hold it tightly in your hands.

Now look at the jewel. What does it look like? What colour is it, what size, do you know what kind of jewel it is? Get a clear picture of this jewel, then, when you feel ready, open your eyes, come back to your ordinary, every day consciousness, and bring the jewel with you.

You might like to draw a picture of this jewel, or write about it in your diary. This jewel is a gift from your superconscious, and you can use it as a magical talisman that will protect you on your explorations into the depths - and heights - or your unconscious. Use it wisely and its strength and radiance will grow with you.

3

THE MULTIPLE PERSONALITY

Psychological life can be regarded as a continual polarization and tension between differing tendencies and functions, and as a continual effort, conscious or not, to establish equilibrium. (Roberto Assagioli)

Life often seems to be an endless struggle between different parts of us wanting different things. The more we look at ourselves, the more it seems we are not whole, but composed of lots of different parts all having their own needs and desires. We are not split personalities but rather multiple personalities. Each of the 'little personalities' within us is called, in Psychosynthesis, a subpersonality. Each subpersonality has a part to play in our lives and we all play many parts, often with conflicting thoughts and feelings about what is good for us, or even of who we actually are.

You might be a 'mother' seeing your children off to school, then the very next minute a 'housewife' washing the dishes. Later that morning you are a 'dancer' in your aerobics class, then a 'friend' for someone over lunch. Meanwhile your 'husband' has become a 'business man' in his office. Later tonight you will be alone together and become 'lovers'.

All of us play such roles, often apparently flitting from one to another part with consummate ease. Yet how conscious are we of these parts we play? Do you easily slip into a part of yourself that blushes and feels shy when in a crowd? Do you become an angry part of yourself just because you missed a bus? Are there times when you get 'stuck' as a housewife or a banker and wish things could change? Or perhaps you are so identified with a role you do not even realise it is a role you are playing. Instead you think it is the 'real' you.

Our personality is rather like an orchestra, and all these different parts or roles we play are like the players in that orchestra. As we become more able to define our lives, and control our processes in a positive inclusive way, we become like the conductor, allowing each individual member to play a part, and working towards orchestrating the personality into a harmonious whole. This conductor is the self or 'I'. As the conductor we will also contact the composer, the transpersonal Self, who will supply us with information about how to play the musical composition of life and also, perhaps, information about each individual players part in the whole.

One way to start learning more about our different subpersonalities is to give them names. Roberto Assagioli suggested naming each of our subpersonalities with humour, both as a way of connecting to their energies but also to maintain a healthy detachment and 'lightness' in this work. So, for example, a rather crazy emotional part of your personality could be called 'Loopey Len'; a bossy part 'Mrs Knowitall'; a rather dreamy little girl 'Alice' (in Wonderland); and so on. By giving our subpersonalities such names, we have identified them as not being all that we are, and have given them a 'handle' by means of which we can interact with them.

Spend some time now thinking about your different subpersonalities. It is a good idea to make a list of the main ones, then see how many you can name. Thinking of your more prominent traits, attitudes and motives will help you start. For each part of you let an image emerge. It may be the image of a human of either sex, or an animal, a mythical creature, or anything at all. Do not 'make-up' these images for your subpersonalities, but rather let them spontaneously emerge from your unconscious.

You can start with the more obvious roles such as husband or wife, partner, daughter or son, businessperson, sportsperson and so on. Then consider subpersonalities that are more based around different states - the miserable old man, the angry cat, the fool, the controller, the top dog, the mystic, the sad little girl, the sensible adult, the shy boy, and so on. The aim is not to have the longest list of subpersonalities in town, but rather to know which subpersonalities you are aware of right now in your life. The list will change, and you can always add more subpersonalities as your work on yourself progresses.

When we first think of our subpersonalities, those we most easily connect with are part of what can be called our 'core personality'. These are subpersonalities we happily include as part of us, included in our sense of who we really are. Some of these will be well integrated and be very helpful to us in our lives. They form the basis of what is sometimes called 'the ego' (though be careful, as there are several different ways of using this term.) They constitute who we believe we are.

Other subpersonalities are more suppressed. They are in the middle unconscious, we know they are there but we don't happily accept them as part of ourselves. Depending upon the conditioning we have had, and various other developmental factors, they might include subpersonalities that represent 'forbidden sexual drives', parts of us that we hide away because we believe them unworthy, powerful parts of us that frighten our sense of who we are. They might also include self-assertive parts, which may become distorted into aggressive subpersonalities. They also include social conditioning, for instance, the 'top dog' who is always telling us what to do or not do. For some people, almost everything they do is accompanied by the voice of an inner 'top dog' telling them whether it is 'right' or 'wrong', whether they should or should not be doing whatever it is. All of these suppressed subpersonalities are often projected onto other people.

Hidden deeper in the lower unconscious are repressed parts of us, primitive parts which are trapped and totally not accepted. They constitute what is sometimes called 'the shadow'. These parts of us can hardly be called subpersonalities, as we know so little of them. They emerge and 'control' us at times, but generally we keep them well repressed. We have to learn to face these parts of us, so we can release the energy we are using to hold them down. When we release this energy, we usually find we have grown and transformed, perhaps only in a small or subtle way, but nevertheless in a very real and tangible way.

Psychosynthesis aims to expand our consciousness to include all three types. We can only transform subpersonalities when we connect with and fulfil their basic needs. Until then we remain fragmented. A fragmented personality might include a part that split off, as if in trance, acting as if it is 'not at home'. Cut off from any true, direct experience, if it does express itself, it is often through pleading for its wants in a very unbalanced way. Or we might include a part of us that finds its identity through others, always wants more, never feeling like it has enough. A subpersonality like this only knows where it stands when in relation to someone (or something) else; otherwise it feels lost, and will generally do anything in its power to avoid these feelings of despair.

We can become so identified with some of the roles we play, it becomes very difficult to let go of them. Imagine a mother whose child has grown up and is ready to leave home. She loves this child and wants the best for him or her, but she is so attached to the role of mother the separation makes her very sad. She is clinging to her role, and it is only through facing the sadness and accepting the loss that she will release enough energy to be able to move on. When she gets through this, and gives up her old role, she finds she has not 'lost' the child at all. And in no longer being so identified with the role she can, paradoxically, play it better.

Or imagine a man who has worked from nine until five in an office for most of his life. He has now retired and, sadly, he has been so identified with his role in his office, he doesn't know what to do with his new found time and 'freedom'. He feels bored, at a loss, and even catches himself wishing he could be back at the office. The retirement he has looked forward to no longer seems so attractive. He will have to find very definite ways to let go of his old role, and cultivate new interests to replace the old.

We all know people who, at least in some aspects of their lives, have not 'grown up'. For example, there might be a thirty-year-old man who still plays with his train set - perhaps when he does this he is really identified with one of his subpersonalities who is still a ten year old boy. Perhaps to avoid some of the painful issues he felt in adolescence he reverts, as it were, to an earlier time. Or imagine a fifty-year-old woman who still acts like an adolescent girl when men are around. We all have examples of such subpersonalities within us. It is as if all our 'little selves' are at different stages of development, some having reached full maturity, others at 'younger' stages, even infantile when confronted with painful or difficult issues.

There is no suggestion that there is anything wrong with having subpersonalities. Far from it, they provide us with the means to interact with ourselves, other people and the world in general. Every subpersonality has an important part to play in our total being. Problems arise when they have got you rather than you having them. You come home after a day's work and you cannot stop thinking about it. Yet to 'disidentify' from the role you might only need to simply take a bath and put on different clothes.

Psychosynthesis offers us techniques whereby we can discover the roles we play and then more clearly choose to either identify with them when appropriate or disidentify from them when that is appropriate. This way our lives become more harmonious and we are more able to make choices about what we really want. Psychosynthesis, in other words, helps us to both become the conductor of our life orchestra, but also to play all the parts in the orchestra that we wish to play.

WANTING AND NEEDING

Our subpersonalities know what they want and are determined to get it. They really look out for themselves. This can be all right in itself, but problems arise when what one subpersonality wants is in conflict with the wants of another one. For instance, part of you might want to go to the cinema whilst a different part of you wants to stay at home. Perhaps one part of you might really need to leave a deadening job but another scared part won't let it happen.

Some of the deepest conflicts can arise between 'thinking identified' and 'emotionally identified' subpersonalities. You feel like telling someone you love them but you think they will laugh at you. Or you know it is a good idea to take regular exercise but part of you feels too lazy. Such inner conflicts can emerge in rather contradictory ways. A man might be a strong 'boss' at the office but at home a 'weak' husband and father. One day you might go out and be the 'life and soul' of a party, the next you are a mass of nerves, frightened of going out to the corner shop. The work in harmonizing the relationship between the thinking and feeling functions can lead, through the methods of Psychosynthesis, to the release of creative energy. This creative energy will be accompanied by the emergence of transpersonal Qualities such as Love, Joy, Truth and Beauty. We will talk of these Qualities in a later chapter.

To harmonise the wants of different subpersonalities, it is necessary to get behind them to the deeper level of 'needs'. Needs are more inclusive than wants: 'I want you to kiss me right now' and 'I want to respect your own choice' might be conflicting wants. When we contact the underlying need - perhaps 'needing more affection in life generally' - then we can find ways to fulfil this need without conflict.

We can make this shift from 'wanting' to 'needing' through simply identifying the initial conflict then accepting it.

We have to accept that if we cannot get away from it, we might as well include it. Once we are able to accept the wants of both sides of the conflict, a transformation is possible.

With all our subpersonalities we need to get to know them. We do this through dialoguing with them, letting them have a voice and realise their wants are being heard. Then we build a true relationship with them in which we attend to the larger needs of all concerned. We can learn to love all our subpersonalities in spite of their faults, and in doing this we give them the space they need in order to grow.

Wants can be harsh and demanding whereas needs tend to be more flexible. Needs are also closer to the essence at the core of the subpersonality. By moving towards this essence you allow the underlying transpersonal Qualities to manifest more clearly. This then fuels the transformation towards unification of the personality.

Many of the conflicts we see between different subpersonalities is an acting out of the dynamic between Love and Will. We can learn more about subpersonalities if we look at them in the light of this dynamic. Is a subpersonality content with simply being, does it want to be loved, or does it want to do, to act, perhaps to control? Does it feel most sad or hurt when it is not getting love or when it is not getting its own way? Is it angry because it feels there is not enough love in your life, or is its anger a power issue?

The way to answer these questions is not through trying to work out the answers intellectually. Instead, you watch and observe your subpersonalities, hear what they have to say, and be aware of what they are feeling. Love-orientated subpersonalities tend to want to be included, listened to and taken care of. Will-orientated subpersonalities want to be able to express their needs, and not be restricted from taking the decisions they feel are right. Part of our work is to ensure these wants are met in harmonious ways.

Subpersonalities tend to be either ones who want everything (that affects them) to change, or ones who want everything to stay the same. These wishes usually interact in a dynamic way with the need for love or power. A love-type subpersonality, for instance, might want change: 'everything would be better if only you loved me.' Another love-type subpersonality might not want change: 'I couldn't live without you.' Psychosynthesis teaches us to co-operate with the process as much as possible - to choose change when that is most appropriate or to choose stability when that is the better choice.

To reach closer to the transpersonal Self, we have to learn to trust in both things that change and in things that stay the same, and at the same time not be attached to either. Awareness has to be coupled with psychological mastery. We can use our will power to stop us slipping mindlessly into different subpersonalities, but instead to be able to choose, at any moment, the most appropriate role to play. We have the ability to become the driver of our car, not just be a back seat passenger. The Qualities that emanate from transpersonal levels become 'degraded' in the personality; trust becomes foolishness, courage becomes foolhardiness, compassion self-pity and so on. Psychosynthesis helps us realise this, and it also helps us reverse the process. Qualities can also be 'elevated' in the personality - our self-pity becoming compassion and so on. The more we work in this way, the less distortions there are in our daily living. Although we might never reach complete unity, the more we move in that direction, the less distortions there are. If we could ever reach total unity in ourselves we would be free of all conflicts and distortions.

When we do any subpersonality work, however, it always releases energy and in so doing allows us to move closer to our centre and our true self. This expresses itself through the increased harmony we then find in our lives. Our multiple personality, our 'orchestra', as it grows and harmonises, becomes the ultimate healer of our divisions and fragmentation.

EXERCISE: THE ROSE GARDEN

In the next exercise you will meet a subpersonality who will take you into a garden of roses. Enjoy the experience of this, and see how subpersonalities are not always in conflict, either with each other or with you.

Either sitting or lying down, take a few deep breaths and relax. Imagine you are in a meadow, and spend some time tuning into being there ... What is the sky like? Is it a sunny day? ... How do you feel? ... What can you hear - bird song perhaps? ... What can you smell? What do you see? ... Be in your meadow as if it really exists.

In one direction you can see a small house or cottage. Walk towards it, feeling your feet on the ground, and remembering to pay attention to really being in your meadow... As you reach the house, you realise it is the home of some of your subpersonalities. You wonder who will live there, and how they will greet you. As you approach the door be aware of your excitement and anticipation.

You tap at the door and wait expectantly ... Greet the person who opens the door to you, and pay attention to what he or she looks like. Is it a man, a woman or a child? Old or young? Fill in as much detail on this figure as you can ... Then exchange some words, asking the figure its name if you like. Find out as much as you are able about this person.

The subpersonality then asks you into the garden of the house. It is a beautiful rose garden. Pay attention to the roses, their colours, scents, and overall beauty ... Allow yourself to be infused with the quality of the roses ... Walk with the subpersonality into the depths of the garden, then find one particular rose to which you are attracted.

Both you and the subpersonality look at this rose, brightly lit by a ray of sunshine. Feel the energy of the rose, its beauty and warmth, transform your feelings and thoughts. Let yourself feel really good to be in this beautiful garden at this time.

Then turn to the subpersonality and see how it has changed. Again engage him or her in dialogue and ask how he or she feels, what transformations, if any, may have taken place. Ask particularly about what the subpersonality needs.

Finally thank the subpersonality for taking you to the garden, say goodbye for now, and bring your consciousness back to your room.

Write about the experience, and the needs of the subpersonality, in your diary. In what way(s) can you express and fulfill this need, or at least some aspects of it in your daily life?

4

SELF IDENTIFICATION

We are dominated by everything with which our self becomes identified. We can dominate and control everything from which we dis-identify ourselves. (Roberto Assagioli)

In the last chapter we learnt about subpersonalities and how, although each of our subpersonalities has an important part to play in our total being, problems arise when we become too identified or attached to any of them. It is as if they have us rather than us having them. There is the mother who is so identified with the role of being a mother that when her children leave home she cannot let go properly. The businessman who comes home from the office and is so identified with that role he cannot relax with his family but finds himself constantly worrying about what happened that day or what he has to do the next day. He isn't sitting there thinking 'oh I wish I could be less identified with this role I play at work'. On the contrary, more often that not he will be so caught up in the role no such considerations will arise. Indeed, we can become so identified with a role that we never take the time to stop and see how we really feel. We might even believe we like being attached!

Another way of looking at how we become identified is through the functions we use to relate with the world - our bodies (and sensations), our feelings (and emotions) and our thoughts (or mind). Of course these three functions are not really that separate and are truly interrelated. If we look for example at our thoughts, then feelings and sensations will be there too. But it is useful to view them separately both to help us understand them and to help us separate ourselves from them.

In our early years, from our birth maybe until around seven or eight years of age, our primary focus for development is on our bodies. We are concerned with survival in our 'physical reality'. There is then a shift to development of our feeling function that lasts up to and through puberty. The emergence of sexuality can be seen as a joining of body and feelings. After this, during our teens we are primarily concerned with the development of our minds and we often go through identity struggles involving the mind, feelings and body. To function most effectively, we need to have all our functions available to us, well developed and not lop-sided, otherwise we will not be able to so effectively channel the rays from the sun (the Self).

To develop our personalities most effectively, we need a good connection with our bodies, feelings and mind. This connection can be best made through differentiation, which quite simply means we have to be able to tell, whatever is happening to us, whether it is truly an experience of sensing (body), feeling or thinking (the mind). We can then get a better picture of which of these functions we use more and which tend to be more overlooked in our everyday life. We find whether we are more mentally, emotionally or physically identified. This will change for different situation, of course, but with most people there is a general tendency to be more thought or feeling orientated.

In Psychosynthesis we try to raise the energy of the less well-developed parts, mainly through inclusion. We also work on bringing more balance to the more suppressed functions. It is a principle of Psychosynthesis that each function must be made whole before it can be synthesized with other functions and fully brought into an integrated personality.

If you feel you need to develop a more balanced relationship with your emotions, for example, is it appropriate for you to go to that wild party tonight? Depending upon your individual circumstances it may be beneficial or not for you. But through bringing such awareness to play, and differentiating in this way, you can make clearer decisions rather than just following whims that might lead you off your chosen path of self-discovery.

Another example might be found in a person who feels they want to develop their mental function but finds it hard to read anything but monthly fashion magazines. Whilst there is nothing wrong with this in itself, that person might do far better choosing to read more mentally stimulating material. Alternatively, mental skills could be applied to the reading of the magazines - analyzing their contents, looking at what is really being 'sold' in the pages between the ads, and so on. Part of the skill in working on developing and balancing your mind, feelings and body is in finding ways you can adapt the current situation, whatever it is, to your advantage in this way. How can you use your setting to aid rather than hinder your development?

It is important that to look at the relationship between sensing, feeling and thinking, asking ourselves how well do they work together in our personality? Then when problems arise, we can see them as opportunities to find out more about what is happening underneath, what is behind the problem. This gives us the opportunity to work on a deeper level. And, it must be stressed, in Psychosynthesis we never wish to bring any function down to the level of a lesser function. Instead, we always work to elevate a weaker function so that it rises up to the level of a stronger one. If you are strong in feeling and weaker in thinking, then the work will be to develop the thinking function so that it is raised to the level of the feeling function. The work on the stronger function will be that of refinement. We cannot have a truly whole sense of who we are unless we are totally there!

Most people tend to be generally more attached to either their thoughts or their emotions, and can thus be described as mentally or emotionally identified. Such identification is useful for it allows us to inter-relate to the world around us. People who are predominantly identified with their thoughts, who are, in other words, mentally-identified, need to increase their awareness, experience and expression of their feelings, rather than diminish or decrease their mental awareness. This is balance through upward growth, and inclusion, rather than through decrease, and exclusion which is both unnecessary and inefficient.

Psychosynthesis uses various techniques to help us get to this deeper level of understanding. These techniques include 'time sharing', which means giving all the functions space for expression in your daily life. If you give an angry emotional part of you space for expression, for instance, it will then not come up inappropriately at other times, but will more readily 'time share' with other parts of your personality.

Another useful technique we mentioned in the last chapter is 'dialoguing', which means allowing different functions to communicate with one another to see what each has to say, both in terms of what they need but also what they can give. Whenever there is a conflict, you can do what is needed through listening to the voice of all the parts involved.

DISIDENTIFICATION

The experience of self-identification, of having an 'I', distinguishes our consciousness from that of the majority of other living beings on our planet. As far as we can tell, other creatures do not have a sense of self-consciousness. No dog will ever think: 'I am me, myself, separate and different from everything and everyone else.' We do not usually experience self-consciousness, in this way, either. It is usually experienced, not as pure self-consciousness, but rather mixed with and veiled by the contents of consciousness, that is, everything we are sensing, feeling and thinking at any time.

In Psychosynthesis, we primarily see this separate unique self as the simplest part or 'unit' of our total being. It is our core. The self, seen in this way, is completely separate from everything else that makes us up - our bodies, feelings, thoughts, desires, all our subpersonalities, the different roles we play and so on. As it is separate, it is a place of unity and individual wholeness from where we can utilize and direct all these other elements that make us what we are in totality. And unlike these contents of our being, the self never changes, but remains the one static, unchanging, ever-present part of ourselves. One minute I am a father, then a lover, now I am feeling, then thinking - but I am always my self.

The self is what makes us who we really are, separate not only from all the contents of our consciousness, but also from everyone and everything else too. As selves we are each have our own individual experience. Of course, we might be identified and see ourselves as, say, a sportsman. This person might then become so identified with this role that he believes it is who he really is, rather than a role he is playing. Or someone might become so identified with their feelings they loose sight of the rest of their functions. Thus the great value of being able to disidentify from all these functions and roles and get to the true central core self. This self is not attached to anything, but is uniquely whole and centered in itself. From this place if you ask yourself: 'who am I?' the answer is not a sportsman, a mother, a banker, an angry person, a thinker, a fool, an actor, or anything other than 'I am me.'

Being identified is a bit like being in a dream where you move from one identification to another without awareness. Some Eastern philosophies compare our waking 'reality' to just such a dream. We don't realize we have, say, a particular feeling, we become the feeling. I don't have sadness, I become sadness. Such identification and attachment limits our perceptions. If we can awaken from this limiting dream, and identify with the self, we can come alive with a new awareness

We are usually attached to or identified with the contents of our consciousness. To make self-consciousness an explicit, experiential fact in our lives, we need first to dis-identify from our bodies, feeling and thoughts, from all our subpersonalities, from everything that fills us up and creates the contents of our consciousness. We have to become truly empty - then we find there is something left, this sense of 'I'-ness, of being a self, or simply being.

Through deliberate disidentification from the personality and identification with the self, we gain freedom, and the power to choose either identification with or disidentification from any aspect of our personality, according to what is most appropriate for any given situation. Thus we may learn to master and utilize our whole personality in an inclusive and harmonious synthesis.

We often find it most difficult to disidentify from our thoughts. We construct our world through our thoughts about it, so it can feel dangerous or difficult to stop thinking about it. Maybe our world will fall apart and we will be left in an unstructured, undifferentiated state. In actuality, however, we find we are left with the self. We find a new clarity in our lives we never knew could exist before. Indeed, when we stop our inner dialogue with ourselves, we find that special and extraordinary aspects of ourselves are able to surface. We can make more creative choices about our lives, and more easily find ways to manifest these choices.

When we disidentify, we can then choose to re-identify. That is the goal. We don't want to be without our vehicles for expression and experience; we want to have them rather than them having us. It is as if when we re-identify with thoughts, feelings or the body, we can take a little bit of our new self-awareness with us. Not only have we found our 'I', the self, and are more able to disattach ourselves from the contents of our consciousness, but also we can more effectively control our being and doing in the world in a positive, life-enhancing way.

From this new perspective, we can truly say 'I am simply myself, and I have a body, and feelings and thoughts in order to experience the world and express myself in it.' With this new strength, as well as being able to bring more clarity to what is happening in our lives, and having the ability to choose what is the best choice for us, we also find we are generally happier and more effective in our relationships with other people. On top of this, we also then have an 'safe anchor', so to speak, which allows us to more easily explore our lower unconscious and sort out some of the blocks, complexes, obsessions and other life-diminishing facets of this part of our being. We have also, through this work, created more space for the influx of transpersonal energies into our personality. We are more able to manifest Qualities such as Beauty, Trust, Joy, Truth and so on.

The benefits of disidentification, then identification with the self, cannot be over stressed. You have already learned in the last chapter what is perhaps one of the simplest ways to start disidentifying from various roles. Through recognizing subpersonalities, and naming them, you are separating yourself from these roles. If you can see, for instance, that part of you is, say, 'a daughter', then you can realize you are not just a daughter. This applies to all our subpersonalities, whatever roles we play.

It is perhaps more difficult to directly disidentify from the functions of thinking, feeling and sensing, but it can be done. It is achieved chiefly through a form of introspection whereby we become the 'observer' of our life. We can look at everything that happens to us as distinct from ourselves. If we are angry, for example, we can step back, become an observer, and see our anger. Then we realize we are not our anger, rather anger is something we have. We awaken from the dream, and see ourselves from a place of grater perspective. We might find it is right to be angry in the present circumstances, or not, but whichever is the case, we will have it rather than it having us.

The most important self identification work we can do is through life situations as just described, when we observe ourselves from a separate place. As we do this more, we start to realize the self as a continuous truth behind all that happens in our lives. But it is always useful to forge links and strengthen our connection to the self, to help and foster this natural process. The exercise that follows helps us to do just that, is the most important one in this book, and is central to the work of Psychosynthesis.

EXERCISE: SELF-IDENTIFICATION

The following exercise is a tool for moving towards and realizing the consciousness of the self. This exercise, called 'self identification', is of vital importance, and should be done with the greatest care. If you feel at all tired do not read on from here until you have at least taken a break. You will enjoy this exercise more if you are fresh when you first try it out.

Relax yourself in the best way you know how, putting yourself in a comfortable but alert position. Take a few deep breaths, and let go of any tensions from the day. Follow the instructions slowly and carefully.

Affirm to yourself the following: 'I have a body but I am not my body. My body may find itself in different conditions of health or sickness, it may be rested or tired, but that has nothing to do with my self, my real I. I value my body as my precious instrument of experience and action in the world, but it is only an instrument. I treat it well, I seek to keep it in good health, but it is not myself. I have a body, but I am not my body.'

Close your eyes, recall what this affirmation says, then focus your attention on the central concept: 'I have a body but I am not my body.'

Attempt to realize this as an experienced fact in your consciousness.

Now affirm to yourself: 'I have feelings, but I am not my feelings. My feelings and emotions are diversified, changing, and sometimes contradictory. They may swing from love to hatred, from calm to anger, from joy to sorrow, and yet my essence - my true nature - does not change. I remain. Though a wave of anger may temporarily submerge me, I know that in time it will pass; therefore I am not this anger. Since I can observe and understand my feelings, and can gradually learn to direct, utilize, and integrate them harmoniously, it is clear that they are not my self. I have feelings, but I am not my feelings.'

Close your eyes, recall what this affirmation says, then focus your attention on the central concept: 'I have feelings but I am not my feelings.'

Attempt to realize this as an experienced fact in your consciousness.

Now affirm to yourself: 'I have a mind but I am not my mind. My mind is a valuable tool of discovery and expression, but it is not the essence of my being. Its contents are constantly changing as it embraces new ideas, knowledge, and experience, and makes new connections. Sometimes my thoughts seem to be independent of me and if I try to control them they seem to refuse to obey me. Therefore my thoughts cannot be me, my self. My mind is an organ of knowledge in regard to both the outer and inner worlds, but it is not my self. I have a mind, but I am not my mind.'

Close your eyes, recall what this affirmation says, then focus your attention on the central concept: 'I have a mind but I am not my mind.'

Attempt to realize this as an experienced fact in your consciousness.

Next comes the phase of identification. Affirm clearly and slowly to yourself: 'After this disidentification of my self, the 'I', from my body, my feelings, and my mind, I recognize and affirm that I am a centre of pure self consciousness. I am a centre of will, capable of observing, directing and using all my psychological processes and my physical body.'

Focus your attention on the central realization: ' I am a centre of pure self-consciousness and of will.' Realize this as an experienced fact in your awareness.

When you have practiced this exercise a few times, you can use it in a much shorter form. The important point is to keep to the four main, central affirmations:
I have a body and sensations, but I am not my body and sensations.
I have feelings and emotions, but I am not my feelings and emotions.
I have a mind and thoughts, but I am not my mind and thoughts.
I am I, a centre of pure self-consciousness and of will.

Some people find it difficult to follow the affirmations in this exercise that say you have but are not your body, feelings or mind, objecting that this may cause a disassociation from these functions. A suggested alternative way of using the exercise, if this bothers you, is to change the disidentifying statements to 'I have a body and sensations and I am more than my body; I have feelings and I am more than my feelings and emotions; I have a mind and thoughts, and I am more than my mind and thoughts.' This is almost as effective, but the original as designed by Assagioli uses the principle of affirmation through negation which can have a particularly powerful effect on creating the required conditions for Self Identification.

You may have to repeat the exercise a few times to start with to get its full flavour, but then you will be able to do it daily from memory. The effort will be well worth it. All the influences that try to capture your attention and demand identification will no longer have the same hold over you.

5

SPIRITUAL GROWTH AND MEDITATION

Everything is spiritual that relates to the unfoldment or true progression of humanity ... The hidden world is becoming as real to us as all that we see, and we are beginning to awaken to the reality of a great Life in which we live. (Roberto Assagioli)

It is possible for us to connect with the transpersonal or spiritual realms of energy. Meditation is one of the many ways to connect with the spiritual realms and we will be looking at this in detail later in this chapter. Other ways include dance, devotion, concentration, loving sex, aesthetic ecstasy, compassion, and shock. There are also many techniques and exercises that have been devised to help us connect with the spiritual, and Psychosynthesis uses many of these.

As well as connecting with spiritual energies, we can also manifest them in the world. It could be argued there is little point in us getting into contact with the spiritual unless we are going to utilize its transforming qualities in ourselves and our world. Psychosynthesis emphasizes this need for the grounding or manifestation of transpersonal energies. A spiritual treasure, whatever form it takes, is only truly meaningful when it is 'brought back to the world.' The rich jewel that an explorer finds is of no value unless he brings it home and shares its splendour with others.

Of course, sometimes just connecting with the transpersonal realms can be enough. We might, for example, feel low and purposeless in our lives, then through a spiritual connection we might find there is hope and meaning after all. Or it might just be to just know something more than mundane reality exists is enough. But even if the spiritual connections we make only transform something inside us, it is nevertheless true that these energies will bring into manifestation better human relations. It is inevitable that if we, as individuals, transform ourselves in some way, that transformation will affect those with whom we come into contact.

When we connect with and manifest the transpersonal, we are more able to do our 'true will', to make our lives more purposeful. The 'higher' or 'deeper' Self that is in touch with the Universal Self becomes more manifest through us, so we are truly co-operating with evolution. Then our own Psychosynthesis can more readily happen, for we are aligned with rather than fighting against this natural current. And, in a truly dynamic sense, we find our everyday lives are improved. We feel more whole, more meaningful, happier, and those around us can share in this splendour.

Sometimes the emergence of transpersonal or spiritual energies is not chosen or allowed in some active way, however. The energies 'burst in upon us', as it were, in a totally spontaneous way. It has already been made clear that one of the aims of Psychosynthesis is to help us to make more connection with the transpersonal. Another aim is to help us deal with the results of more spontaneous emergences of spiritual energies.

When energy comes upon us unexpectedly, it can be a very positive experience. We may experience transformative 'highs' or quite simply feel a silent 'grace' pervading our lives. Sometimes, however, when such energies emerge unexpectedly, it is as if they are too much for the personality to cope with and we are 'blown out'. If we are fairly well prepared we can withstand these blowouts and find ways of utilizing the energy. If we are not prepared, then such energies can lead to all sorts of strange distortions of attitude and behaviour. We might think we are literally 'god', we might believe we are 'chosen' in some way, we might become inflated in our sense of self. In extreme cases, this can even lead to dangerous behaviour both to ourselves and to others. Many murderers say they have been 'spoken to' in some way. Perhaps in some cases the initial contact was genuine enough, but the personality was not able to cope with the energy and consequently it was channelled into a distorted message. Because of this danger, even if only manifested in a mild and fairly harmless way, as is usually the case, Psychosynthesis emphasizes work on the personality. The clearer we become in our personalities, the more able we are to deal with and constructively utilize our emerging transpersonal energies, whether chosen or spontaneous.

WAYS OF CONTACTING SPIRIT

Once we realize the great benefits to our world and ourselves when we contact the transpersonal realms, we want to know how we can do it more often and more effectively. As has been said, there are many ways of achieving such a connection and Psychosynthesis uses many of these when it is suitable to the unfoldment of any individual's Psychosynthesis. It is best to find ways that are appropriate for the person involved - 'different strokes for different folks' (or 'different scenes for different genes'!)

In the last chapter, we learned how important Self Identification is, and the exercise offered a good way of disidentifying from the personality and identifying with the self. This technique is one of the most effective ways of connecting with the spiritual. In the first instance, by disattaching in this way, we are bringing ourselves to our centre that in itself opens us up to such energy. Then we are also 'calling in' or 'invoking' the self, our distinct and unique 'I'. When we move closer to becoming 'a centre of pure self awareness and of will' then we are moving more into the spiritual realms are are thus more able to channel this energy into our personality and, through us, into our world. When we are the self, we are aligned with the Self and are thus making the ultimate individual connection to the Spirit itself.

It is important to distinguish the Self from the superconscious. The superconscious is a section of the whole unconscious and is, in fact, a rather artificial division. Our experience tells us that in reality the unconscious is not divided into sections. But for convenience it is most useful to make the three distinctions as is done in the Psychosynthesis map. The 'superconscious' (or 'higher unconscious') is a description for that part of the unconscious that 'contains' energies of a higher frequency than those of the contents of the lower unconscious. This is not saying that one is 'better' than the other, but merely making a distinction to aid understanding.

The Self, on the other hand, is the central reality of a being, the innermost centre where he or she is completely individual and at the same time connected to everyone and everything else. The experience of this spiritual Self gives a sense of freedom and expansion to the individual. To experience the Self is of great value for it brings connection, revelation and spiritual maturity.

The Self never changes in essence; it is 'that which remains when all else is gone.' The superconscious is constantly changing, however, both as the Self radiates energy into it and then, in turn, it radiates energy into the personality. If we say the Self is like the sun, then the superconscious is the sun's rays, flowing to earth and giving life. We may each have our own individual experience of the sun, but in reality it is one sun that illuminates us all.

The Self is constantly radiating Qualities into the superconscious. These 'Soul Qualities' include: Love, Truth, Beauty, Joy, Courage, Trust, Ecstasy, Delight, Unity, Calm, Compassion, Peace, Loyalty, Freedom, Risk, Power, Simplicity, Vitality, Understanding, Humour, Patience, Service, Wonder, Eternity, Vitality and so on.

In the superconscious, all these Qualities remain in their 'pure form', undistorted in any way. As they come through to the middle unconscious and the personality, they become distorted. In Psychosynthesis, when we talk about the 'distortion' of Qualities, we do not mean they 'go wrong' or are 'bad' in any way. It is simply that, in our usual personality state we do not either experience or express these Qualities in a clear way. How often have you given or received totally unadulterated, pure Love or Trust? We might be close to the pure experience, but there will still be something else operating at the same time. If a Quality becomes even more 'distorted' it can take on a 'negative' form. Love can become possessiveness, or jealousy, for example, or Trust might become jealousy or slavery.

At first sight, we might think that the distortion of Qualities in this way is a very negative experience. On the contrary, however, Psychosynthesis teaches us that it is, in fact, very positive. If we can face our possessiveness, for instance, and deal with it appropriately, then it will transform into its underlying Quality, or at least, some of the transforming energies of that Quality will be made manifest.

Someone might, for example, have a very devious subpersonality. Through subpersonality work, disidentification and various other Psychosynthesis techniques, this angry subpersonality might grow a little and feel that its needs are being better met. Then there is space, as it were, for the emergence of the underlying Quality, which in our example might be 'Truth'. With the emergence of this Truth, a transformation can take place and the subpersonality - and through it, the whole person - can grow even more. Work on the Psychosynthesis of the personality is thus a natural, on-going spiral of increase once the process is truly and clearly set in motion. Luckily for us, however, we never come to the end of this work - luckily because this means we have an endless reservoir of material we can transform. It is this process that allows us to ground or manifest our true creative Spirit, the Self.

GROUNDING

If we attempt to manifest any transpersonal energy or Quality into the world, it is ineffective so long as it is not grounded through the personality. Nothing can happen without a connection to ground. We have to clearly connect with our transpersonal energies and find ways to effectively bring them into the world. However bright or illuminating our insights and realisation might be, if the light is not radiated then it cannot help light our path let alone anyone else's.

If we can understand the difference between motivation and intention we can learn to ground our energies much more effectively. Intention essentially comes from a connection to the Self. Motivations, on the other hand, come from our reactions to the outside world, and are 'chosen' by subpersonalities. Motivation and intention can actually be the same thing, or at very least be closely connected, but usually they are not.

Motivations are usually exclusive and are what push us into partial, un-centred and often ill-considered decisions and actions. They are a response, and often a victim kind of reaction at that. Intentions, on the other hand, are more about getting our deeper needs fulfilled. These needs are not so exclusive and are more about manifesting the Self and our True Will or Purpose. If I am motivated to want a banana then nothing else will do. I will get angry or upset if I don't get it. If I can contact my inner need more clearly I might find it is actually for fruit. I can now happily eat an orange and fulfil my purpose.

Whether we are dealing with the deepest intention of the Self or a simple desire or motivation from a subpersonality, we need a definite plan to fulfil it. This plan will tell us how we can go about manifesting or grounding our desire. This plan might include a need for us to be strong willed or we might just have to let go and accept what is. We might need to be single-minded, or we might need to deal with some emotional state before it can happen. Once we have done the preparatory work we are then able to ground our transpersonal energies.

There are several easy ways to ground energy, which include:
• simply expressing the experience;
• writing, and/or drawing;
• evening reviews (going over the past day and looking how you performed, not as a judgemental exercise but in order that you might function more effectively through knowledge of how you habitually perform);
• meditation, either on the object of the will itself or a symbol you have constructed to represent the will;
• evocative word cards; sometimes called 'self-advertising' - you write your desire (in words or symbols) on postcards and stick them up around your home in places where you will frequently see them - just as with commercial advertising, constant exposure has an effect on the unconscious;
• free or automatic drawing;
• creating a mantra and constantly chanting or repeating it to yourself;
• specific acts in your life, for example going to beautiful places;
• finding an object to represent what happened.

The aim of grounding is, ultimately, to co-operate with our personal and transpersonal evolution. We can help in that process by taking responsibility for the creation of our life, using our abilities to fulfil our real inner needs, and to ground our inspirations and insights. The most effective ways of grounding energy come from your own life situations. If you have never gone fishing there's little point (in the short term anyway) of grounding a need for fish through fishing. You'd do better to fit the need into your life situation and experience, that is, go to the local supermarket!

Fear is a major block to grounding - it may manifest as fear of responsibility, of loosing individuality, of impotence, of being a victim, of disrupting your life, of loneliness, of inadequacy, of being rejected, or even as the fear of success itself! Whatever gets in the way of our ability to manifest whatever it is we wish to do; the best way of dealing with it is to connect with who we are through Self-Identification. At the same time, we have to be willing to work through the blocks to our success with Psychosynthesis and other similar techniques. Meditation can be particularly useful in that it helps us concentrate, connects us with our spiritual essence, and aids us in finding ways of expressing our inner truths.

MEDITATION

Many different meanings are given for the word meditation, and there are many different types of meditation and meditative techniques. At the simplest level, if we concentrate on something - anything at all - we are meditating. The more we discipline our thoughts, feelings and sensations to not intrude upon this concentration, the more deeply we can enter the meditative state. Many spiritual disciplines consider this work to be of prime importance.

It is often imagined that meditation is primarily an abstract activity, involved with turning inwards and somehow transcending the 'ordinary world'. In fact, meditation does involve concentration, reflection, understanding, being receptive and so on. It also includes, however, ways of bringing these connections into outer expression and it is thus also a very active and outer directed technique. Meditation could be defined as the conscious and deliberate use of inner powers and energies to fulfill a specific purpose.

As a prerequisite to most types of meditation is to be able to still ourselves, the first action in meditation is to perform some acts that do this. We might slow our breathing down, sit in a particular posture, visualize a calming scene and so on. We have to shift our attention from its normal outward orientation towards the stillness of our inner world. To do this effectively, we can relax physically, enter a state of emotional peace and direct our thoughts to either stop or be one-pointed. Luckily for us, however, it is possible to meditate without achieving complete success is these preliminaries. The 'secret' is to centre ourselves as best we can (perhaps through the 'Self Identification' exercise), and then simply trust that the wisdom of the Self will lead us towards that with which we need to connect.

Psychosynthesis uses a form of meditation called receptive meditation. To truly be able to receive, however, we need to firstly clear our minds of all our thoughts about whatever it is we wish to meditate upon. This is done in Psychosynthesis through a process called reflective meditation that, therefore, usually proceeds receptive meditation. There would seem to be little point in connecting with the spiritual if we do not bring our new energy, connection and insights back to the mundane, material world. To find ways to achieve this, Psychosynthesis uses a technique called creative meditation.

At times, of course, Psychosynthesis uses many different forms of meditation, including contemplation, silent meditation, active meditation, one-pointed focusing and so on. But when we usually think of meditation and Psychosynthesis, this threefold type of meditation - reflective, receptive and creative - usually springs to mind.

Reflective, receptive and creative meditation allows, if done in its entirety, for many levels of our being to operate and be active in our meditation. Each of these three 'types' of meditation can be done singly and often it is appropriate to do just that. If we combine the three together, however, it gives us the opportunity to meditate in a very thorough ways that not only connects us to our inner being but also helps us express that connection in our everyday world. Both reflective and receptive meditation help us increase our spiritual awareness and thus deepen our ability to serve both ourselves and our fellow human beings. Indeed, all meditation is a form of service for as we make inner connections and express them outwardly we increase the overall level of awareness in the collective consciousness of our race.

The following exercise shows you how to do all three and to connect them together, grounding the resulting insights. It can easily be adapted to any subjects upon which you wish to meditate, or adapted to create different methods of meditation.

Exercise: Meditation

The first requirement for meditation, as for most of the exercises in this book, is to be able to relax. The most effective ways of relaxing and centering are ones you find for yourself. You might like to choose as quiet a place as possible. It is usually preferable to sit rather than lie down, unless the exercise specifically asks you to lie. Choose a sitting position, either on the floor or in a chair, where you are upright but not rigid, your spine erect but not forced upright, and with your feet flat on the floor. For meditation, you might like to have your hands loosely clasped in your lap and have closed eyes. Before starting the meditative process take a few deep breaths and consciously choose to quiet your whole body. Through centering yourself, eliminate as much as possible from your consciousness (all thoughts, emotions, desires, plans, fantasies and so on).

Reflective Meditation

Reflective meditation could be called 'directed thinking'. For this exercise we will use the subject of 'Peace', but you can use any other subject to meditate upon as is appropriate for your evolving process.

Take a sheet of paper and put a circle in the middle with the word 'Peace' clearly written in it. Now quite simply think about this subject. Any words, images, ideas and so on that come to you as you think as one-pointedly as possible about this subject, put on lines radiating out from this circle.

When you feel you have exhausted your thoughts on the subject of 'Peace', continue for at least another five minutes. This allows you to delve deeper than you normally might, accessing deeper recesses of your mind. Your knowledge of the subject, through this kind of reflection, is stretched.

Receptive Meditation

With receptive meditation, you tune into your unconscious and receive intuitions, inspirations, messages, energies, and stimuli about your chosen subject. The most important requisite for receptive meditation is silence, as without it you cannot hear what your inner world is telling you.

Perform your receptive meditation in as quiet an external place as possible, and make your inner world as silent as possible also. Hold the concept of 'Peace' in your consciousness and try not to think of anything else. Be one-pointed in your determination to shut off all extraneous thoughts, feelings and sensations. Just be.

Do not do anything; just see what comes to you. Meditate in this receptive way for at least fifteen minutes.

Before continuing, record anything that came to you during this meditation.

Creative Meditation

Now consider what you have learned about 'Peace' from both your reflective and receptive meditations and in particular how you could put this knowledge and understanding into action. Try to find which of these ideas are the most relevant to you in your life right now, then choose one item from your meditation that you would like to put into action.

Consider this one concept and find ways of acting upon it. Be precise and practical, so for instance, if you choose 'to be more loving' as the action, find ways to do this actively and practically. You might want to express your love to someone very directly, or alternatively you might simply want to do something for someone you know will please them. Even the simplest acts, rightly performed with intention, can be very effective.

6

PURPOSE AND THE CREATIVE WILL

Since the outcome of successful willing is the satisfaction of one's needs, we can see that the act of will is essentially joyous. And the realization of ... being a self ... gives a sense of freedom, of power, of mastery which is profoundly joyous. (Roberto Assagioli)

Every choice or decision we make is an act of will. We might not be aware that we have chosen, and may even feel like a total victim with no choice at all. Nevertheless, wherever we are and whatever we are doing, it is our choice. Without making a choice, we could not stay where we are or move anywhere else. Without making a choice, we could not either stop what we are doing or continue doing it. Every time we make a choice, we perform an act of will. Our will power is the dynamic energy that brings us into this world and if we consciously connect with this energy it gives us the ability to be and do and become whatever we wish.

We have many different inner powers and the right use of these powers can enable us to make the best choices both for our own well-being and the world around us. We can only make these choices, however, through developing these inner powers in a balanced and conscious way. The discovery of our will and its subsequent training is the foundation of this work, which can be best achieved through direct experience. If we make a comparison with a car, the first thing we have to learn is that there is an engine through which we can choose to move the car. Then we have to find ways of using that engine so that we can travel in the direction that is best for us at any given moment.

Of course, a lot of the time our actual experience is very different from this. Even if we are aware we have a car, it certainly doesn't feel like we are in the driving seat! We are drifting or muddling along as if we are the victims of our circumstances. We see ourselves as the victims of where we are or who we are, of poverty or depression, of failure or even success! We are the victims of other people who made us whatever we are, or stop us doing what we wish. We feel as if we are not really free to choose what we want. Since childhood we have been told by parents and teachers and other 'well wishers' that we need to face the 'reality' of life. The message, that we cannot have everything we want, easily becomes one that says we cannot have anything we want.

If someone asks us to do something, the two obvious responses are yes and no. We can say we will or we will not. Yet usually we have a third choice available to us - 'not for now'. We do not have to limit ourselves by saying yes or no when 'not for now' is more appropriate. Sometimes it is right to make quick and immediate responses. The question at hand needs a fast response, or it is so obvious which choice is needed. Often, however, we can take the time to consider our choices and make them in a more centered, balanced way. The more consciousness we bring into our decisions, the more we are able to choose what are the right decisions for us.

In Psychosynthesis, we consider that any act of will actually takes place through six clear stages:
• investigation (finding out what it is we wish to do);
• deliberation (considering all the different things we wish to do at any time and selecting the acts most relevant to our current situation);
• decision (deciding upon the one act that is most important to us at the present time, and clearly formulating and stating this desire);
• affirmation (staying connected to this decision through constantly re-affirming that this choice is what we really desire to achieve);
• plan (thinking about the different ways we can actually make whatever it is happen);
• execution (doing it, finding ways of carrying out the intended plan, either in entirety or step by step.)

Every choice we make involves these six stages to a greater or lesser degree. It might be that for a particular choice we know what we want, hardly have to deliberate over it at all, and are able to quickly plan and execute the action necessary to succeed. For example, our choice to go to a nearby shop to purchase something we need. On the other hand, we might not really know what we want, and we might endlessly deliberate over the choices and never actually decide what to do. Or we might know exactly what we want and yet not know how to go about planning and executing the necessary actions. Our desire could be something well worked out, but for which the execution needs to take place at a particular time. If we choose a sunset, we will only be able to make it happen at the right time of day.

Whilst our acts of will always include all the six stages, they rarely do so in a linear fashion. For instance, whilst planning we may need to go back and deliberate further when we discover that we have not quite got the choice right. Often we need to keep going back to our choice to affirm it over and over. Constantly returning to the affirmation stage to focus on and strengthen our choices is usually a good technique as it reinforces the planning and execution of our desire.

We also have to consider that every choice we make affects everything and everyone else. If I choose to eat this particular orange right now, you will never be able to eat it either now or at any other time. That may not seem so serious - after all, there are plenty more oranges. In other circumstances, however, such knowledge takes on much more significance. For example, someone may choose to ignore their knowledge that lead-free petrol is better for the environment. That they continue buying leaded petrol seems to make no difference, because after all what difference can one person make? Yet in reality the situation will surely be worsening.

We must make our choices clearly and with heart, and be aware of this global effect, yet we must not allow such knowledge to make us impotent. Rather we must try to align ourselves with the flow of nature so that our choices add to rather than subtract from the evolution of consciousness on our planet.

THE STAGES OF WILLING

Although the process is, in actuality, continuous, as individuals we can experience the will as having four stages. The first stage could be described as 'having no will'. It is a common human experience to feel like a victim to outside forces, other people or the circumstances in which we find ourselves. At many times in our lives we all experience a sense of impotency, frustration and an inability to act. Instead of doing what we wish, we become totally reactive to the circumstances or the environment. We feel as if what we are, and what we are able to do or not do, is totally dependant upon what happens outside of us.

At these times we act like a victim to our repressed urges and desires, to basic drives, or to people or events outside of us. When we are coming from this state, when we believe ourselves to be 'will-less', our primary motivation is desire. We do not see ourselves as having any control, but instead experience ourselves as 'slaves of desire', whether we are fully conscious of this or not. Our one wish is to get our desires met and to avoid as much struggle, effort and pain as possible. If we have to manipulate people we will so long as our desires are met. As we reduce our responsibility in this way we become even more a victim and we can easily sink further into this deadening trap.

In reality, however horrible the situation you are in may truly be, you can make of it what you will. You could be unjustly imprisoned and, as a victim, spend your days bemoaning your fate. You might plot revenge on those who unjustly imprisoned you, those to whom you are a victim. Or you could undertake some other plan of action - you could meditate, write, use the time to make detailed observations of yourself or your fellow inmates, and so on. There are many stories of people doing just this. Assagioli, the founder of Psychosynthesis, when imprisoned by Mussolini, spent his days developing and 'fine-tuning' his system of psychology. In other words, Assagioli, in this unjust situation, chose to take responsibility for himself and not sink into a victim role.

Of course, we do not have to be in such an extreme situation to feel like a victim. Think of times right now when you feel like a victim. Perhaps you are a victim to your boss at work, or to your partner, your parents, or even your children! Perhaps you feel like you are a victim to the unjust society in which you live. The key to releasing yourself from this victim consciousness is to realise that, whatever is happening to you, you are creating the situation. We all re-create our worlds afresh each and every moment.

The next stage of the will process is coming to an understanding that 'will exists'. We might still feel we cannot actually do it, but we know, whatever it is, that it is possible. We realise we have a choice. This choice in any situation is always, as we have already discussed, 'yes', 'no', or 'not for now'. Of course, we may have reached this stage with a part of our personality but be less developed in other parts. Even if this stage of the will is only partially experienced, however, it leads to a shift in awareness from unconscious desires to active, conscious wishes. We might still feel separate, but there is a beginning of responsibility, the knowledge that some choice is possible. We are starting to develop our personal power.

Once we know that the will exists we are able to start working on developing it within ourselves. There are two basic aspects of will power that we can develop and, in Psychosynthesis, we call these 'the strong will' and 'the skilful will'. Strong will is the energy to choose whilst skilful will is the knowledge of how to use that energy. The strong will is like a car, the skilful will the driver. We can learn to develop both strong and skilful will. In most of us, one will be developed more than the other, but there is usually room for improvement in both.

One of the best ways to develop the strong will is to find ways in your daily life of being strong willed. You may hate washing up, for instance, so to develop your will you could choose to do it regularly and with positive attention. You could choose to make physical acts into acts of will. If you were gardening, for instance, you could do it consciously, being aware that each spade full of earth you move, or each flower you plant is an act of will. You might do aerobic exercises, or dancing, and do this not so much just for the exercise value, but because each movement you make you are consciously choosing to make. You could choose to read stories or watch television programmes about great heroic deeds performed against all odds. You can easily devise other techniques for strengthening the strong will, but above all perform these techniques playfully, cheerfully and with interest.

You can also develop skilful will through acts in your daily life. When washing up, for example, you might ask yourself what is the most skilful way to do this, to make it most efficient and with the least expenditure of unnecessary energy? Should you wash the greasy pans or the glasses first? The development of skill is accomplished not only through what you actually do but through the attitude you have to the act being performed. It's not what you do, it's how you do it. Part of this skill is being aware of how much energy you put into doing something. If you put in too little energy, it's like using a spoon to move a mountain; using too much energy, like taking a forklift truck to an egg! Later in this chapter we will discuss further the technique of using daily life to help us develop all aspects of the will.

Once we have developed our will, at least to some degree, we pass to the next stage of the will which in Psychosynthesis we call 'having a will'. When this stage or level is attained, it can be experienced consciously or unconsciously, but it happens, usually, through a gradual awakening. We start to become a 'director' in our life. When we have chosen to play a particular role, we hold both an awareness of the self or centre, and the role that we are playing. We switch between them as appropriate.

At this stage of the will, that is when we consciously realise we have a will, there is a distinct move towards integration. There is less fragmentation and more clarity of choice. We realise that we have a will and we can choose with it. We start to feel more connected to our 'purpose' for being alive on this planet at this time. From this place we truly take responsibility for our acts. Of course, we may not be responsible and conscious in this way all of the time, but the amount of time we spend in this state gradually starts to increase.

In Psychosynthesis we call the fourth and final stage of the evolution of the will in the individual 'being will'. When this stage is reached there is alignment with the transpersonal Self and the deepest, most spiritual aspects of will. We are connected with our innermost understanding. We can reach this level of consciousness through meditation, through silence, or simply through turning inwards and allowing this energy of the Self to permeate through us. Once we have reached this stage, even for a moment, it is inevitable that we will desire to express this deep and meaningful connection in the outside world. Indeed, it is the sign of true 'spiritual attainment' not when the person involved can sit for hours in a yoga posture, or perform 'miraculous' feats, but rather when this energy is expressed in the world in a way that brings healing and sustenance to his or her fellow beings.

SPIRITUAL PURPOSE

When we start using our will from a centred place, we find we are the source or cause of what happens in our life and are not just an effect or victim to circumstances. We discover there is a distinction between our 'true will' or Purpose, which can be defined as the will of the Self, and the energies, such as drives and self-centred desires, that come from subpersonalities. Of course, this is not to say that subpersonalities should not get what they want, their needs have to be met fully before they can truly be transformed. But their wishes are inevitably in conflict with the wishes of other subpersonalities. We experience no such conflicts with the 'true will' for this originates from the deepest, innermost core of our being.

We can only truly discover our true will or Purpose when we consciously and actively take steps towards its manifestation. That may seem obvious, but too often we forget this and, instead of following our path a step at a time, we try to leap ahead, not paying attention to what is happening in the present moment. The next step is always of utmost importance, and, in actuality, the only step we can make. Even physically if we try to take four steps at once we are more likely to fall over than succeed. This is even truer when we are talking about inner Purpose. We find it is easier to stay on our path if we pay attention to our immediate position, rather than worrying about something way ahead.

We may have little or no idea of what our true will or Purpose is, but if we reflect upon what Purpose means to us, and what we would like to manifest in our lives that has 'real meaning', we can start getting at least an inkling of it. You might like to try some reflective, receptive and creative meditation on 'Purpose'. Remember that Purpose always follows the rule of non-interference - it cannot be your real Purpose if it involves you interfering with or altering someone else's Purpose.

When we have connected to our Purpose - through meditation as suggested above, or through any of the other methods used in Psychosynthesis or other ways to self-realization, the next step is to decide how to manifest this Purpose. The techniques for grounding that we have already discussed can be most helpful in this, but the most important thing is to find your own individual ways of manifesting your Purpose. This is where it is often most helpful to have a good guide who will be able to not only help you connect with your Purpose but also help you to find ways to manifest it.

The Good Will

The will is not only active, not only involved with 'doing'. You could choose, for example, to just be, to pass some time 'doing nothing'. Indeed, one of the greatest distortions in our thinking about will power is to believe it has to be an effort or strenuous, or that it depletes or uses up energy in some way. On the contrary, when we make conscious, definite acts of will rather than ending up with less energy, we feel energized, more alive, more 'present' in the world.

We need to be flexible and be able to find a balance between active and passive acts of will. Both can require strong and skilful will. To say 'no' to something, for instance, might require a tremendous act of courage if friends are encouraging you to do it. Or to exhibit patience in waiting for something you madly desire can require great reserves of strong will. The more centred we become, the more able are we to make acts of will, either active or passive, strong or skilful, as the situation requires.

One result of moving towards our centre and making our acts of will more conscious and purposeful is that we find there is another aspect of the will, sometimes called 'the good will'. Acts of will that are made from the heart, that are filled with sympathy, love, understanding and warmth, are all manifestations of the good will. When we have good will towards someone, whether we act upon it or not, we are connected the energy of the will with the energy of love.

Psychosynthesis theory describes the good will as a synthesis of the archetypes or energies of love and will. An act of good will made towards someone is a dynamic and joy filled process that fosters understanding and co-operation. When we tune into the good will we recognize that whatever we do, it is part of the greater whole of human relations. The good will has also been described as 'love in action'. In terms of human relations, so long as we only do to others what we would have them do to us, we are tuning into the energy of the good will. The good will, however, is not just being soft and nice, it is dynamic and active.

Imagine what we would be like if we had no good will at all. We would not be able to actively express love, we would take actions that promoted our own interests at the expense of others, we might be suspicious and defensive, judgemental, prejudiced, indifferent to the suffering of others, isolated and so on. On the other hand, we could have too much good will. People would walk all over us, or we might be overly helpful to the point of interference, or we might never be able to say no. We would be so nice we would be really sickly.

With just the right amount of good will, however, we create a true balanced between both love and will, we are co-operative and helpful and exhibit all the qualities of 'right human relations'. At each and every moment, all of us have the choice as to whether we want to exhibit good will or not. As always we have three options - yes, no, or not for now. Right now we can choose which of these options we wish to take. If we choose to say 'yes' to the good will, there will naturally be times when we do not succeed. But whenever this happens, we can always choose to come back to it, centring ourselves again and becoming once more infused with the energy of good will.

THE WILL IN DAILY LIFE

In our daily lives we have lots of opportunities for developing all aspects of the will. Perhaps as a definite act of will we might rise in the morning a quarter of an hour earlier. If we have a special reason for doing this it is, of course, an act of will. But we can also choose to do it simply as a way of training our will, or of developing our power. Each time we utilize a situation from daily life in this way, we strengthen ourselves and become more able to then use our will when we really need it.

As mentioned earlier in this chapter, we might develop strong will through doing the washing up, and skilful will through doing it in an effective way. It might be an act of good will to do it for someone else. Whatever we do in this way to develop our will power we can do with an attitude of joy and interest. We will find then that we will accomplish not only these 'training' tasks but all the other tasks in our life with greater effectiveness and ease, without tension and exhaustion.

It is also worth remembering that everyone with whom we come into contact can help us in developing our will, even without their knowing it. If another driver cuts you up, or the traffic is heavy, for instance, it is an opportunity to develop patience and serenity. If your boss at work is always dominating and short with you, you can use his energy to help you develop your force and proficiency. We best succeed in these ways through our attitudes and awareness. We can see our life as a laboratory in which we can both experiment with and develop our will.

The best ways to develop the will through daily life

are those that we discover and invent for ourselves. This might include doing something we wouldn't normally do, or not doing something we normally do. We could, for example, do something today we were planning to leave until tomorrow, or leave until tomorrow something we believe to be urgent. Whatever we choose to do, it is important to do it simply because we want to do it. Then we will find our will power is increasing for once the energy of the will is in motion it generates more and more energy. If we don't try too hard, but let our desire to be successful flow from our true sense of self, then we succeed with clarity and ease.

Exercise: The Value Of The Will

Relax and centre yourself. Think of times in your life when you have missed an opportunity or caused pain to yourself or someone else through your lack of will. Picture these events as vividly as possible and allow the associated feelings to affect you.

Now write down a list of these times in your life with which you have just connected. Let yourself really desire to change yourself so that you have more will.

Reflect on all the opportunities and benefits there would be both for yourself and others if your will was strengthened. Think clearly what these advantages would be, then write them down. Allow the feelings aroused by these anticipated advantages to really affect you. Feel the joy that these opportunities could give you, the satisfaction you would feel if you were stronger willed. Let yourself really feel your desire to become stronger in this way.

Finally picture yourself as having a strong will. Imagine yourself acting in every situation with firm decisions, focused intention, and clear awareness. Visualize yourself walking, talking, sitting and simply being in a way that exhibits your mastery over the will. You are strong, yet subtle, firm yet kind, acting with skill and discrimination.

Realize you can use this technique to strengthen your will whenever you choose.

7

THE POWER OF IMAGINATION

Imagine the conditions of the world when the majority is concerned with the good of others and not with its own selfish goals. Realize the part that you can play in building this world. Visualize the spirit of goodwill as a ray of light reaching out from you ... to all people, problems, and situations that are your immediate concern. (Roberto Assagioli)

Imagination is our ability to form images or concepts of external objects that are not actually present to our senses, or are even nonexistent. We can imagine a unicorn, for example, yet it is unlikely many of us have actually seen one! Imagination is thus the basis of the creative faculties of the mind. Anything that is created, whether artistically, scientifically or in any other way, is initially conceived of in imagination. In Psychosynthesis, we use imagination to explore our unconscious, inner processes and to stimulate our personal, interpersonal and transpersonal growth. We also use imagination to express this inner learning and growth in our outer world in creative and life-enhancing ways.

Imagination offers us a symbolic connection to our unconscious, and can help us connect with all our unconscious processes. Once we make this connection, transformation is possible. Imagination can also help us to understand and express our inner wisdom in a stimulating way. Through using imagination to connect to our inner processes, we can bring underdeveloped parts of ourselves out into the open where they can gain independence. In fact, our imaginative faculties not only offer us a symbolic connection with our inner world, they can help us transform all our inner and outer relationships.

Although some images may be seen as universal, each one of us has our own world of imagery. To many of us today a white dove may symbolise peace, yet it may not only symbolise 'food' but actually be an item of food to someone. In the West we may wear black to a funeral, yet in other parts of the world white may be worn. This is not to deny the importance of universal symbolism, which can be rich and rewarding to connect with. But it is of utmost importance we find our own images and symbols inside and trust in our own inner processes. What something means to you has infinitely more meaning than any interpretation put on it by someone else. In Psychosynthesis we always encourage people to find their own imagery and find their own personal connection to symbols and myths.

When we start exploring the images that come up from our unconscious, it inevitably expands our awareness. There has to be a balance between this awareness and the will, however. The new images that emerge may expand our awareness about ourselves and our world, but we need the will to do something about this awareness. If we do not integrate our increasing awareness we run the risk of becoming 'image junkies', always on the look out for new images and symbols as if they were a drug feeding a false sense of 'self' which inflates and separates us from any true connection to the transpersonal. On the other hand, if we do not explore the realms of imagery and symbols, but try to rely on what we already know, see and feel, then we run the equally dangerous risk of becoming rigid and sterile.

There are many ways to use the imagination. For example, in imagination we can try things out in a symbolic way. Both real and imaginary situations that frighten us can be accessed and worked on before the actual situation (for example, an interview) happens. We can use our imagination to change our relationship with different aspects of ourselves. Indeed, the many different ways of using our imagination to help us grow are only limited by the powers of our imagination. Anything we can imagine could possibly happen - and we can imagine just about anything.

Another use of imagery is to relive past experiences (whether 'highs' or 'lows'.) If we allow ourselves to relive a traumatic experience, for example, and fully experience the feelings, emotions and sensations that accompany the images associated with the experience, there is a possibility of transformation. When an old pattern is removed we can 'make space' for a new pattern. If you relive, through imagery, your birth, for instance, and clear out some of the pain and difficulties associated with this experience, you could then use images and symbols to re-create a 'new birth' that is healthy and more life-enhancing. Such use of imagery, so long as it is genuinely accompanied by the associated experiences, can have a profound transformative effect on our personalities.

The power of the imagination is well known to advertisers, big business, politicians, and all those who would control or manipulate us in some way. If we see the same advertisement many times over and get bored with it and think the advertiser would do better to change it, then we are missing the point. Even if we consciously resist it, anything that is repeatedly presented to our senses has an effect. We may not think we bought a certain product as a result of advertising, yet in many cases we have done just that, albeit totally unconsciously. All images and symbols that we see or imagine tend to produce the physical conditions and external acts that correspond to them.

The fact that images repeated over and over sink into our unconscious, as it were, and affect us, can be used to our advantage. If we are affected by adverts in this way then we can choose to create our own adverts and respond to them. For instance, if you wanted to have more love in your life you might write a suitable affirmation on some cards - 'I am worthy of love' perhaps - and place them around your house where you will frequently see them. You won't have to consciously look at these messages for, just like other 'adverts', they will work on an unconscious level. Then, if you become more worthy of love, it is quite likely you will get more of it!

Through images, it is also possible to manifest positive qualities in your everyday life. If we used this power to contact, say, the quality of Joy and manifest more of it onto our planet it would be most positive. Symbols can help us discover and utilise our power, which can help us to choose what we want and reject what we do not want. In using our power in this way we need to use our discriminative faculties to ensure we only manifest what is 'for the highest good'. When we truly own our power, and align ourselves through our sense of self with our Purpose, as described in the last chapter, we find we naturally discriminate with an easy inner wisdom.

We can use our imagination to manifest our power in many different ways. We can start, for example, with a given image, like the meadow or the mountain found in many of the exercises used in Psychosynthesis. Sometimes we might just like to relax and let the images flow, trusting in the wisdom of our unconscious to bring up what is right for us at any given moment in time. Any way we choose to use images to aid our growth is effective if it comes naturally and is not forced. As our imagination is so rich we need never force anything, but we do have to learn to trust in ourselves.

Real joy can be found in moulding the contents of the unconscious, controlling our inner world in a positive way, not so that we have 'power over' anything or anyone, but so that we have 'power with' the true nature of our inner being. When we start finding our inner freedom, when we are no longer controlled by images and fantasies but are able to use them for our own advantage, in an unselfish way, we are becoming psychologically mature.

All kinds of images, positive and negative, are continuously emerging from our unconscious. We can react to them or we can act upon them. In other words, we can have them or let them have us. If we have them then we can do what we want with them. We can feed upon the positive images, letting them grow bigger and stronger, and we can disperse the negative ones, not letting them take us over. For instance, we can quite simply take a positive image that is emerging from our unconscious, and consciously choose to make it grow bigger and bigger, letting it overwhelm us and fill us with its positive energy. On the other hand, when a negative image emerges from our unconscious, see we can cause it to grow smaller and smaller until it disappears. We could even imagine it is totally consumed in the light of a burning, cleansing sun.

If we let ourselves go and trust in the emerging images from our unconscious, we can have a sense of being 'new born' in that we are more able to connect with the 'newness' of any situation without becoming identified or attached to what is happening.

THE ESSENCE OF SYMBOLS

Symbols have been called the 'language of the unconscious', and when we start communicating with our inner world, we do so through symbols. To be truly understood and integrated, however, symbols cannot just be understood on an intellectual level but must also arouse feelings and sensations. Neither can they be understood or interpreted out of context. A plane dropping bombs and a plane delivering needed supplies not only involve different concepts of 'plane' (although the same plane can do both jobs,) but also arouse totally different feelings. To truly understand a symbol we have to get behind the outer form, which can veil and hide the inner meaning, and tune into the inner truth, the essence of the symbol.

In Psychosynthesis, we are not so concerned with cold, rational analysis of symbols but rather choose to approach the essential inner form. Some of the ways of achieving this include:

• simply considering the outermost form of the symbol, seeing what it shows you on its surface without any analysis or interpretation at all. It is often surprising and illuminating to discover that the symbols that emerge spontaneously from our unconscious often tell us so much just in themselves, without us needing to interpret or judge them in any way.

• allowing the feelings and emotions that the symbol brings up to be fully experienced. Again we can do this most effectively when we suspend judgement and interpretation. Feelings are truly about values, so when we allow ourselves to 'feel' a symbol we discover its true value.

• using our intellectual skills to discover what a symbol teaches us, penetrating into the deepest meaning of the symbol. Without having to rationally analyse a symbol we can use our thinking function to bring our knowledge into play and interpret the symbol in a clear and non-judgemental way.

• letting the symbol's inner or deeper meaning intuitively emerge. Behind any of the sensations, feelings and thoughts we may have about any symbol is its more abstract, 'bigger' meaning, an understanding that goes beyond our individual concepts about it. We cannot learn to be intuitive; we can only 'let it happen'. When it does we are then tuning into levels where we are more deeply in tune with the Purpose of our soul.

• identifying with the symbol, to discover the quality and purpose of a symbol. The form in which a symbol manifests may obscure its deepest meaning or it may not, but in either case, through identifying ourselves with the symbol we can start to connect with its deepest essence. To do this effectively we have to be centred and relaxed, and not attached to any of the thoughts, feelings or even intuitions we may already have about it. For example, you could do the Self Identification exercise and then consciously imagine you are the symbol under investigation. What then do you think, feel and sense?

We can change both our inner fantasy world and the outer 'reality' on an individual and collective level. The symbols we need to work with never have to be suggested from outside, as our unconscious will invariably send us the right messages. When we can trust these messages from our inner world, we find they are transformative both to us as individuals and, through us, to our world as a whole. We can re-own symbols so they are part of the life-enhancing process of growth and evolution rather than leave them in the hands of those who would use them to control and manipulate others for their own selfish ends.

Dreaming

Because dreaming does not 'actually happen' in the outer world but, by its very nature, only happens in imagination, we can see that it plays an important part in how our unconscious speaks to us. As with all the work we do with symbols in Psychosynthesis, although there are times when we need to analyse the symbolic content of our dreams, we often find we learn best what they are trying to tell us about ourselves if we use other, less directly analytical methods.

We can take any item from a dream, whether a person or an inanimate object or whatever, and have a conversation with this item, letting it speak and give us useful information. Try remembering a recent dream right now and, taking any item from the dream, speak to it and then see what it has to say back to you. Another way of working with dreams is to consciously continue the dream's contents. This is particularly useful if a dream feels incomplete in any way. We can allow ourselves to imagine what happens next, letting the 'story' of the dream unfold until it comes to a positive, life-enhancing conclusion.

It is sometimes useful to draw or paint images from dreams. Doing this, we often receive deep insights into the meaning of our dreams without imposing any kind of intellectual interpretation. For instance, we might start to recognise recurring themes in our dreams, which may help us to see things that we are attached to or which we need to work with further in some way.

When we 'awake', as it were, within a dream and become aware that we are dreaming whilst still in the dream is called lucid dreaming. Within lucid dreams, unlike their more usual counterparts, we can make deliberate acts. Perhaps the simplest method to induce lucid dreaming is if we tell ourselves, as we drop off to sleep, that we are able to have lucid dreams! This affirmation is then planted in our unconscious and helps create the conditions for lucid dreams. We cannot expect it to happen every time, however, and we may need to continuously repeat the formula for many weeks or months before success is achieved.

Whether we have any lucid dreams or not, it is always useful to watch dreams, looking particularly for patterns in the events of dreams that help us understand our relationship to our unconscious. Keeping a dream journal in which we record our dreams upon awakening also increases our perception. When we realize that we spend a third of our life in sleep, it becomes almost second nature to accept that the events we remember from dreams are worthy of our attention. Dreams are messages from our unconscious realms. Most dreams, it is generally believed, are simply re-plays of 'stuff' from our lower unconscious, based on past incidents and events which our consciousness is trying to understand or restructure in some way. Working on these dreams can be a potent way to work with our lower unconscious, therefore. Occasionally we have dreams whose origin appears to be the superconscious. These dreams often have a particularly luminous quality to them, and we feel subjectively different about them. When we get such dreams, which can include prophetic visions and deep spiritual insights, it is not so much a matter of working with them, but rather of holding their vision and allowing ourselves to see it unfold in a natural, organic way.

EXERCISE: THE HOUSE OF THE SELF

When we use any kind of imagery, we are making a connection between the conscious and the unconscious. To make such a connection real in our everyday lives it is important to connect all these images with our body. We can also use our bodies as a source of symbols and images. How does your body feel at this moment? We can use the body as a starting place or source of images, and then use these images creatively in our personal growth. In the following exercise, we will use our imagination to see our inner world in a concrete form. So long as we keep it on this level, however, it will not be as real as if we find ways to ground our insights and understanding through our bodies and out into the world.

Make yourself comfortable, relax and centre. Imagine you are a house. See yourself as a house. What kind of house are you - a cottage, a terraced house, a grand mansion or what? Take some time to imagine what sort of house you are in as much detail as possible.

Picture this house in front of you and imagine you enter through the front door. This is no problem, for it is your house. You can explore the rest of the house some other time, but for now we will visit the basement or cellar.

Find the way down to the basement, and consider what it is like. Go into as much detail as you can, from assessing the condition of the foundations, the walls of the basement, the damp level, what junk might be stored there, and so on. Assess whatever comes up so you get a good, clear picture of the full state of your basement. Really be as honest as if you were a surveyor checking the house for possible purchase.

Now recall it is your house and choose to do with it whatever you like. Change the basement in any way that seems suitable to you. Perhaps you need to reinforce the walls, or dry it out, or paint it, or throw away junk - take some time to make your basement into the sort of basement you would most like to have. The power of your imagination will even allow you to add or remove rooms, completely change the shape or style of the basement, make of it what you will.

If you think about the Psychosynthesis egg diagram and relate this to the house you have just imagined, it is quite easy to see how by exploring the basement in this way you have been exploring some aspects of your lower unconscious. At other times you can explore other parts of the 'house' (including 'going upstairs') to examine your superconscious. Remember, however, that whatever you may find upstairs or downstairs, it is most useful when you bring it into your every day life, the 'living room' of your house, and use it in a way that assists your growth and development. What did you discover in your basement that it would be useful for you to bring up to the living room and utilize in some way?

8

ACCEPTANCE AND CHANGE

In accepting pleasure without craving for it and attachment to it, and in accepting pain, when unavoidable, without fearing it and rebelling against it, one can learn much from both pleasure and pain, and 'distil the essence' which they contain. (Roberto Assagioli)

If we become attached to change and try to make things in our lives change before they are ready, we are fighting a loosing battle. Similarly, if we become attached to things staying the same and resist all changes in our lives, the battle is similarly hard and ultimately pointless. On the other hand, if we learn to accept what is happening without being identified either with things changing or staying the same, this creates the space in our lives for things to either change or not as appropriate.

Two primary, archetypal energies in life are 'change' and 'maintenance'. Both are equally necessary, and both form part of a dynamic polarity of energy with which we can either co-operate or not. When we accept either, then these energies can manifest in a relatively undistorted way. Change can then be seen in terms of progress, evolution, transformation, and freedom. Maintenance, in this clear form, manifests as timelessness, rhythm, patience and a sense of eternity.

When we fight either change or maintenance and do not accept things as they are, then these energies start manifesting in a more distorted way. Then change can be purposeless, lead to the dissipation of our energy, make us insensible to either our needs or the needs of others, be destructive and leave us without proper and clear boundaries. Maintenance, once distorted, leads to inertia and laziness, closed-mindedness, rigidity, cowardice and fear of the unknown, and a strangulation of the flow of life energy.

It cannot be over-emphasized that there is a need for both change and maintenance in our lives. When we talk about acceptance of what is, and allowing both of these polarities to manifest in our lives, this does not mean we have to blindly accept some predestined fate, or make ourselves victims to circumstances. On the contrary, when we learn the value of true inner acceptance, this frees up our energy so that we can either change or not as is best for us in any particular set of circumstances. Of course it is not always so easy, but it is for us to balance ourselves in a way that excludes neither change nor maintenance, but includes the best of both.

Everything changes all the time. This is a basic truth of life and it has been said that the only thing we can be absolutely sure of in life is just this, that everything changes. If we could accept this 'truth', then we would not become so fearful when events in our lives do not appear to be changing fast enough - or appear to be changing too fast. We would be able to see that, as everything changes, these things too - whatever 'these things' are - will pass away. We might feel trapped in a relationship that no longer serves us - but everything changes. We might feel alone because we cannot find a good relationship - but everything changes. We would be able to tune into the natural flow of life and accept what is. Then we would be able to act from this place and let things come, let things be and, when appropriate, let things go.

This is all very well but, in reality, for most of us most of the time we become attached or identified with our desire for certain things to change and certain things to stay the same. You have a good relationship - well, of course you don't want it to change, but if you hold onto it and don't let it grow and change in its natural fashion then it will become rigidified. Then it will not be the same relationship anyway, and the chances are it will change, perhaps now in a way you wouldn't want. Or maybe you are not in a relationship and you want things to change so badly you become attached beyond anything else to the idea of having a partner. You yearn for it and, at every opportunity, you make allegiances and try so hard to make it work. Often people doing this find that they are trying so hard it just doesn't happen, or if it does, the relationship doesn't last. Once more the attachment has led you astray, and life isn't 'working' again!

Once we let go of our attachment to anything changing or to anything staying the same, however, we start to see it for what it really is. Once we have this new vision of how something is, then we can choose to change it or not from this clearer perspective. But this true acceptance has to be really felt, really lived, it cannot just be an intellectual position. Then, once acceptance is experienced in this way, transformation can take place. It has been said that acceptance always precedes change or transformation. This has to include the acceptance that it may be right for something to change or not. True acceptance includes acceptance of things that change and of things that stay the same.

When we accept things in this dynamic way, not simply resigning ourselves to the circumstances but actively and consciously realising we are choosing them, we are more able to understand their inner meaning for us. When we accept something in this way we see it for what it is more clearly. We then have the choice of either letting it happen or fighting it in a more effective way.

We cannot ever totally get rid of unwanted experiences in our life so we may as well learn to accept them. Indeed, it is many people's experience that if they fight against unwanted experiences the situation just becomes worse. On the other hand, if we accept what is, if we accept that life does include pain and failure, unpleasant experiences and times when we have to do things we would rather not do, we take control of the energy and can use it for us rather than against us. For example, if you accept a depression you are more able to effectively deal with it than if you do not accept it and try to shrug it off.

We cannot always change the outer conditions but we can always work on the inner conditions. It may seem paradoxical if we simply think about it, but once we act upon it we find that the one way we always have available to us of causing change is through an act of acceptance. When we accept what is, we are open to learn. Understood this way, acceptance is one of the most major tools for transformation.

If we think of a recent experience that we really enjoyed and recall all the features of this experience, the pleasure associated with this good experience, whatever it was, will come up into our consciousness. It is possible to re-live pleasurable experiences, to feel them inside as if they are still happening. This is a healthy act, something that can give us pleasure and make us feel good. Problems arise, however, once we become so attached to it that it is all we want and we devote all our energies to making it happen again.

On the other hand, if we recall a recent 'bad' experience, something we did not feel good about at the time, and spend some time recalling all the sensing, feeling and thinking associated with this experience, we can also feel this experience as if it is still happening. This, too, is a healthy act because, although we might not want to remember unpleasant or upsetting times in our lives, if we allow ourselves the space to do so it can help us deal with the associated issues.

Both apparently 'good' and apparently 'bad' experiences in our lives can be viewed as having value. Indeed, it is often the learning we get from the supposedly 'unwanted' experiences that helps us to grow the most and become able to express who we really are and what we actually want in life. To really delve into the depths of our past and bring to the surface traumatic or upsetting experiences is work best done in the presence of a good therapist or guide. But as we learn to accept the value of both types of experience, we become more complete in ourselves, and more able to face the future whatever it brings us.

THE POWER TO ACCEPT AND CHANGE

We can use the power of our will and our imagination to make things change, or to accept things as they are. To do either we have to have the will to make it happen, whether actively causing change or passively letting things unfold. We also need imagination so that we can create the new worlds into which we wish to move, or change the old patterns from our past. We have learnt about using both these powers in previous chapters of this book. They are sometimes described as the powers that give us the ability to cause change to occur in the way we want it to. They are also the powers that help us to accept times when it is right for things not to change, too.

The other powers we require to make this work effectively are the powers of love and awareness. Without awareness how could we know whether our choice is 'right' or not? And without love how could we be sure we were making the 'right' choice in accordance with the needs and energies of other people? These four energies - love, awareness, will and imagination - are those we use throughout our lives to aid us in taking the actions we want and that are in accord with the evolution of consciousness on the planet.

These energies become particularly important to us

when we are at a time of pain, crisis or failure in our lives. Experiencing such times is often what lead us to find help from a Psychosynthesis guide or from some other kind of therapist or counsellor. In Psychosynthesis we do not attempt to 'patch up' the pain, divert the crisis or ignore the failure. On the contrary, we realise the value in such experiences. It is often through accepting pain, in all its guises, that we come to realise more about ourselves and unleash creative energies.

We all have the experience of failure at some time or another in our lives. Many people experience failure so often that they start to see themselves as 'a failure'. Then it is as if failure has got them rather than them having it. No longer does a person in this state say, 'I have a situation in my life where I have failed,' but the experience takes hold and they say something more akin to, 'I am a failure'.

When we experience failure it can cause us to cut off from our potential energy. For example, we may be angry, bitter or disappointed. It is fine to feel these things, but it is also important, when we are ready, to move on, to allow the creative potential to flow once more. We can take the initial stage towards achieving this through simply accepting the initial failure and the resultant emotional turmoil. We may try then various psychosynthetic techniques to help us.

One of the most powerful techniques for doing this is called 'blessing the obstacle'. In order to accept the failure, we make a conscious act of blessing whatever has stopped us from succeeding. Once we have done this, not just through paying 'lip service' to the concept but through actually taking on this attitude as completely as possible, we are ready to move on.

When we consider what we have learned from the apparent 'failure', then the idea of 'blessing the obstacle' is not such a strange concept. For instance, the failure will have given us the opportunity to do whatever it was we 'failed at' again, only better this time. If it were some act that could never happen again, then through blessing the obstacle we can come to the realisation that it obviously was not meant to happen. In doing this we are not subordinating ourselves to some impersonal fate, but rather we are making an act of conscious control and decision-making.

Everything we do in our lives, whether we are conscious of it this way or not, we decide. Even if that is not an actual 'truth' there is nothing to stop us believing it is true. If we choose everything in our lives, then if it doesn't happen, we must have decided upon that, too. This can be hard to grasp and accept in our everyday consciousness, as our personalities have not been conscious of the process and certain subpersonalities may even want to hold onto the pain or failure. But in Psychosynthesis we always believe that at the level of the self or soul we decide upon everything that happens to us in life. From this perspective life takes on more meaning and we can tune into our deeper sense of purpose more effectively. Of course, as you have already learned in this book, one of the most effective ways to achieve this 'healthy disattachment' is through the self-identification exercise.

If we can learn to surrender to pain and failure, rather than sinking deeper into it and become overwhelmed with the experience, what we find is that it brings us through it quicker. But the first stage has to be so surrender to the experience, to let it happen completely. This is easier said than done, of course, but once we achieve this we can consciously choose to move on. Then, instead of being a victim to pain or failure we always have the ability to ask ourselves: what use is this to me? What can I learn from it?

The crises we experience in life, although we may not see it so clearly when we are in a crisis, actually put us up against our growing edge. Crises usually happen when we have an old pattern of behaviour or belief that no longer truly serves us and it would be better for us to let go of. It is usually some kind of fear that stops us doing this naturally. Then the energy builds up until, if we are still resisting the change, we enter a crisis. It is as if the crisis, or at least its energy, originates in the superconscious and then 'knocks at the door', as it were, of the personality. We can either open the door or resist, and the longer we resist, the stronger the energy becomes until finally, if it is necessary, the energy will burst the door open anyway and we will enter into a life crisis.

Any new energy that is trying to emerge into our awareness has to be first accepted, then grounded and expressed. We often hold back from this out of fear. We may not exactly like things how they currently are but we'd rather face the devil we know than risk unleashing the unknown. We create blocks to the expression of our new, emerging energies, blocks that are often no more than simply fear of change. So the energy of crisis is really our survival energy that has been energized as a resistance to the new experience. It is only when we get far enough into it that we realise our survival truly requires us to change. Then we are able to accept the new situation and move on.

The most important aspect of this work is often not what is happening but our reaction to it - so turn and face it, whatever it is. At the same time disidentify from the situation to gain a better perspective and a sense of right proportion. See both successes and failures for what they are - events in the unfoldment of who you are. Gain a sense of perspective and proportion when you consider either, and always ask yourself: what choices can I make? How can I improve this in terms of my unfolding creative potential?

THE TRANSFORMATION OF ENERGY

If we do not accept pain, failure and crisis in our lives we often find energy building up in us that then may start to discharge itself in inappropriate ways. We may become overly aggressive, for example, and explode at little things, totally out of all proportion to what is actually happening. Or we may project our aggression, fear and pain onto other people, particularly members of our family, friends or work colleagues.

We all have the tendency in such situations to project onto other people our attitudes, impulses, and feelings. If we feel hostile towards someone, for instance, it is easy to project this hostility onto them and believe it is them who are being aggressive, not ourselves. We then in turn become defensive and threatened and a vicious circle is set up. If we perceive this happening we must take action to 're-own the projection.'

We have to accept the basic truth of life that everything depends upon our attitude. If we are feeling hostile to someone, or we perceive (correctly or incorrectly) they are hostile to us, the only way we have to change this situation is through changing ourselves. We have to realise we have free will and can make the decision to be ourselves without making demands upon others or without projecting our 'stuff' onto them. We are then free to relate to them from a more centred position. When we do this we often find the situation transforms and the conflict is resolved.

It is often surprising to find how effective this can be. We may, for example, quite simply share how we are feeling with the other people involved. If we are honest and let ourselves speak freely about our fears, our feelings, and our thoughts on whatever the conflict or issue is, we find the energy transforms. Suddenly we are friends again, sharing in the common plight of all humans, of being alone in essence and yet connected to everyone and everything at the same time. Such moments of true spiritual realisation, which can emerge out of the simplest act such as speaking up about our feelings, are truly transforming and enriching to our lives.

The important point in all this is that we get to discharge the energies involved. It is the same if we feel true physical aggression. We do not have to go round to that person's house, for example, and get into a physical fight. The unconscious will accept a symbolic gratification of the desire and we can quite simply beat hell out of a cushion. The satisfaction from doing this, coupled with the actual, physical discharge of energy, will clear our consciousness and we will be able to move forward with clearer choices and more awareness.

Exercise: Blessing The Obstacle

Choose to sit somewhere where you are relaxed but not so relaxed you will fall asleep. Take a few deep breaths and centre yourself in whatever way you choose.

Remember a recent time where you experienced pain or failure in your life. Really consider this time in depth, allowing yourself to recall and experience all the associated thoughts, feelings and sensations. Let yourself really experience the pain associated with the experience.

Now imagine you step out of this experience so you can see its elements laid out before you. Say out loud: 'I bless this <whatever it was you experienced as pain or failure>.'

Continue to look at the components of this experience as if you are a detached observer of the pain, failure or whatever it is. Make the blessing statement out loud a couple more times, and now as you do this see and feel the memory of the experience change. Let it become lighter and less attached to you.

Be aware of what you have learned from the situation, and then consciously choose to move on.

9

BODY AND SELF

The body and psyche can be transmuted by means of a regenerative transformation. This produces an organic and harmonious unification ... a bio-Psychosynthesis. (Roberto Assagioli)

One of the major and most valid criticisms of Psychosynthesis in the past has been its exclusion of the physical body as anything more than a vehicle for imagery and grounding. Assagioli said that Psychosynthesis must include the body, however, and even stressed that it should really be called Bio-Psychosynthesis. Many modern Psychosynthesis practitioners with a more holistic vision are now including varied body techniques into their practice. These include the more 'traditional' psychosynthetic use of the body as a source of images with which symbolic release may be achieved. They also include more direct, body-related techniques, including ones borrowed from bioenergetics, integrative body psychotherapy and other body-orientated methods of growth and development. It is also possible to use dance, massage, internal martial arts such as t'ai chi and other quite distinct methods of body awareness in a Psychosynthesis context. Some of the most imaginative guides, as with all areas of Psychosynthesis therapy, are constantly devising ways of integrating body work directly relating to the needs of their individual clients.

It has been argued that the Self Identification exercise which says 'I have a body, but I am not my body' involves a denial of the body. This is not the case, however, as it is used in a context where the feelings and thoughts are treated in the same fashion not to deny them but so that the individual can have a direct experience of disattached awareness. In fact, it is always stressed by good Psychosynthesis guides how important it is to re-identify with the thoughts, feelings and body. Although people who tend to be a bit 'up in the clouds' and out of their bodies are often attracted to it, this position is most definitely not encouraged in Psychosynthesis. In the Self Identification exercise it clearly includes the body when it says: ' My body is my precious instrument of experience and action in the outer world ... I treat it well, I seek to keep it in good health, but it is not myself.' Indeed, we cannot truly dis-identify from something unless we truly have it first. In other words, it is actually the case that unless we have our bodies (as well as our feelings and thoughts), we cannot truly dis-identify from them, therefore cannot truly achieve a personal Psychosynthesis.

People sometimes neglect and deny their bodies a proper place as 'the temple of incarnation.' It is only through having a body that we can be here in the world, being and doing whatever it is we choose to be and do. But this neglect is a symptom of modern life generally, and not just Psychosynthesis. The general trend in our Western societies is to eat convenience foods and unbalanced diets rather than listen to our real body needs. We are often more concerned about the outer appearance of our bodies and current fashions rather than the real health of our bodies. Exercise, if taken, is a fashionable fad rather than an essential part of healthy living.

We not only neglect the body, we often have distorted awareness about it. We become conditioned in childhood to associate shame and guilt with our bodies and various of our bodily functions. How often are children labelled 'dirty' for simply discovering an interest in their natural bodily instincts and functions? How often are children given conscious or unconscious messages of denial when they discover their natural sexuality? How often are we all denied access to the pleasures of the world of sensation? Yet it is so patently true that if we reject our bodies or have distorted beliefs about our bodily sensations and functions, we will not be able to either fully disidentify from or identify with our bodies.

When we are children we depend upon our parents for our basic physical survival. We know our parents tried to do their best to love and protect us, but this does not deny the truth that they also hurt us physically and emotionally. We found ways to protect ourselves from this hurt. One of the chief ways we discovered for doing this was through building for ourselves a physical 'body armour'. This could not only protect us from physical hurt but also emotional and mental pain too, inflicted not only by our parents but by other people as well. We needed this armour to protect us but unfortunately we still wear it as adults. We are so encased and entrapped within it we can only lift it off a bit at a time, and then with great effort.

Psychosynthesis can teach us that we do not have to be attached to these defense mechanisms, this armour, for we are no longer children. As conscious adults we can choose to sense, feel and think without fear of denial or disapproval. Or if we get these reactions from other people we can accept their position without letting it overcome us and make us feel vulnerable. If we want to have a certain feeling, whether it makes us happy or sad, then we can have it without fear or guilt. So long as we do not harm anyone else with our actions, then we are truly free from these restrictions.

We can perform everyday physical acts, such as cleaning the house or doing the cooking, with the new awareness if we are more able to be in our bodies. Psychosynthesis won't actually help us cook a meal, say, in the actual physical sense. But holding the vision of Psychosynthesis and making our physical actions, whatever they are, from the consciousness of this vision, can help us cook, clean, make love, dance, be strong or be weak as is right for any given situation. We can use Psychosynthesis techniques not to sidestep physical reality or disattach from it, but to really be present in it by choosing to identify with it clearly and consciously. This is perhaps the clearest spiritual statement anyone can make. The spirit in Psychosynthesis is seen as both transcendent and immanent. On the transcendent side we may like to sit and meditate and so on, but to 'do Psychosynthesis' in everyday life we have to bring a sense of the immanent self into our lives. Then everything we do can be illuminated by consciousness.

The essential Psychosynthesis view is that we are incarnations of the Self. Our energy is embodied and made individual in that we are here in our bodies. We cannot deny the body without denying our very existence as 'little sparks of the spiritual Self'. We can only do this by including not denying the physical body with all its sensations.

EMOTIONAL ACCESS

We access our emotions through our bodies and every emotional experience is truly a body experience, not an intellectual one. There is a constant interaction between our bodies and our emotions. Try to image experiencing fear or anger without the body. How could adrenalin give us the energy to flee or fight without the body to do it with? Or try to imagine loving without a body. How could we truly express love without arms to hold someone?

For one reason or another, most of us have an excess of emotional energy held within our bodies. This can be released through cathartic techniques, many of which are used in Psychosynthesis. When we discharge emotional energy through catharsis, however, it is important to remember we do not do this just for the sake of it, but rather we do it as part of the overall process of personal development. The basis of catharsis is simple. We live again, as realistically as we possibly can, events or situations from our past that created emotional disturbances within us. If we really re-live these experiences to the fullest degree, we can now discharge the emotions that perhaps we could not discharge at the time. This way we release some of the emotional holding in our bodies and 'dissolve' as it were some of our bodily armour. We can repeat the catharsis for any experience until it no longer holds an emotional charge and thus free ourselves from the imprisonment of this past episode.

If we just effect catharsis, however, without dealing with the causes behind the original trauma, then as with all 'dis-ease', the symptoms will return. We have to get to the root cause behind the problem, and this is where other Psychosynthesis techniques, including visualization, can be very effective. In fact in re-living the original experience we are using the imagination to re-create the visual, auditory and kinetic aspects of that time. It is clear, therefore, in this context, that it does not really matter whether what is remembered actually happened or not, just that the person re-living it believes this is what happened. For a full and effective cathartic release, the client must have a clear contact with the guide. This does not mean there has to be actual physical contact, but for the sense of well-being that comes after catharsis to last, the guide must be fully present physically, emotionally and mentally for the client.

When we deny our natural emotional need for experience and expression, and whenever we deny our natural instinctual impulses, we develop anxiety and neurosis. This is particularly true for repressed sexual energy, emotional or physical. If we repress this energy then we loose touch with our sensitivity. Whilst this may mean we feel less pain when we are hurt, it also means we feel less pleasure when we are pleased. When we are repressed we experience tension and muscular contraction. Our bodies in this state can shrink, contract, and become fixed and rigidified. For Psychosynthesis to be effective, we have to treat these conditions not only on the symbolic level of imagery, but also directly on the physical level. If we release repressed emotions and sensations directly through the body, we free up a lot of energy. This allows us to be more alive, more real, more centered and connected on a transpersonal as well as a personal level. Indeed, it is with this free flowing energy that we can truly experience the fullest, most manifest sense of the Self.

Through having a direct body experience, we can more readily access and, if we wish, change our emotional life, but it is true that we can only release the quantity of energy that we have built up in the first place. When the charge is high enough to get us deeply into the release of the energy, we may have a peak experience where we enter spiritual or 'transpersonal' realms. When this happens, we are contacting the Self through our bodies, and realising who we really are.

BEING HERE

When we try to really incarnate into our physical bodies and express ourselves in the physical world, there are subpersonalities within us who do not want us to really be present in this way. Some subpersonalities appear to be actually in a state of not wanting to be incarnated, not wanting to be here on the planet. They take the line that it is difficult being alive, and it is far easier - and safer - to stay in a state of undifferentiated bliss. When we hear a voice within us say things like 'why do I have to be here?', 'I'd rather kill myself' or 'I want my mummy' we can be fairly sure it is a part of us that fears coming into the world fully. Subpersonalities with such fears of incarnating can hold us back from being fully present and expressing our true purpose.

It is important that we consider all the ways that we avoid incarnating fully. We have to watch for 'yes but...' responses to things we could do which would manifest our purpose more clearly. We have to look for those times when we never quite made up our minds, when we avoid making decisions that would help us grow and develop and express ourselves in the world more clearly and more fully.

When we are in such states, one of the best ways to move forward and release some of the held back energy is through expressing ourselves directly through our bodies. This might be through finding some underlying emotional blockage and expressing it in anger or sorrow, for instance. But often all we need to do is simply move - walk, dance, jump, run, it does not really matter - and the actual physical movement will bring us more clarity and help us make the decisions or take the actions we need.

Through physical work and the release of energy blockages in the body, we may express true transpersonal consciousness, a sense of the Self. It has been said that a new born baby is whole, complete in itself, and free from all restriction and fear. We can re-live and truly feel in our bodies all that we knew and felt as babies. This can include the free flow of energy, a sense of connection to the Self and to the oneness of all life. Our bodies may be armoured, but when we start to release this armour, we find our bodies also carry all the knowledge and understanding we have of the transpersonal or spiritual realms. Our internal truths can be remembered, lived and re-lived through our bodies. We can appreciate this when, for example, we see a dancer who is no longer dancing but has become the dance. We can appreciate this most when we are the dancer ourselves.

If we believe there is a part of us that continues beyond our physical life, how much better to directly experience this in the body than just have it as a mental construct. Bodywork in Psychosynthesis gives us the opportunity to master, channel and ground spiritual energies in our lives so we can truly live our purpose for incarnating.

It is a basic mystical truth that there is nowhere to seek the Self except inside oneself. The true esoteric traditions stress this is a physical truth, not a metaphysical conception. Inside our bodies we can find the Self. Outside of ourselves we can only find otherness not the Self, illusion not reality, glamour not truth. And when we find ourselves inside, we tap into an endless source of creative energy which we can express easily and healthily through not only our bodies, but also our emotions, feelings and thoughts.

Another basic mystical truth is that the only time that

exists is the present moment, everything is 'here and now'. After all, how can we be anywhere else but 'here' when if we move somewhere else, and someone asks us where we are, we answer that we are 'here'? And how can there be any other time than 'now' when at any and every moment the only time we can actually experience is this 'now'? We can remember yesterday or imagine tomorrow but can only experience this memory or fantasy in the present moment.

However we conceive of this 'here and now' experience, and whatever concepts we create around it, we can only really experience it in our bodies. When it is directly experienced it becomes a living expression of spiritual truth. To the person having such a transpersonal experience, time physically stops and space physically becomes alive and glowing with energy. Thus the true mystical experience is not something we think or feel, but something we live as a physical reality.

ENERGY CENTRES

Along with all the Eastern and Western methods for growth and development that include an understanding of the transpersonal, Psychosynthesis utilizes knowledge of the more subtle levels of energy in the body than just the physical ones. No one could deny the physical energy we have in our bodies, but once we start looking into ourselves we find there are other levels of energy within us, too. These 'subtle energies' have to be included in our work if we wish to achieve the fullest understanding of ourselves.

Of particular importance with this work is making a connection within our physical bodies to the energies that either help us ground or hinder us from doing so. Many people who are drawn to spiritual work do not easily connect with their ground of being and can easily spend too much time with their 'head in the clouds'. A strong stable base is needed if we are going to start using the more subtle energies within our bodies. Psychosynthesis, in working with the body as well as in all its other techniques and methods, stresses the importance of clear, firm grounding.

Inside our bodies we have seven major energy centers or 'chakras'. Each chakra is a power centre within the body, involved with the experience and expression of energy particular to its individual function. Chakras are all also interconnected and we really only describe them separately to help our understanding of them. Each chakra within our body may be either closed or open, and when it is open it gives us powers of perception and creativity. These seven major body chakras are located at the base of the spine, the genitals, solar plexus, heart, throat, middle of the head (or 'third eye'), and at the top of the head.

Imagine what would happen if you were driving a car fairly fast when suddenly a large lorry pulls out in front of you. Most of us will feel a pain, a strong sensation of some kind in our belly or solar plexus area. This is the contraction of the chakra located at that point. The belly chakra has many functions, as have all the chakras. For instance, we can consciously radiate energy out from our solar plexus and belly. If we view someone as a 'bad' person in some way, for us they will be just that. On the other hand, if we radiate energy as light from our solar plexus, and start to see that same person in a positive way, then they are 'free' from the box we had previously put them in and are able to move on and change. We are also free too, for when we put someone in a box we restrict ourselves as much as we restrict them.

Imagine the sensation you sometimes have in your heart when someone you love is unhappy or sad. They might be said to 'pull at your heart strings'. This would be an experience of the heart chakra, which is connected with the experience and expression of love. On a deeper level, however, it is also involved with the interaction between the energies of love and will and for it to operate most effectively these energies have to be balanced. The heart is also associated with 'deeper' feelings and values such as service to others and altruistic feelings. Humanity as a whole is said to moving in the current age towards a new connection and awakening of the heart values.

One aspect of chakra energy we particularly like to look at in Psychosynthesis is the dynamic between the three lowest chakras, the base of spine, sexual and solar plexus centres. Males often make a strong connection between the base of spine and sexual chakras, connecting power with sexuality. Women, on the other hand, tend to connect the base of spine centre more strongly with the solar plexus. Whether, in both cases, this is because of conditioning or is genetic is not certain. It leads to confusion, however, when these centres are not properly functioning, and the energy required for the proper functioning of these three grounding energy centres is distorted. Because of these connections, there is a tendency for men to express their power imbalances through their sexuality, whereas women tend to do so through their emotions. If we can distinguish between these energies and 'tease them apart' as it were, then they can be given the space to function properly on their own level. The interaction between them can then lead to a release of energy that helps clarify rather than cloud our personal issues regarding being here in the world, sexuality and power.

The upper and lower chakras connect to each other and they all revolve around the heart, at the centre of the system. The heart, on this energy level, is equivalent to the personal self or 'I'. When our energies centre on the self through the heart in this way, there is connection between our different levels and the possibility that we can express ourselves on any level we wish in a clearly harmonious way. The personality revolves around our central core identity, and the soul is clearly heard, seen and felt in our lives. This is one of the major aims of Psychosynthesis.

EXERCISE: A BODY OF SENSATION

Take a few deep breaths and start to become aware of any sensations you currently have in your body. Let your awareness focus on your body. Does it feel hot or cold? Are you heavy or light today? Where do you sense tensions and pain? Where do you feel loose and relaxed? Focus as clearly as you can on the sensations in your body. Use as many of your senses to do this - can you hear your breath or your heartbeat? What do you see inside your body today? Do you feel there is too much or to little energy in any parts of your body?

As you become aware of each sensation that becomes foreground for you, bring your full attention to this sensation. Without becoming attached to it, look at what it is saying to you. Do you need to stretch or to move your body in some way? Observe all these sensations carefully, and honour their 'messages'. What do you need to do in your life to improve your relationship with your body?

Now expand your awareness to include all of your body. Become aware of your entire body and whether it is feeling cold or warm, tingling, alive or dull, in pain or pleasure. Allow yourself to feel your body. If you feel pain or tightness imagine, as you exhale, that you are breathing out through that part of the body and the tension or pain leaves with the breath. If you feel numb or 'dead' in any area, imagine you bring living energy into that area of your body as you inhale. If you feel generally tight and unaware, then let your in-breath bring you energy. If you feel over-excited or agitated, then allow excess energies to flow out through the palms of your hands with your out breath. Use your imagination to move energy around your body and 'heal' yourself.

Finally, feel yourself in your body as fully as you are able. Really be in your body. You might like to stamp your feet a few times to really feel the earth beneath you. Breathe in and out and be aware how your breathing roots you to earth. Decide to continue paying close attention to your body and to look after it in the coming days. Your body is your precious instrument of experience and expression, it is your temple in which you incarnate and choose to do your purpose in this life. Choose to treat such an important part of yourself with the respect it deserves.

10

LOVE AND CONNECTION

We are in continuous contact with each other, not only socially and on the physical plane, but also through the inter-penetrating currents of our thoughts and emotions ... A sense of responsibility, understanding, compassion, love, and harmlessness are all links in the chain of right relationships which must be forged within our own hearts.
(Roberto Assagioli)

Psychosynthesis is not only involved with the individual, but also with groupings of people of all kinds. This encompasses our relationship with our parents, our children, our lovers and partners, our friends and colleagues and, on a wider level, all the groups to which we belong, including the whole of life. Psychosynthesis, understood as a natural process, encompasses all life and one of the main aims of Psychosynthesis is to create 'right relationships' between all beings.

In this chapter we will look at some of the major aspects of interpersonal Psychosynthesis, particularly as it relates to the individual and his or her primary relationships. The principles that we apply at this level, however, are the same ones we apply in Psychosynthesis at other levels, suitably adapted. If we hold to the vision that we are not isolated but are part of one family of life, we are sharing in the vision of Psychosynthesis. When we filter this down through the different levels of relationship, we can still hold to the vision - one family of human beings through to the families into which we were born and which we have subsequently created with loved ones. The Psychosynthesis view of family is an open one that encourages its members to find themselves and then express this knowledge and understanding in an attitude of loving awareness.

At some times in our lives it is better to keep ourselves to ourselves and not share our energies. Psychosynthesis encourages us to respect our inner wisdom when such times occur in our lives, and not to think or feel guilty if we choose to be separate or alone. At other times we feel more like exploring who we are and what we do as it relates to other people (and other beings.) Psychosynthesis offers a wealth of techniques and principles that can help us to facilitate this inner process. The very best way to explore our interpersonal expression, however, is quite simply through expressing ourselves. A good part of interpersonal relating is always trial and error and it is through taking risks and exploring this arena that we can truly learn and grow and play a more active part in our 'family'.

Sometimes we do not express ourselves at all as we would wish. We start to express ourselves then, depending upon the reaction we receive, we may stop altogether, suppress elements of our expression, or totally change direction. This applies not only to individual situations but to how we interact overall with other people. Some people are 'stopped altogether' most of the time and find it really hard to express themselves. Most of us suppress many different aspects of our inner world and do not express the totality of who we are with other people. It is a major principle of interpersonal Psychosynthesis that the first step to success is to accept ourselves for what we are. We learned the importance of acceptance in Chapter 8. Once we accept ourselves without judgement or censorship then we can simply express who we are without holding back. Then we open up the possibility of change both individually and interpersonally.

This does not mean we cannot or should not have secrets and, indeed, to respect the power of silence. Sometimes we share aspects of our growth and development too soon and thus dissipate some of the energy. Sometimes our 'need' to relate makes us share things more from a level of deficiency rather than inclusion. Our secret inner world needs to be cherished and fostered, and kept secret. Then, when we are choosing to be intimate we can allow others to share in some of this world, the power and awareness of which can be one of our major strengths.

The second major principle of interpersonal Psychosynthesis is not to label people or 'put them in boxes'. If we want someone to stop seeing us in a certain way we have to stop seeing him or her that way. How often do we find ourselves saying something like 'you should be like me', or 'you should do what I do', instead of accepting the other person as he or she is? We can easily slip into seeing people in 'boxes'. We then start relating to the box instead of the person. Then we don't have to be really present or take any real risks in opening ourselves up, for once we put someone else in a box we put ourselves in a box too. Boxes are not noted for having great interpersonal relationships with one another! Fortunately, however, the opposite is also true: if we accept someone for what they are and do not label or box them, then we give them the space to treat us similarly well.

Sometimes we rightly feel we should not be demanding, should give the other person more space, more love, or whatever. It is also important, however, to be aware of our own needs and openly express these too. So long as we can choose to accept the response to our demand, whether it be 'yes', 'no', or 'not for now', we are then entering into an active inter-relationship that allows both parties room to both express and receive love. Also it is true that people tend to match our expectations. If we decide another person is going to say no then they will tend to do just that. We always get what we put out - so the more we label someone else the more we become labelled ourselves. The more we expect of someone the more is expected of us. And - luckily - the more we love someone and allow them to be themselves, the more we are loved and allowed to be ourselves.

When we acknowledge another person and honour their uniqueness and individuality, we set the scene for true love to emerge. We also open up the possibility of change, which is often why we find it so scary to do this. If things change we imagine we might loose out in some way so we cling to what is as if our lives depended upon it. Of course, in a sense, this is true, for when change occurs our lives do change. If we take the risk of letting others truly be themselves, though, then the likelihood is the change will be life enhancing and positive. This is not always so easy, of course, but at least through trying we can move ourselves forward in a positive direction. This leads us towards the third major principle of interpersonal Psychosynthesis which is the understanding that to be loved, the only thing we have to give up is the experience of not being loved.

PROJECTION AND PERCEPTION

We have a tendency to project onto other people or the world in general all the ideas and images, fantasies, feelings and thoughts that we have about other people and the world. This projection can take place consciously or unconsciously. In this way, each of us creates our own reality, different, by the nature of this projection, from everyone else's reality. Thus, for instance, a dog to one person may be an emotional comfort, a trusted companion whereas the same dog, to another person, may be a dangerous beast best avoided. Similarly, we may be angry about something another person has done and through projection see them as being angry at us. The energies that we project onto others then gets attracted back to us, and we believe we were right all along.

It is of great importance that, wherever possible, we re-own all these projections and relate to people in a more direct way. One way of re-owning projection is to start honouring ourselves and trusting that what we feel is okay. We can then start to honour other people in a similar way. When we give ourselves the right to be, to grumble and moan if that's what we need to do, to be angry or loving, or whatever we need, then we create the space in which we can allow the same for others.

For any relationship to work to the fullest degree, the other person or people in it have to be willing to do the same. But it is a basic truth of interpersonal relationships that it really does only take one person to change it. If we start acting in this way then we create change. We are not victims to other people or circumstances and always have the ability to change what we wish to change. Some of the best ways of creating such change include appreciating the differences between ourselves and other people, being willing to hear the good things people say about us as well as the bad, and giving people good feedback when they do things that clearly honour us for who we are. We can also treat any of the problems that arise between us and other people as blessings that give both us and them the opportunity to grow.

Basically we have to accept the other person for who they are, even if we cannot accept some aspects of their behaviour. There is a major difference between who someone is and what they do. Once we start relating to who they are then we are relating to them at a level of soul rather than personality. At this level all conflicts and disharmonies are growthful. If we would like aspects of our relationship to be different then we cannot really blame anyone else but ourselves. Even if we could genuinely blame another, blaming someone is never a positive way forward, it just builds another barrier between them and us.

Of course, our personal reality is not just projection, there are many other components too. It has been said that our personal reality is primarily a combination of projection and perception. What we have to work with in any relationship is our perceptual reality. All we ever can do, really, is to work on our end of a relationship. We create and live by our own beliefs and actions. If we can learn to stop projecting our anger or sadness and start accepting it as ours, then we have taken a major step to improving our relationships. We are then in a position where we can start seeing the other people involved for who they really are. The relationship moves then towards more of an 'I-Thou' relationship where we can express ourselves clearly and allow the clearer expression of the other person or people involved.

The first step has to re-own our projections, however. There is a simple technique for starting to do this. We start by recalling a difficult situation with another person and taking some time to really picture and feel this situation. Then we imagine ourselves as if we were actually the other person. We imagine ourselves seeing the situation from their viewpoint. After taking some time doing this, coming back to ourselves, we imagine we toss the other person a rope and, lassoing our projections, we slowly bring them back to the centre of our body. The more energy you put into feeling this is really happening, the more effective it is. We can choose to truly be ourselves and let others be themselves.

THE PRIMARY SCENARIO

The 'primary scenario' for all our subsequent relationship is the one we experience in our families with our parents or guardians. It is useful if we can distinguish what actually happened in our primary relationships from what we imagine happened or simply believe without consideration. One way of doing this, discreetly if necessary, is to ask the other people involved how they view what happened. What your mother, for instance, saw happening in those early days of your relationship with her is no more 'the truth' than what you saw happening. But having different perspectives on the primary scenario can help us get a clearer, more complete picture.

We can also use our imagination and visualization to help us re-create and learn from these early days. For instance we can simply relax, close our eyes and allow a symbol to emerge that represents our primary family relationship. If we trust that the symbol which emerges is right for us at this time, and without judgement or censorship, simply allow such a symbol to appear in our mind's eye, then we can use this symbol to learn more about ourselves. If the symbol were a house on fire, for example, what might that tell us about the relationship? And, if the symbol was this, what could we do to change it? We might put the fire out perhaps, or allow the fire to run its course and then re-build the house anew, but this time better than it ever was before.

We can also meditate upon our primary scenario and see what reflective and receptive meditation brings up for us. We might, for instance, meditate upon the roles we played in our family. What skills did you learn from your family that are useful to you as an adult? What role models did you have in your family that aid you now? What roles did you play in your family that have meaning for you now (for example hero, peacemaker, troublemaker, joker, etc.)? Once we start finding the answers to these questions and consequently raising our consciousness in this way, we can then creatively find ways of changing not the actual family as it is now, or the events that 'actually' happened in the past, but our way of relating to this. We might even start to think of our families as chosen by us, and as having given us exactly what we needed.

The primary scenario forms the basis of all our future relating. Emotional patterns are transferred from parental relationships to personal ones. Perhaps our mothers or fathers exhibited over-development of their maternal or paternal roles, and were overprotective. Perhaps, at the other extreme, they were over strict and restrictive. We can ask ourselves if we follow these patterns? Perhaps our parents were prone to do their living their children. Are we repeating this pattern? Perhaps within us there is an over-development of romantic ideals. Perhaps we are obsessed by sex? Where did we get these ways of relating from?

We learn the ways we relate from our parents. If our relationship with them was clearly formed, then we know it is okay to be ourselves (to love ourselves) and it is okay to change (to empower ourselves). If these relationships were not so clearly defined, and in most of us this is exactly the case, then we exhibit corresponding distortions. We need to ask ourselves exactly what did our parents teach us about love and power? And we need to remember that were not victims to some 'horrible ogres' whose conscious or unconscious aim was to cause us pain in later life. It is always true that, whatever we do, it is the best we can do at that time. This is equally true of other people, including our parents or guardians. Realising this brings acceptance, and true acceptance, as we have already learned, brings clarity to our ability to be ourselves, and our ability to be both loving and wilful.

Just as we can bless any apparent obstacle to our growth and development, so we can bless our parents for doing the best they could. Forgiveness removes any lack of wholeness. Forgiveness brings love - both to the person forgiven and to the forgiver. We can never have enough forgiveness.

THE EXPRESSION OF LOVE

We can love ourselves or other people either from our sense of self, our centre, or in a more partial way, perhaps from a needy subpersonality. There is nothing wrong with loving someone in a partial way so long as we do not become identified with it in a way that does them or us a disservice. When we love from our centre we can be more objective, genuine loving without attachment, caring but not overwhelming, strong but not manipulative.

To love from a subpersonality usually involves various aspects of need - I love you because you give me something or other. It depends upon the response - I won't love you any more unless you continue giving me whatever it is. To love from the self is to be proactive rather than reactive, to love someone for who and what they are rather than what they do. To be able to say I still love you despite what you are doing. Love from a subpersonality is usually shallower and more whimsical whereas love from the self is deeper and more lasting. Love from the centre is whole rather than partial, complete rather than fragmented. It is a synthesis of love and will, thinking, feeling and sensing. In this way it is complete and gives a sense of freedom rather than bondage.

We may try to understand love through analysing it in this way, but it is still love, however. Love quite simply just is. If it comes through a subpersonality it may be less whole, more needy, more reactive, but it is still love and we have the power within us to change it, to transform it into a more centred love. As we discussed in the chapter on subpersonalities, if we consciously work on meeting the needs of a part of us it can change and become more self-sufficient. When this happens, the love this subpersonality expresses can also become more self-sufficient. Parts of us that feel little or no love can have their 'love element' expanded whilst parts of us that have lots of love but express it in a distorted way can have their 'love element' refined. This is a basic principle for all Psychosynthesis work, that we can elevate or expand energies we have too little of and refine or purify those energies of which we have too much.

When we realise and express love, we find its qualities abound. True love, of ourselves or others, gives us the energy for creative acts, it gives us insights and confidence, it strengthens and nourishes us, and, perhaps most importantly, it allows us to discover more about our true, inner selves. Often it is more difficult to realise and express self-love than it is to express love to others. Yet how much richer and more meaningful our lives become if we allow ourselves some self-love. This does not mean narcissistically becoming enamoured of our bodies, our emotions, feelings, thoughts or even our deepest soul connections. What it does mean is to accept ourselves for what we are, in totality, and realise we are what we are. When we accept ourselves in this way we realise the greatest love within and are more able to express it.

Love in itself is often not enough, however, and it has to be coupled with understanding otherwise it can blindly cause problems where it aims to release, can maim and spoil where it intends to free and encourage, can become sentimentality instead of simply being itself. Love to be truly helpful has to be applied with wisdom and understanding.

If we see only our own viewpoint and do not truly see the position of others, then we are obscuring the free flow of love. If we assert ourselves at the expense of others, in an artificial, excessive or inappropriate way, then we block love. If we have prejudices and preconceived ideas about how love should be expressed then we block love that way too. But if we let love be, let it flow through us as if we are channels for its greater energy, and if we work on making ourselves more conscious and more efficient channels for this energy, then love is our sustenance and salvation.

There is no such thing as an 'ideal relationship' but we can all consciously choose to create a reality in which we move towards rather than away from such a goal. In an ideal relationship we relate primarily in a holistic way. This means we include all parts of our personality, including the darker parts. We see the other person or people involved as equally whole and love them unconditionally. We own our shadows, and not project it onto others. We would love without need or deficiency. We also would be willing to surrender to how the relationship evolves. We can move towards this ideal in all our relationships, but for it to become the primary focus we have to work at it, not because we think we should but because we really want to.

SEXUAL RELATING

To isolate sex in a relationship and try to understand it out of context is not a very effective way to do this. We can better understand sex if we see it as part of a whole picture that includes all the other components of the relationship. It is very rare for sex to be a purely biological act, for it always involves feelings, emotions, thoughts, fantasies, all our resistances, our attachments, our fears and so on. Sex is often used in a relationship as means to a different end than the obvious one. It can be used to avoid difficulties, to avoid boredom, to overcome other difficulties in the relationship, to have power over the other person, and so on.

On the other hand, sex can be viewed as spiritual, as a holy act of union between people. When one and one come together sex does not give us two, it gives us a newly formed, ecstatic one again. Our inner desire for Unity can be met and fulfilled through a positive attitude towards sex. Books abound on sexual techniques, but the most important technique is in bringing awareness into our sexual lives. We can apply all the principles we learn for improving ourselves to improving our sexual relating. Awareness in sex brings vast amounts of energy for us to use in whatever way seems appropriate to us at the time. Used wisely, the energy of sex continues to increase, and can promote our successful Psychosynthesis.

Most sexual problems fall into either or both of these categories: not operating sexually (too little), and only operating sexually (too much). As with anything of which we have too little or to much we can apply the principles of elevation and refinement. When we explore our sexuality with a Psychosynthesis guide we explore such questions as: What are the inner qualities behind the forms in which we relate sexually? Do we live out emotional patterns from the past in our sexuality? Are we attached to sex in such a way that our self-image is dependant upon our sexual relating? Are we able to both disidentify from and identify with our sexuality when it is appropriate to do so? What meaning has sexuality for us? How has our attitude to sex been conditioned, especially in the primary scenario?

The exploration of all aspects of our interpersonal expression, including sexuality, is perhaps the most exciting aspect of our existence in this life for it gives us the opportunity to know ourselves not only singly, as ourselves, but in combination with other people. We can extend our explorations to include all the beings on the planet earth, or we can focus on ourselves and our most intimate relationships. But however we explore our love and connection we can come to realise both our uniqueness and our total interdependency.

EXERCISE: THE RELATIONSHIP WHEEL

Using a large piece of paper, draw a circle in the middle of it, quarter the rest of the space and put the names of four people with whom you are currently involved at the corners of the four boxes.

Using the circle at the middle as a focus, tune into your centre and clearly self-identify. Then choose one of the four people and do a free drawing in their 'box' to represent the relationship. Do not just draw a representation of the person, but tune into what the interaction between you feels like and try to represent this in your drawing. You can do this with a pencil, colours and as complicated or as simple as you wish; the important thing is to get down a representation of the current state of your relationship with this person.

When you are ready, tune back to your centre (the circle in the middle), then choose to go into another box and do a drawing for the relationship with that person. Repeat the process until you have a drawing in all four boxes.

When you have four drawings, spend some time tuning into your centre then look at the four relationships and see what differences you can find in the drawings, and what common elements there are. You can look for colour, shading, broken or unbroken lines, shapes and patterns as well as what is more obviously depicted in the actual shapes drawn. You might like to share this with someone else, perhaps one or more of the people involved.

11

THE SPIRIT OF SYNTHESIS

Let us feel and obey the urge aroused by the great need of healing the serious ills which at present are affecting humanity; let us realize the contribution we can make to the creation of a new civilization characterized by an harmonious integration and cooperation, pervaded by the spirit of synthesis. (Roberto Assagioli)

Just as in the last chapter we saw that Psychosynthesis comes alive and reaches some of its most meaningful insights when it is applied to relationships between individuals, we also find that Psychosynthesis can have a vital part to play in the totality of interdependence between all living creatures. No one really exists as an isolated individual, anyway, for we all have involved and intimate relationships with other people and beings and our world in general, and thus we are truly interdependent. If we look at the whole of life in this way, we can see the potential, at least, for one family of living beings that co-exists harmoniously within itself and within the world it inhabits. On a spiritual level we can imagine the transpersonal Self as that which includes all the individual parts that make up the collective totality of existence and which is beyond each individual part. It is a general principle of Psychosynthesis that the whole is greater than the sum of the parts.

If four people stand around a heavy object and they try to lift it into the air they may manage it but there is a lot of effort involved and the whole procedure will appear clumsy and uncoordinated. If before they try to lift the weight they breathe together, matching their breathing to a common cycle, then they count from one to ten together and all lift at the same moment, they will find the weight is remarkable easy to lift. There is nothing strangely mystical or magical about this. The four people trying to lift the object together but in an uncoordinated way are 'the sum of the parts'. Their lifting capacity is the sum of the lifting capacity of all four of them minus what they loose through not being synthesized into one 'lifting unit'. If they perform acts to bring their action together then they become a 'whole that is greater than the sum of the parts'. The lifting becomes easy, and, you will find if you try this with some friends, is accompanied by the release of much energy. What was an effort before is transformed into a pleasure.

We all form groups like this to perform our various tasks in life. These groups include our family, groups we form locally in our town for various purposes, our work groups, social classes, unions of various kinds, our national groups, and so on through the group we call the entire human family to the group that includes all living beings. If we can apply this principle of synthesis to all these groups to which we belong then we find that the tasks become easier and there is a release of positive energy which can be used not only for the good of the group involved but also for other associated groups as well.

It is rarely that simply, however. Problems arise between individuals within groups and between groups that are not dissimilar to the problems that arise within the individual. As we have already discussed, as individuals we are composed of many different subpersonalities and the people in any group can be compared to subpersonalities. The methods and techniques used in Psychosynthesis to harmonize the inner world can be well applied to the outer world, too. Indeed, the drive towards unity we feel inside when we touch into the deepest aspects of our nature can be seen and applied to outer groups and situations as well.

When we make this connection we start to realise that the Self creates diversity from unity in order that all beings can find their own way to realise the unity from whence they came and to which they are returning. We are divided for the sake of love, for in love we can find ourselves again and, in finding ourselves, discover that our separation was an illusion. We have the opportunity from this place of division to form a union, to come together with another being and be at one with him or her, or even to come together with all other beings and realize a total union. Without the division no such knowledge would be possible. Whilst we are in this illusion of duality, however, we can help bring more beauty and harmony into the world through our clear consciousness of loving what we do and doing what we love. Then we help move the whole of life towards that final goal, the supreme synthesis where all the parts of life come together and realize the whole that includes all yet transcends each individual part.

It is important to stress here that this is not an ungrounded, 'mystical' view of life or the place of individuals within the unfoldment of the universe. Of course, no one would want to deny the reality of a mystical experience which separates an individual from their mundane, earthly existence and, in a state of bliss, leads them to temporarily forget all outer reality and the environment. If we become attached to such experiences, however, we fall into the mystical trap. Psychosynthesis stresses the importance of avoiding this through always paying attention to bringing all transpersonal energies back to ground and finding a way of expressing them in the 'ordinary world'.

The mystical experience should not be seen as an end in itself but rather a step along the way from which the individual who has the fortunate to have such an experience, can draw creative energy, and enthusiasm. The true mystical experience also brings with it the desire to come back into the world to express the energies involved and help one's fellow human beings to also experience this enlightenment. The 'mystic' who remains spaced out has missed the boat, as it were, that carries us all, irrespective of our experiences, towards the final goal of fully realized and consciously shared unity.

The other mystical trap is to believe that once one has reached some sort of blissful state, or received some sense of enlightenment, that this is all there is to it. It is the experience of all the great mystics that enlightenment os neither an end in itself nor, as such, does it last forever. Nothing remains the same, everything changes, and the enlightened state is no exception to this cosmic rule. Everything that is alive is in a constant state of movement, constantly renewing itself as it moves from moment to moment. If you stop moving, quite simply you die (and even then this is an illusion for in death we may find at the very least decay and a return to an energy state and perhaps more.) Each revelation has to be grounded and expressed and also not clung to. In Psychosynthesis we see the true mystic as the one who is working to express the energies with which he or she has connected, not the one who remains connected and has nothing left to say, do or feel.

THE PRINCIPLE OF SYNTHESIS

It is worth stressing the principle of synthesis: that the whole is greater than the sum of the parts. If we look at a painting and analyze it into its component parts we may find the different colours, brush strokes, shading and light, figures and background, we may even find beautiful scenes depicted within it, trees, people, places ... but we have to see it as a whole, in its entirety before we can realize the value of it as a great work of art. What comes out of that synthesized whole is something beyond any or all of the individual components, perhaps something that even transcends the artists original conception.

In the psychological application of this principle of synthesis, we stress the importance of each part being made whole in itself before it can be truly synthesized with other parts. If one of your subpersonalities is not 'whole', if it has wants at odds with your true purpose, if it has unheard and unmet needs, if its true qualities are obscured, then how can it take its true place as part of the whole personality without creating disharmony? It is so important, therefore, that we do not short change our work on the personality, which is, after all, the 'vessel' through which we express our innermost spiritual truths.

Synthesis is, in fact, an organic process. We cannot force it or make it happen, but what we can do is co-operate with and facilitate the process as it organically unfolds. One way of achieving a move towards actualizing this potential that we all have is to work at balancing and synthesizing the opposites that exist within us. If you are a man then you can work at bringing out the 'female' within you to create more harmony and balance. If you are an idealist then perhaps you need some practicality to help balance your personality. If you are attached to the spiritual path then perhaps a little sensuality may lighten your load. Each of us as individuals has our own inner connection, our own inner world of opposites. The work of synthesis, in this area, is to find these opposites within ourselves so we can balance them and create a clearer synthesis.

If for example, you were very at ease with your intellectual powers, at home in the mental world, so to speak, you may want to make more connection to your feelings. If your mental side, was, say, the size of a football and your feelings the size of a tennis ball, the technique of synthesis would not be to make the mental connection smaller until it was the size of the 'tennis ball feelings'. The opposite would be the case, to elevate your feelings until they match the size of your mental attributes. At the same time you could be refining this mental side to make it, in itself, clearer and more harmonious. The work of synthesis involves, therefore, a continuous process of elevation of the smaller element of any pair of opposites and the refinement of the more developed polarity.

A further principle of synthesis is that we can never solve a problem at its own level. If we take the example of two subpersonalities who are in disagreement, perhaps about whether we should take a certain decision in life, then so long as we remain on the level of their argument it will continue. Both the parts are fighting for their rights, even for their very survival. Each part knows what is best for us and is going to 'damn-well' make sure we do just that. If we can gain a perspective from a different level, however, we may be able to find a way to overcome the difficulty. One part of you wants to go out right now and another part wants to stay in. From a third place of greater perspective we might find that a compromise can be reached - you'll stay in now but go out later, for example.

Once we have disidentified from both of the parts in this way, we have moved ourselves, if not actually to the place of the self, at least to a clearer space. We are no longer caught in the problem at its own level. Once we are thus placed, we can then start looking for a synthesis, perhaps through asking ourselves what it would be like if the two parts not only found a compromise but actually came together. We can do this at least partly through not being too attached to fulfilling the individual wants of each part but looking towards finding out what their real needs are. When we do this we are moving these parts a little towards unity, towards the synthesizing centre that is the Self.

Such a synthesis is not only possible, it is desirable. We can be both loving and strong, intuitive and logical, spontaneous and disciplined, idealistic and practical, spiritual and sensual and so on. Indeed, what we usually find is that when we start bringing opposites together we again get a whole that is greater than the sum of the parts. A new reality is created. I am still loving but now I can be strong when it is necessary and not allow people to just walk all over me, taking advantage of my good nature. I can still be a spiritual person and can better express my connection to the transpersonal not in spite of but because of my new connection to the world of the senses.

When we create synthesis in our lives, when parts within us come together into a new relationship, or when we find a way of moving closer to someone or something else in this true synthesizing manner, then we not only grow individually, we add to the total growth of all sentient beings. We also free up energy that was previously blocked and involved in conflict, energy we can then put to creative uses. The more we move towards our personal synthesis, the closer we move the whole of creation towards the time when there is a universal synthesis.

COLLECTIVE RESPONSIBILITY

Everything we do in our lives makes a difference not only to ourselves but to everyone and everything else. Until fairly recently in human history it would have seemed unthinkable, on moral as well as practical terms, to imagine that what even the collective totality of humankind can do could make a really appreciable difference to our home planet. Yet now we realise that everything we do not only makes a difference, but those things we do carelessly and selfishly can put the lives of all the creatures on this planet in jeopardy. We have evolved into 'planetary people' and to fully honour this growth we have to take responsibility for our individual actions and the actions of our race as a whole. Everything we do can make an enormous difference, from that single squirt of an aerosol spray to closing our eyes and ears to the plight of many our fellow human beings, let alone the even sorrier plight of many of the other species of life on this planet who, in reality, have an equal right to be here.

Both our knowledge about what is happening in the world around us, with its wars, disease, disharmony and ecological unbalance, and a sense of inner inadequacy, can make us believe that there is nothing we as individuals can do to change the world in any way. When we connect with our innermost nature, with a sense of Self, however, we find we are also connected to everyone and everything else. We are part of a collective consciousness that is totally inclusive and infinitely caring. Realising we are a part of this collective shows us that everything we do does make a difference.

Some of the more spiritual connections we make in

Psychosynthesis work can help us realise that all life forms, not just human beings, are part of a totally interconnected and inseparable energy field. Whilst most of us may spend a large part of our lives imagining that we are separate and disconnected, once we start to explore the deeper aspects of our being we discover the underlying truth of our connection. We may not be able to 'be there' all the time, indeed it may not be right for us to stay in such a state, but once we have the intimation of its real existence, once we actually experience it in ourselves, there is no looking back. We have 'set our sights' on the clarity and connection that comes from such realisations and we try to make each move we take a step in that direction.

When we realise we are connected to everyone and everything else, we start to have a different perspective on time and space. In reality we are no less connected to an ant on a distant island in the South Pacific than we are to our noses! While it may be very rare for us humans to realise this connection, we can start moving our awareness in that direction. We can start to cultivate within ourselves a sense of this 'global consciousness'. We can realise our individual consciousness is a small but significant piece of the total consciousness of life on our planet

Many of the exercises and techniques of Psychosynthesis can help us have an inkling of this awareness and, perhaps more importantly, ground this awareness in our everyday lives. When we ground this awareness it helps us take actions that move the total collective consciousness forward in its positive evolutionary path. It is not an exaggeration to say that one small act made by one individual at one moment in time can make a profound difference. When we care for others, both those immediately within our field of awareness and activity, but also to all living and non-living things generally, we are grounding this consciousness. When we care for our environment, both locally and generally, we are also grounding this consciousness. Every conscious act we make that includes such caring furthers the cause of global awareness in this way. We can find many different ways to contribute to this cause and each way adds to the richness of our experience. Perhaps such awareness will bring about some cures for the ills which currently threaten not only our individual existence but the existence of life as we know it on our planet.

SOMEWHERE IN TIME

At school many of us were given a misleading view of evolution. We were either told directly, or it was suggested to us indirectly, that the human being is the apotheosis or pinnacle of evolution. Everything that had come before was designed to simply lead to the human race and, in creating us, evolution had fulfilled its task. The evolutionary process could be condensed into a twenty-four hour day. In this model, life appears a little before noon and the whole of human history only takes place in the last half second before midnight. This interesting but false description of evolution suggests we are somehow 'the end'. Quite what is meant to happen when midnight strikes is not described.

A better model is created if we map the sun's expected lifespan onto the twenty-four hour day. This lifespan is currently estimated at around twenty billion years. In this model, the time is now around eight o'clock in the morning and the whole of life has been around for just the last couple of seconds. Human existence so far amounts, therefore, to a split second around eight in the morning. Seen in this light our perspective on evolution changes.

It would be possible to take this second model of the evolutionary process and say: why bother then? If we are such a small, insignificant moment in the time of our planet, even if we destroy ourselves and all life with us, it's only a couple of seconds out of a whole day. The planet will survive and go on without us, and if we're lucky it may even get round to giving us another chance!

On the other hand, why not bother? Look out of your window and see a piece of the beautiful blue sky, listen to the sounds of birds simply singing in a wood, touch one hand against another and feel the wonder of life, present in your every moment. Why not bother - after all, we've come this far in a couple of seconds, let's see what we can make of the next hour or two.

EXERCISE: THE INNER GUIDE

Relax and centre yourself in the usual way. Imagine you are in a meadow where the sun is shining and the birds are singing. Spend some time really feeling your presence in this meadow. Notice what you can hear, what you can see, what you feel.

At one edge of the meadow is a hill with a path leading up to the top. Start to walk in that direction, really feeling your feet on the ground beneath you. Start an ascent up the hill, taking your time to really enjoy the sights and sensations you experience on your journey.

As you reach the top of the hill become aware that you are about to meet someone who is intimately involved with the evolution of your life. This person is your inner guide - you might see him or her as a wise old person, as a guardian angel, or simply as someone whose eyes express great love and care for you. However you visualise this person, let the image of him or her appear clearly before you. Allow yourself to fully experience the excitement and interest such a contact invokes.

You can now engage this being in a dialogue and, in whatever way seems best to you at this time, ask about any issues, questions, choices or problems you currently have in your life. The dialogue may be verbal or non verbal, it may take place on a visual or symbolic level, but however it occurs really relish this time you are spending with your inner guide.

Also ask about global awareness and the state of our planet and what you can be doing to help the current precarious situation. Let your inner guide's wisdom and understanding help you realize your connection, your ability to love and your power to cause change to occur.

When you are ready, thank your guide for having appeared to you and, returning back down the hill, enter the meadow and once more feel your feet firmly placed on the ground. Bring your consciousness back to your room and spend some time considering what you have learned and how you can put this learning into practice in your life.

PART 2

BEYOND THE ELEMENTS

12

THE ROOTS OF PSYCHOSYNTHESIS

Only the essence in us can begin to discover the secrets we are looking for, and attain a conscious contact with the Existence of which we are an inseparable part. (Roberto Assagioli)

The early part of the Twentieth Century was an exciting time for someone interested in the workings of the human psyche. Many new ideas were being discovered whilst, at the same time, older spiritual and esoteric traditions were revealing their secrets. In his prime during this period, Roberto Assagioli, the founder of Psychosynthesis, was an eager young psychiatrist. He was excited at discovering what he thought was lacking in psychoanalysis. Returning to Italy after his training with Freud, and already having a deep interest in esoteric subjects, he had the vision of bringing together his spiritual pursuits with his interest in the workings of the human psyche.

Freud's psychoanalysis delves into the past, looking for events, particularly from childhood, that have affected how the individual relates to the world. Assagioli agreed with this, clearly seeing the importance of such work. In an attempt to be 'scientific', however, Freud had cut out all reference to spiritual or mystical matters. They could not be quantified so were best avoided. Assagioli considered that by cutting out these aspects of the human psyche, the whole person was not being addressed. As well as the 'basement' of the past, we all also have an 'upstairs' of potential, of future possibilities. So he put them together and formulated Psychosynthesis. As an antidote to the over-rationalised world view held by psychoanalysis, Assagioli's work was a vital presage to the opening up of spiritual and esoteric realms that now we almost take for granted. For the age in which he was working, he took the best possible course. He put together the psychological and the spiritual, then somewhat disguised the esoteric background of some of his ideas so as not to put off the straight, scientific community who, in the early stages of this century, were still deeply rooted in materialistic scientific values.

As the century progressed, however, things changed and the idea of soul and spirit is included by very many psychotherapists in one form or another (even if it is not openly addressed as such.) The acceptance of the transpersonal in the human psyche is becoming the norm rather than taboo. Of course, the work of Jung has played a major role in this, particularly in understanding that we have to address all aspects of the working of the unconscious, whether brilliantly lighted with spiritual energy or endarkened by the repression that characterises the shadow. Assagioli's intention was for Psychosynthesis to deal with all aspects - analysis itself, deep personal psychotherapy that includes all aspects of the psyche, and of course, access to and expression of creative and spiritual energies. Psychosynthesis has the potential, therefore, to be a truly integrative and holistic psychology, perhaps of increasing importance in the new century.

Psychosynthesis clearly has roots in the esoteric traditions in which Assagioli had a life-long interest, a fact glossed over or ignored by some practitioners. It is sometimes stated that he was a friend and colleague of Alice Bailey, and that he incorporated ideas from Raja Yoga into the Psychosynthesis conception of the Will, but that is as far as it usually goes. Jean Hardy in her book 'A Psychology with a Soul' does much to uncover the 'secret' origins of Psychosynthesis and adds to our understanding of what is central to Assagioli's intent. His interest in Theosophy and the esoteric doctrines of Alice Bailey grew out of his abiding wish to create a synthesis out of the Western and Eastern approaches to personal and spiritual development. He believed Theosophy was the best attempt at this that was available in his day. Whilst he was probably aware of some of the limitations of Theosophy, he supported it whole-heartedly.

Being aware of the prejudices of the scientific community during his life time, being Jewish, and wishing Psychosynthesis to have a solid and acceptable ground in the Western psyche, led Assagioli to position many of his more esoteric ideas and practices behind a 'wall of silence'. These were only to be revealed to those who proved themselves 'safe'. This chapter will explore the esoteric roots of Psychosynthesis, focusing particularly on the Western Mystery Tradition with which Assagioli imbued his life and work. The principles and practices of Psychosynthesis not only make more sense but 'come to life' when understood from this perspective. Indeed, some Psychosynthesis exercises, in both content and delivery, embody many of the esoteric principles that we will be exploring.

A typical Psychosynthesis meditation opens by asking the listener to reflect on what is going on for her or him in that particular moment. The subject is asked what they are feeling, thinking and sensing. They may be asked to let this content of their awareness alone, not trying to stop it but to bring attention to their breath, or the heart. They are then asked reflective questions concerning their thinking and feeling about the subject of the reflection. This helps open the individual and group to the process being discussed, including both their more mental and their more feeling related associations. Right from the beginning, in other words, a typical Psychosynthesis exercise will employ sound esoteric practice: to still the mind and body as a prerequisite to deeper work.

THE 'SCIENTIFIC' BACKGROUND

Roberto Assagioli felt it was vital to keep apart the 'scientific' and 'esoteric' strands of Psychosynthesis. This was most probably so in his day, and there is still a lot of suspicion and even hostility between scientists and esotericists. Behind this, however, Assagioli's pragmatic approach was informed by his hope that Psychosynthesis would be a medium for communication between the scientific and esoteric communities and, hopefully, offer a platform for their synthesis. When we reflect that modern science has largely grown out of roots in alchemy, and when we consider the work of Jung and many Jungians to interpret alchemy from a psychological perspective, Assagioli's hope does not seem so far-fetched.

Before considering the influences from the mystery traditions in depth, consider for a moment the 'scientific' influences on Psychosynthesis. Obviously, Freud and Freudian thought was a major early influence on Assagioli. Like Jung, however, Assagioli found Freud's approach far too limiting - particularly in excluding the higher ideals and values of human endeavours, and particularly the religious and esoteric. Indeed, Freud is on record as warning Jung against 'occultism' when referring to spiritual experiences.

The first sign of Assagioli's independent genius was in

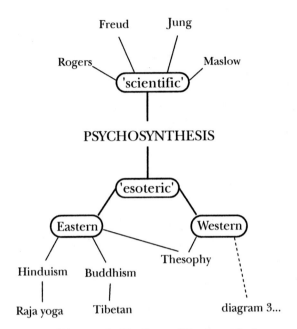

Diagram 2: The Roots of Psychosynthesis

breaking from Freud. We could say the second sign of his genius was in taking with him the best ideas from Freudian psychology and leaving behind its limitations and prejudices.

Jung also broke away from Freud, and Jung and Assagioli had a life-long friendship (although they rarely met.) In a later chapter we will explore some differences between the Jungian and Psychosynthesis approaches to human development, but in this context the similarity of their desire to include the superconscious and the realms of spirituality and the esoteric is more relevant.

Assagioli read widely and continuously, annotating many books as he read. His wide knowledge and understanding led him to adopt many ideas and techniques from a variety of sources. In the later years of his life, particularly as his contact with America progressed, he remained open to ideas which he felt could further the work of Psychosynthesis. He was clearly influenced, for instance, by the work of Carl Rogers and the person-centred approach to healing. Rogers' central themes of unconditional positive regard, congruence and empathy, whilst they may not have originated from esoteric sources, are thoroughly in line with this approach. Assagioli was particularly excited by the work of Abraham Maslow, the 'founder' of transpersonal psychology and the advocate of the investigation of what he called 'the further reaches of human nature'. Maslow was a great synthesizer and was himself much influenced by esoteric thought.

One of Maslow's most useful concepts involves what he called 'deficiency needs' and 'being needs' (shortened to d-needs and b-needs.) Deficiency needs are primarily those for food, warmth, and shelter, the basic needs that have to be met for us to be alive and well. Maslow spoke of our different needs existing in a hierarchy. Once a human's d-needs are fulfilled, he or she may then start considering their b-needs, which include the need to understand life and oneself, to consider the origins of consciousness, where we come from and where we are going, and the meaning of life.

Obviously if you are not fed, are cold, and in fear for your continuing existence, the concerns of being needs are not uppermost. Assagioli fully understood and concurred with this, not least because it coincided with his own approach. He had always stressed that to be effective Psychosynthesis has to include ways of dealing with the difficulties of life and living. For him, d-needs included psychic deficiency - feeling hurt, shame, pain, fear, anger and so forth, and the notion that these needs also have to be met appropriately. Someone with unexpressed anger, in Assagioli's view, could not effectively approach divinity; someone who is suffering repressed fear and shame because they have been abused as a child needs to work with that area of their intrapsychic life in order to effectively be able to meditate, perform rituals or simply and fully appreciate the beauty of nature. Of course, Assagioli was not saying that until you are completely healed you can't approach deity! Indeed, he always stressed that the work of 'personal Psychosynthesis' (working with the d-needs) is a continuous life-long process; and that it happens alongside 'transpersonal Psychosynthesis' (working with the b-needs), not that one follows the other.

When we reflect on our own 'deficiency needs' and 'being needs' and how these needs are met, it may help us to become clearer about the life choices we make - a central aim of both Psychosynthesis and most esoteric practice. The Psychosynthesis subpersonality model, for instance, stresses that our needs bring us closer to ourselves than do our wants. The model says that the more we identify and fulfil our needs, the more we are exhibiting and expressing the deepest qualities at our heart. This is a result of good mystical and magical practice. Interestingly, Psychosynthesis correctly stresses the importance of recognizing 'the mystic' subpersonality as a potential distortion of a clear connection to the Self.

The two primary strands of influence on Psychosynthesis are the 'scientific' and the 'esoteric'. Whilst focusing mainly on Western approaches, we need to consider the Eastern influences on Psychosynthesis. Assagioli's adult life encompassed most of the first two thirds of the 20th century when many Eastern approaches to spirituality were being introduced to Western thought. Assagioli found this exciting and stimulating, and was particularly moved by many Buddhist concepts. Being pragmatic in his approach to spiritual growth, however, he was especially drawn to what he learned of the Tibetan Buddhist and Bon-pa approaches, and to the more practical aspects of Hinduism, especially Yoga. It was these interests that led to his deep involvement with Theosophy and the work of Alice Bailey. A major aim of Theosophy was clearly stated as being the synthesis of the Eastern and Western ways.

Yoga has many different branches. For instance, the well known 'hatha yoga' primarily focuses on the physical body for spiritual attainment (or 'union' which is the etymological origin of the word 'yoga'); 'gnana yoga' focuses on attainment through knowledge; 'karma yoga' on attainment through practices aimed at clearing past karmic patterns; and 'raja yoga', sometimes called the 'royal yoga', spiritual attainment through the correct use of the will. The importance of the will in Psychosynthesis cannot be over stressed, and Chapter 16 will return to the subject of the will, and how we can understand it more fully. For now, though, picture the young Assagioli, only too aware of the importance of the will for healthy psychological functioning and of its denial and denigration by mainstream psychological thought, discovering raja yoga!

Although it has been suggested that Assagioli stole some of his ideas about the will, and the functioning of the will, from raja yoga, there is no real evidence for this at all. What is patently obvious, however, is the 'permission' such a discovery would give the young explorer. If the great Eastern traditions had held the will in such an elevated position ('the royal path) then he felt supported and encouraged to continue with his explorations. He had already discovered the central importance of the will in Western esoteric thought where it is given equal primary position with the imagination, his other passion.

THE WESTERN WAY

To explore Psychosynthesis in the light of the Western Mystery Tradition, we have to be aware that there are many different strands to this tradition as diagram 3 shows. Some of the branches of influence shown may have meaning or connections for you.

Diagram 3: Psychosynthesis and the Western Mystery Traditions

CHRISTIAN MYSTICISM

One of Assagioli's main interests was in what is nowadays called 'Christian Mysticism', a thread running through the Christian church and religion that has often been kept so secret that people have doubted its existence. The Crusades and Inquisition, in trying to stamp out all opposition to the 'official line', and particularly in their slaughter of Gnostic Christians and Cathars, attest not just to their paranoia, but also the power of what they were trying to stamp out. After all, if it isn't powerful it isn't a threat. In Gnosticism and amongst the Cathars we find the roots of Christian Mysticism.

Assagioli found many of the practices of the Jesuits, following the strict will-developing exercises of St Ignatius Loyala, very instructive. In his writings, he mentions both the Jesuits and St John of the Cross, who represents the more mystical, feminine approach to Christian mysticism. His main focus in this area, however, was on the work of Dante, which he felt synthesized the masculine and feminine approaches. He saw in Dante's Divine Comedy an archetypal description of the processes each individual goes through in their developmental journey through life. Indeed, he says: 'The central symbolic meaning of the Divine Comedy is a wonderful picture of a complete Psychosynthesis.'

The Divine Comedy follows a three-fold pattern: descent, purgatory, and paradise. Descent is equivalent to birth, purgatory to life, and paradise to 'death' in the sense of the death-and-rebirth of the individual after times of transition and crisis. In the Psychosynthesis egg diagram, descent equates to entering the lower unconscious, purgatory to living life (in the middle unconscious, as it were) which is basically controlled by the material in the lower unconscious, and paradise as finding ways of bringing the energies of the superconscious into this everyday existence.

The two main characters in the Divine Comedy, Virgil and Beatrice, offer a clue to Assagioli's thinking on this subject. Analysis has to come before synthesis. Virgil represents 'reason' which equates to analysis - a necessary stage but one that can only take one so far. Beatrice then represents 'beauty', the stage of synthesis which can take one further, to living a life of soul. In Chapter 5 of Psychosynthesis, Assagioli devotes a section to the Divine Comedy, which subsumes his understanding of Christian mysticism as presented by Dante. Assagioli suggests exercises based on imagery such as the blossoming of a rose, the cycle of wheat, the growth of a seed into a tree, and so on. They all follow the alchemical theme of descent, purgatory and paradise, for instance the planting and growing of a coffee seed; it's grinding and firing to make coffee; and its stimulation of the drinker!

Even the familiar pattern of meditation used in Psychosynthesis has the three-fold aspect that can be related to descent, purgatory (or life), and paradise. After reflection on a chosen subject, one exercise used in Psychosynthesis groups asks the course members to imagine they each have a clear crystal bowl balanced on top of their heads. It is suggested that all the words, concepts, idea and so on from their reflection fill up this bowl, and that they can feel the weight of all these ideas on which they have been reflecting heavily pressing down on their heads. The participants descend and enter into 'purgatory'.

Then the Psychosynthesis practitioner tells them to imagine the sun comes out above their head and a single ray of light shines down onto the bowl, dissolving all the words, ideas and so on in the bowl. It is slowly suggested that all the contents of the bowl evaporate until the bowl is completely empty. We start our ascent. The sun keeps shining and now the bowl itself dissolves, and the sun shines right through into the heart of the subject. From the heart, the light from the sun fills up each person's whole body. They are told that if thoughts, feelings or sensations intrude, then they should quietly and easily return to the sense of the light from the sun entering their heads, charging their hearts, and filling them up with light.

Of course, after such an 'ascent to paradise', the practitioner will gently guide the group participants out of their trance-like state and suggest ways for each person to ground whatever they have connected with. This might simply be writing about the experience in a journal, or sharing the experience with other group members, either in pairs, small groups, with the whole group, or even all three. Thus course participants are led through all the necessary stages for an experience of the central aim of Christian Mysticism, ended appropriately with an interpersonal shared experience, helping to build relationship and a sense of community, or belonging.

CLASSICAL GREEK INFLUENCES

Assagioli was interested in the ideas of the classical Greek philosophers, especially Plato, whose concept of a cave in which we live and the possibility of awakening to 'reality' (realising one is within a cave) fits well with the Psychosynthesis notion of awareness. The central core statement of the Psychosynthesis Disidentification exercise can be summarized thus: 'I am this, I am more than this (whatever 'this' is), *and I have a choice.*' This is a very brief summary of Plato's philosophy.

A Gestalt exercise may ask you to close your eyes and say: 'I am this' to whatever it is you are experiencing, then open your eyes and say: 'I am more than this' (staying with whatever you experience.) Then you repeat the first sentence (I am this) with eyes open, then the second statement (I am more than this) and close your eyes. This is repeated several times, creating a kind of 'shuttling' between states of eyes open and eyes closed. Psychosynthesis ensouls this exercise by adding a final stage. The subject is asked to finish with their eyes closed, and to ask himself or herself: 'Who chooses to close my eyes?' Then they open their eyes and ask: 'Who chooses to open my eyes?'

The neo-Platonist view of the world is closely allied to the Kabbalistic worldview and, not surprisingly, Psychosynthesis. One central theme to this worldview is that we live within Seven Dimensions. This is of particular significance in understanding Assagioli's ideas and his adoption of the 'Seven Rays' model from Theosophy. The world can be experienced in many different ways, and each of these ways can be true for any particular individual or group at any particular time. One method for investigating this is through understanding what esoteric science calls 'the seven dimensions.' We will return to this later in Chapter 14.

GNOSTICISM AND THE CATHARS

The Cathars were a heretical sect of Gnostic Christians who inhabited the South of France until the Kings of France and England, in league with the Pope, the head of the Roman Catholic Church, sent armies of 'crusaders' into their area and massacred many hundreds of thousands of people for 'having the wrong belief.' Of course, the 'real reason' for the slaughter was that these 'heretics' were seen as a threat to their power base. Despite these terrible times for these (generally) very gentle people, their beliefs survive.

The Cathars believed that each person had to find their own connection with 'God' (Deity). This entailed experience, as opposed to faith only, which was seen as useful but only as a means towards experience. The Roman Christians maintained that faith was enough, and that faith does not need experiences to support it, that it should be enough in itself. The Cathars' beliefs also led to each person finding her or his own visions and values, which means they are less controllable, so power based politicians and rulers tended to support the Catholic position. For the Cathars, just because someone had found self awareness did not mean they were perfect, of course. Perfection is found in being just what you are, with all your foibles and idiosyncrasies, and so on, and the Cathars called their priests 'Perfecti' meaning just this. The Perfecti consisted of both men and women, something else the patriarchal powers in Rome found threatening.

One way the Cathar message was communicated, preserved and spread was through the songs created by the Troubadours who are popularly known as singing Knights and romantic Courtiers to Queens and their Ladies. Their songs encoded the beliefs of the Cathars and, at the same time, through the use of music and sound, were intended to create the effect of 'illumination', the moment of experiencing oneself at one with Deity.

In his book *Psychosynthesis*, whilst writing about Dante's Divine Comedy, Assagioli makes mention of troubadours, particularly in reference to the imagery of the rose (which is also used by Dante.) His comments dispel any doubts as to Assagioli's understanding of and belief in Psychosynthesis as carrying the same message as the Cathars: 'Psychosynthesis definitely affirms the reality of spiritual experience ... it appreciates, respects and even recognises the necessity of [faith] but its purpose is to help to attain the direct experience.'

The 'blossoming of the rose' exercise is intended to engender such an experience. The procedure described by Assagioli involves the individual or group participants imagining they are looking at a rosebush, then one individual bud. The bud is green because the sepals are closed, but at the tip a rose-coloured point can be seen. The sepals start to slowly separate, then the petals follow suit until 'a perfect fully opened rose is seen.' They exercise goes on to ask the subject to expand their awareness to the whole bush, then to the life force that arises from the roots, then to identify with the rose, or as Assagioli says, correcting himself: '... or more precisely, let us introject it into ourselves. Symbolically, we are this flower, this rose.'

JEWISH MYSTICISM

The influence of Jewish Mysticism and Kabbalah on Assagioli was considerable. The Kabbalah (and its development in the Qabalah) is the central key to the whole Western Mystery Tradition. The link with the Kabbalah is the main factor allowing Psychosynthesis to incorporate many other systems and techniques into its fold without being diluted or corrupted. The Psychosynthesis egg, like the Kabbalistic Tree of Life, on which it was modelled, is an excellent synthetic container for understanding and working with the psyche from an experiential perspective. The next chapter explores the relationship between Kabbalah and Psychosynthesis in some depth.

The wider Jewish mystical tradition also affirms the importance of experience as well as faith, and Assagioli, who was Jewish, was steeped in its warm, heart-full intentions. One of his friends was Martin Buber who has been called the father of Jewish Mysticism. Buber's masterful work expounds the importance of what he called the 'I-Thou' experience. The 'I-Thou' experience is opposed to the 'I-it' experience in which the other person in a relationship is made into an 'object'. The 'I-Thou' relationship transcends the projective and reflective limitations of 'I-it' existence (which can hardly be called relationship in comparison.) What Buber was describing matches the 'illumination' experience of the Cathars.

ROSICRUCIANISM AND FREEMASONRY

Both Rosicrucians and Freemasons have very close links with hermeticism and magic, the beliefs of the Cathars and the troubadours. In Psychosynthesis, Assagioli aptly sums up the particular interest of the Rosicrucians when he mentions: '... the rose at the centre of the cross that forms the symbol of some religious orders.' These orders are, of course, the rosy-cross-ians, or Rosicrucians.

The central core in the inner teachings of both these groups is living life to the full in service to one's sense of one's own deepest spiritual Purpose for being incarnated. Life is a preparation for death, for 'how we behave' at the time of death affects what subsequently happens to us. That the soul is weighed, or we meet St Peter at the gates of heaven, however it is expressed, is a common theme for many religions, whose major concern is the time of transition and crossing into 'the next life'. This might even include coming back here, being re-incarnated appropriately to your karmic position, depending upon your 'deeds' in this life. Thus the importance of good deeds, which should not, of course, be done just with this selfish aim in mind. Writing about modern man, Assagioli pokes fun at many of these beliefs, in his compassionate way, when he says: 'His belief in a future 'heaven' if he conceives of one, is altogether theoretical and academic, as if proved by the fact that he takes the greatest pains to postpone as long as possible his departure to its joy.'

One of Carlos Castaneda's books sits on the shelves in Assagioli's library in Florence. I bet Assagioli enjoyed this book, because he was very familiar with many of the themes and ideas presented by Castaneda. One of the central teachings of don Juan, Castaneda's teacher, is that we can bring ourselves most fully into the moment, and truly 'see' the world as it really is, through 'using death as an advisor.' In a practical way, don Juan suggests to Castaneda that the warrior always remembers that death is waiting just over the left shoulder, with hand poised, waiting to tap the shoulder and announce its presence. Turning to see who it is, the warrior sees death moving in. The only chance is to start to dance, for death waits until a warrior has finished a last dance. Connecting with this metaphor, we can use death as an advisor in each moment, remembering to live life to the full, knowing that at any moment death might tap us. Our whole life then becomes our last dance.

The importance Castaneda placed on having an on-going relationship and awareness of the presence of death is the same as that of the Rosicrucians. The rose flowering at the heart of the cross signifies the same. The suffering of life (i.e. hanging on the cross) is borne through the knowledge that it is the suffering itself that leads to the opening of the heart (the blossoming of the rose.)

A basic component of Rosicrucian and Freemasonry teachings is that it is necessary to descend before you can ascend. This can be understood through the concept of 'light in extension' which is equivalent to LVX, (or Lux) another word for the 'Philosophers Stone' or 'Gold' that the Alchemists sought. Descent is the stage of analysis and ascent is the subsequent synthesis, not as a hierarchy - analysis then synthesis - but as a constant on-going process. We need both at all times. This is reminiscent of the Taoist yin-yang symbol and implies the same. It is also the descent, purgatory and paradise of Dante mentioned earlier. All different parts of us are at different stages in the process, and working with this differentiated energy is the true Alchemy of the Self. All these different parts of us are what Assagioli named subpersonalities, and William James 'our little selves.' The work of Psychosynthesis, with its analytical and synthetic components, is then a true flower of Rosicrucianism and of Alchemy.

Lux, incidentally, is an interesting formula that can also tell us more about the Psychosynthesis process. It is described as 'the curative of the death of Osiris' which means the way to undertake the journey through the underworld (that is, the world of earth). The different letters of this Gnostic god-name, LVX, have specific correspondences: L represents Isis who corresponds with nature and descent (through the sorrow of loss). V represents Typhon who is the destroyer, full of energy (expressed through anger). X is Osiris Arisen, the redeemer whose ascent is filled with Joy. In the Hymn to Osiris from *Awakening Osiris* by Normandi Ellis, it says; 'Whatever I am, woman, cat or lotus, the same god breathes in every body. You and I together are a single creation ... As the houses of earth fill with dancing and song, so filled are the houses of heaven... I am a sojourner destined to walk a thousand years until I arrive at myself.' Assagioli, familiar with earlier translations of the Egyptian Book of the Dead, would have surely relished this poetic translation.

THESOPHY

As mentioned at the beginning of this chapter, amongst all of Assagioli's esoteric interests, best known is his involvement with Theosophy and particularly the work of Alice Bailey with whom Assagioli had a long standing friendship and many shared interests. Assagioli became a theosophist primarily because he saw it as the best attempt at a synthesis of Eastern and Western approaches to spiritual development. However, through including the work of analysis, and the depths as well as the heights of the human psyche, what Assagioli achieved with Psychosynthesis was a better synthesis than that attempted by Theosophy, and Psychosynthesis surpasses Theosophy through bringing a synthesis between empiricism and pragmatic practice. The marriage of scientific and esoteric approaches to the human psyche has been the aim of many practitioners.

Central to Assagioli's attempt at synthesizing Eastern and Western approaches is the emphasis on the will which is what clearly aligns Psychosynthesis with the Western mystery traditions. Eastern systems tend to focus more on the 'love' side of the will-and-love dynamic. There are of course many exceptions, but this is a fair description of the basic leanings of the two approaches. An emphasis on love tends to produce mystics whereas one on the will side tends to produce magicians.

A typology that Assagioli borrowed from Theosophy is called 'the seven rays'. He adapted it to work as a psychological and spiritual typology, calling it, instead of the 'seven rays' the 'seven ways to transpersonal realisation.' Towards the end of his life he also recognised the notion that there is an eighth ray, one of transcendence and immanence. Whether there are seven or eight ways to transpersonal realisation, they are not sharply divided and, in fact, frequently overlap. Each of these ways is associated with a particular Soul Ray which emanates from the Universal Spirit. In other words, each individual soul is 'charged with' or 'informed by' the energy of one or more of these Soul Rays. Each of us has one or more of these rays manifesting through different aspects of our being. In essence (on the level of the Spirit) we are connected to all of the rays, but in terms of our soul and personality some of these rays become foreground to our particular stage of evolution.

The seven ways are called: the way of Will (or Power); of Love (or Wisdom); of Activity (or Action); of Beauty (or Harmony); of Knowledge (or Science); of Devotion (or Idealism); and of Ritual (or Organisation). In the Psychosynthesis version of this model, most people are said to have two primary influences, one for the Soul and one for the personality. Then, within the personality, one ray will be found to particularly influence the mind, another the feelings, and a third the body and senses.

The 'height' of the ray is how it manifests in its 'pure' form; the 'depth' of the ray is, to a greater or lesser degree, how it manifests through the personality. The task, once a ray's influence has been identified, whether in its 'height' or 'depth', is to elevate it. This means to use techniques to create dynamic balance between the various components involved in the manifestation of that ray. This might take the form of personality work, meditation and visualisation; always, however, it will involve a deep-rooted connection with Soul energy through specific exercises. Chapter 14 explores the seven ways to transpersonal realisation in greater depth.

Spiritual Growth In The 1960s And 1970s

Although Assagioli was very aware of the dangers of an unbalanced approach that goes too far towards love or will, he also recognised the need for emphasis on 'the love side' during the period in the 60s and 70s when young people were discovering new ways to view the world and many revolutions of various kinds were being attempted, and sometimes succeeding, throughout the world. Assagioli, although getting older, exulted in these times, delighting in the energy of youth in its discovery of itself. His visits to the USA and contact with many Americans, who were deeply involved in the counter-culture movement of the time in one way or another, deeply affected him.

As the 60s revolution brought many more people to an exploration of the esoteric and occult, so also throughout the 20th century many religions and systems of spiritual attainment have been opening up and revealing their secrets, as if ready for the increased attention and interest (and perhaps, on a more shadowy side, in fear of their impending demise, or even the coming end of the human race.) From his books and contacts, we know that Assagioli was familiar during this period, if not before, with teachings that originate from Sufi traditions (the older, Islamic Sufi tradition and the more modern 'born-again' Sufi movement), Gurdjieff and his followers including Ouspensky, Crowley and his successors in the darker side of the occult, and Steiner (who was an accomplished occultist himself.)

Assagioli was also influenced at this time, of course, by the many Eastern philosophers and gurus who were introduced to the West. This includes Sri Aurobindo with whom Assagioli apparently spent many hours in spasms of endless laughter. They recognised in each other a deep spiritual understanding. All of this contact added to Assagioli's abilities to make Psychosynthesis a system able to hold the width and breadth of both Eastern and Western methods of attainment.

ALCHEMY, HERMETICISM AND MAGIC

In discussing the various influences on Psychosynthesis, I've kept alchemy to last because in many ways the symbols and descriptions of alchemy offer a precise and clear level of insight into the processes of synthesis. Jung recognised this and spent many years of his life translating alchemic texts, writing commentaries and psychological discourses on their meaning and - most importantly - practising what he preached. Assagioli, too, recognised the unique importance of the message of the alchemists.

There are many different versions of alchemy but they all generally agree that 'a common substance' is subjected to a series of operations to obtain an end product called the philosophers stone, medicine of metals, the elixir of life, or just simply gold. This final product has qualities of a living being rather than a thing. In other words, alchemists take a dead thing, impure, valueless and powerless, and transform it into a living thing, active, invaluable and transformative. This exactly describes the work of Psychosynthesis, too.

The alchemists believed that to make gold, you have to first have some gold. In other words they were working to bring each substance to the perfection of its own proper nature. This is the same intention we have already discussed, as for instance with the Cathar's belief that perfection is found within living one's life as it is, with both its heights and depths.

In alchemy the aspirant to initiation is sometimes described as the first matter. This 'first matter', assailed by complexes, plunged into ordeals (which act to break up the impurities) then becomes what is called 'the black matter'. This is the substance of analysis which is necessary to lead to the final synthesis, the transformation of 'lead' into 'gold'. One of the key 'instruments' in the alchemical process is the chalice. A chalice is a magic cup, so the Holy Grail is a particular form of a chalice, as is the cup in the Tarot. The chalice is usually described as being feminine in nature (as opposed to the wand or sword, which dipped into the cup, are usually described as male.) Being female it is receptive in nature and it contains 'drops of blood', which represent the aspirations of the initiate (and, as in the story of Jesus, the blood that brings healing.)

Hermeticists believe that the two most important powers of the human psyche are will and imagination (both properly tempered by the greatest cosmic force, love.) Imagination is what we use to create the world in which we live, and will is the force by which we create and maintain it. So magic can simply be defined as making something intentional happen. The key is using your intention aligned with transpersonal Intent (True Will or Purpose.) As Assagioli so succinctly put it: 'The strength and the power to express compassion according to wisdom; the wisdom and compassion to use power for the greatest good.'

Assagioli, in *Psychosynthesis*, quotes Goethe: 'Reality is that which is effective.' This is the hermetic philosophy in a nutshell. Assagioli goes on to say: '... in so far as these phenomena - whether termed spiritual, mystical or parapsychological - change the inner reality and outer behaviour of an individual they are real.' This book returns to this theme in later chapters.

A medieval magical treatise called 'The Magic of Abra Melin the Mage' is based around the notion that to have 'knowledge and conversation of your guardian angel', the equivalent to 'illumination', it is essential to first go into your depths, to face 'the demons of darkness', and bring them under your control. As already discussed, a basic principle of Psychosynthesis is that that with which we are identified controls us, and that from which we can disidentify is brought under our control.

Assagioli quotes St John of the Cross regarding the 'dark night of the soul', who again stresses the necessity of this stage, without which it is impossible to bring more light into the world (that is, serve humanity in its collective evolution.) Then, concerning exploring ourselves, Assagioli states: 'we have first to penetrate courageously into the pit of our lower unconscious in order to discover the dark forces that ensnare and menace us.' From a Psychosynthesis perspective, we can come to understand and experience that the light of the Self can be found shining in the lower unconscious and, when found, its light, brighter for being experienced in the darkness, may illuminate us.

EXERCISE: THE CRYSTAL BOWL

Reflect on the meaning of synthesis, creating a spider chart with synthesis as your seed subject. Spend at least ten minutes on this reflection before continuing.

Relax and centre yourself, then imagine you have a clear crystal bowl balanced on top of your head... All the words, concepts, ideas and so on from your reflection fill up this bowl, and you can feel the weight of all these ideas on which you have been reflecting heavily pressing down on your head...

Now imagine the sun comes out above your head and a single ray of light shines down onto the bowl, dissolving all the words, ideas and so on in the bowl ... all the contents of the bowl evaporate until the bowl is completely empty...

The sun keeps shining and now the bowl itself dissolves, and the sun shines through into your heart ... from your heart the light from the sun fills up your whole body... Keep to this sense of the sunlight filling every inch of your form.

If thoughts, feelings or sensations intrude, then quietly and easily return to the sense of the light from the sun entering your body and filling you up...

Imagine yourself within your communities (those of family, friends, loved ones; and wider, those of town, nation, planet, etc.)... Keeping your connection with the light which is filling you up, be aware of the web of energy of which you are part... Project good will towards those within your communities and those without... then very clearly and distinctly, bring your self back to ground.

13

THE EGG AND THE TREE

Essential divinity... is a living reality which must be experienced, an inner revelation, an illumination. To realize it means we awaken to an existent but unrealized aspect of ourselves – the highest aspect, the true essence of our being. (Roberto Assagioli)

The Kabbalah (or Qabalah, an alternative transliteration) is the key to understanding the Western approach to spirituality, and therefore to really understanding Psychosynthesis. To those who practice both Psychosynthesis and Kabbalah, the many correspondences between the two are striking. Although Roberto Assagioli does not directly mention the Kabbalah in his writings, it is clear he was strongly influenced by it, both directly through Jewish mysticism, and more indirectly, although perhaps more potently, through mystical teachings from other sources. Assagioli had books in his library by Gershom Scholem (the founder of modern Jewish mysticism), a friendship with Martin Buber (whose interest in Kabbalah is well known), and a general interest in esoteric subjects and philosophies, the works of Alice Bailey and Theosophy, Plato and Dante, and a lively, inquiring mind. It is virtually impossible to imagine him not having knowledge of the Kabbalah.

Writings by Assagioli on Judaism and Jewish mysticism have been found amongst his papers. Most striking is a piece which mentions a psychospiritual description of the psyche that uses terminology from the Kabbalah: '...the traditional Jewish teaching of the human psychological condition consisting of three elements: nefesh, ruach, and neshamah ... my main endeavour has been to give scientific proof of the existence and activity of the spiritual soul (neshamah) with the psyche (ruach) as an inspiring and unifying factor.'

So what is the relevance of these terms nefesh, ruach and neshamah? They describe quite complex ideas that have whole Kabbalistic books written about them. Put simply, nefesh corresponds to the lower unconscious (including the basic activity of subpersonalities); ruach corresponds to the middle unconscious (including the personal I); and neshamah to the higher unconscious (including all the Soul Qualities familiar to Psychosynthesis practitioners, and the Self.)

These three parts (or perhaps more correctly, activities) of the human being have been compared to a candle flame. The blue/black part of the flame, at the bottom nearest the candle, constantly changing, invisible to regular sight, is the nefesh or animal soul. It corresponds to the id and ego, being reactive, and based on inner and outer desires. The middle, more usually visible portion of a candle flame, the yellowish glow in the centre, is equivalent to the ruach. It burns with a steady light, and conveys a sense of continuity and certainty. The light at the top of the candle is the superconscious, and the white flickering edge of the flame, corresponds to neshamah, the higher Self.

These three aspects, nefesh, ruach and neshamah, correspond exactly to the three divisions Assagioli assigned to his diagram of the human psyche, the well-known egg diagram. It is interesting to note that the shape of the egg is suggestive of a candle flame in itself. By being egg shaped, it also brings the Psychosynthesis model into alignment with Western esoteric teachings that describe the energy bodies of a human being as being egg shaped. The Kabbalistic diagram known as the Tree of Life, which is also divided into these same three divisions, is often drawn as enclosed in a vesica or egg shaped container.

At the time of developing and formulating Psychosynthesis, Assagioli followed the stance of his contemporaries Freud and Jung in aiming at a scientific exposition of psychology. In those pre-Quantum days, these pioneers in psychology believed that to be taken seriously they had to place their investigations in a scientific framework. Perhaps this is why Assagioli generally avoided talking about the esoteric foundations of Psychosynthesis, and specifically did not mention the Kabbalah. Also, in the first half of this century, founding a psychology on Jewish mysticism may well have led to negative repercussions that Assagioli understandably would have wanted to avoid. Anti-Semitism was rife even amongst the so-called more enlightened esoteric and psychological circles. Anti-Semitic attitudes have even been uncovered in the writings of Jung himself.

Further to this, the Kabbalah was traditionally a secret

doctrine, its practitioners avoiding revealing their source of inspiration for fear of contaminating the source with cultish, personality distortions. Assagioli may well have subscribed to this viewpoint. However, despite this avoidance of quoting mystical sources, Assagioli, in creating Psychosynthesis, constructed a psychological system that is clearly in tune with the ancient wisdom of the Kabbalah. Many of the main principles of Psychosynthesis reflect those found in Kabbalistic teachings, especially the central importance attached to the act of will, and the inclusion of a transpersonal will (or Purpose) as well as the individual will.

It is clear that the main Kabbalistic diagram, The Tree of Life, is at the core of the spiritual psychology in which Roberto Assagioli, the founder of Psychosynthesis, had a life-long interest. It is therefore not surprising that Psychosynthesis easily interfaces with the Kabbalistic Tree of Life to create a model that can be effectively applied in many areas, particularly in the fields of healing, counselling and psychotherapy. Indeed, an understanding of the Kabbalistic Tree of Life is useful for practitioners of all types of therapeutic work. The larger, synthesising context of the Kabbalah enables different models to be included without any subsequent loss to the integrity of each system.

The Kabbalah can particularly enable practitioners of Psychosynthesis to deepen their knowledge of the human psyche and to understand their basic models in a simple yet deeper and wider context. The Kabbalah helps practitioners to develop their own style in accord with universal principles, develop relationship in line with these principles, and apply methods relevant to each situation. Both the basic Psychosynthesis model and the Kabbalistic Tree of Life are systems of stunning clarity and simplicity. Using the two approaches together creates a meaningful synthesis that adds new depth to our work in service to others.

The Tree of Life

Perhaps the most inspiring aspect of the Kabbalah is that so much wisdom can be expressed through something so apparently simple. Whilst the ramifications and intricacies of the Kabbalah are undoubtedly many, it is nevertheless something that is simple to learn and to start using. I've discovered over the years that keeping the Kabbalah simple leaves space for insights to emerge,

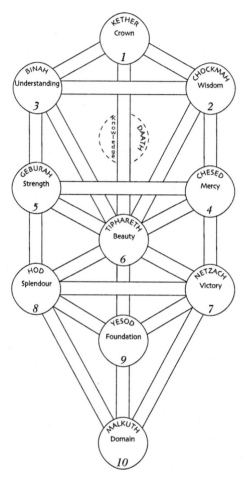

Diagram 4: The Kabbalistic Tree of Life

and it gives you the opportunity to make the system your own. Roberto Assagioli, albeit from a freethinking family, must have felt deeply that the Kabbalah connected him to his Jewish roots. Solomon, quoted from the Book of Proverbs in the Bible, says of the Tree of Life: 'She is more precious than pearls; and all the things you value are not equal unto her. Length of days is in her right hand: in her left are riches and honour. Her ways are ways of pleasantness, and all her paths are peace. A tree of life is she to those that lay hold of her: and every one that firmly grasps her will be made happy.'

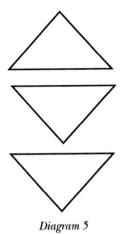

Diagram 5

Although steeped in mystery, The Kabbalah at its simplest is a method of personal and spiritual development based on the map called the Tree of Life. The purpose of this map is to help us sort out different aspects of our psyches so we can more clearly work with heart energy as well as with intellectual knowledge. When you first look at the Tree of Life it looks very complicated (see diagram 4), but it really is very simple. You can start by imagining an upright triangle. Then imagine two triangles, one upright, one underneath that is upside down. Then add one final triangle so you have three triangles, the top one the right way up and the two underneath ones upside down. These three triangles are the basis of the whole Tree of Life image.

So long as you can recall these triangles you will never forget the Tree of Life. Of course, the Tree of Life is little more complicated than that. At each of the corners of the triangles there is a sphere, and there is one extra sphere between the top two triangles and one extra one inside the bottom triangle. That's it, the whole image of the Tree of Life. An image without meaning, however, is fairly useless. So what does this all mean? What's the point of these triangles and the spheres at the corners?

The three circles on the bottom triangle of the Tree of Life (see diagram 6) represent our sensing, feeling and thinking functions, the familiar body, feelings and mind of Psychosynthesis. The bottom one, called 'kingdom', corresponds to the world or earth and the physical body. It represents our physical presence on the planet. When you spend even a moment aware of your physical presence and yet neither thinking nor feeling anything, that is this sphere in its essential form. You might have experienced this if you walk, dance, go running or swimming, and have pushed your body until you are no longer thinking or feeling anything. It is our absolute physical presence before we do anything with it.

The two spheres above the bottom one represent our feeling and thinking processes. So with these three spheres we cover the three modes we use at any moment to express ourselves or to experience what is happening. Usually, however, we do not just sense something, or just feel something, or just

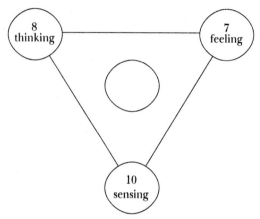

Diagram 6: Sensing, Thinking, Feeling and the Tree of Life

think something. All three modes operate in combination. For instance, some people are thinking most of the time, or are 'mentally identified'. We call these people intellectuals, and their thinking is their most developed function. We all know some people like this. Their sensations and feelings are simply more buried underneath. Some people, on the other hand, are more focussed on their feelings, or are 'emotionally identified'. Their feeling function is the most developed but, of course, they too have thoughts and sensations.

Assagioli drew the field of awareness in the centre of the egg diagram as a circle, and of course this is elegant in its conception. I have taken to changing the circle to an amoeba because our field of awareness is, as it were, constantly changing shape just as an amoeba does. This 'amoeba of awareness' moves about, most of the time, between the three spheres that represent thinking, feeling and sensing. Right now because I'm writing this, my 'amoeba' is pretty much centred on the thinking sphere. But I'm sensing some hunger so there is a little pseudopod (or arm) coming down to my belly saying: hey, tea soon? I'm also feeling a bit sad about something that happened earlier, so there is another pseudopod from the amoeba stretching out to the feeling sphere. Later this evening, after work when I'm relaxed, the 'amoeba' (my awareness) will move over to the feelings sphere. I'll be in a good, warm space, I won't be thinking much at all, or at the very least, I won't be aware of thinking very much.

These three sensing, feeling and thinking spheres, taken

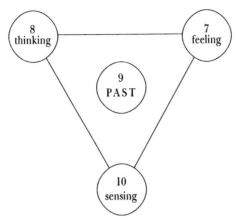

Diagram 7: The Past and the Tree of Life

together, represent what we have to experience life with and to express ourselves with, in the present moment. Here we are, here and now, with these three modes somehow or another activated within us and activating us.

The sphere numbered 9 in the centre of these other three spheres corresponds to lots of other things as well, but the easiest way to understand it initially is as representing the past (diagram 7.) Within any present moment we are always carrying the past within us. What happened to us in the past is affecting what's happening here and now. All the feelings, emotional reactions, thoughts, and senses we experience are unique to each of us, or at least somewhat different from everyone else's experience. At least partly, each of us has different experiences because of the different experiences we have had in the past.

Everything we do with the Tree of Life starts off from the physical earth sphere so the Kabbalah is clearly not a path of transcendence. It is not about saying: hey I don't like it here, there is something wrong with this planet, I'm going to do everything I can to shoot off somewhere else, let us tune in and go to the higher spheres. What Kabbalah teaches is that if we want to visit higher spheres, fine, but then we bring that energy back to earth to ground it. We find some way to make our connections manifest on the planet, otherwise there is no point incarnating in the first place.

An important part of being able to be here in the present moment, and fulfil our purpose, is dealing with the events that have happened to us in the past. It is vital to deal with this because otherwise our energy is depleted, our heart energy is not moving, and we are not living our lives in the best way we can. No one has dealt with all their past experiences, no one is perfect. We all experience different aspects of this, depending upon our past. For example, people who are working with spiritual energies are sometimes in danger of spiritual pride, spiritual inflation, or glamour. 'I connect with a great spirit and this spirit speaks through me alone.' Of course, this might be really important work and the spirit might really be real and might want to speak cosmic wisdom through this person. But if the 'channel' that the spirit is manifesting through is unclear in one way or another, then the message becomes distorted.

As well as the past, the other factor that affects us in the here and now is the future, our inner potential. Everything that is potential can happen in the future. The upper part of the Tree of Life represents the future; it is the potential we carry round in us, that is able to manifest at any moment. Most of the time, though, we are not aware of it. We might be so caught up with experiences from the past, or so busy in the present moment, we forget about our potential. It is still there, however, always manifesting.

Visualisation can be a powerful tool for connecting to potential energy. Once in the trance state brought about through focussing on imagery, we become disidentified from our everyday concerns, and align ourselves with the channel through which inspiration can manifest. We then usually experience this intuitive energy as it comes through in our thoughts, feelings or senses. We might have it as a flash, an inspiration, or an 'aha' experience, the potential shows itself through our thoughts - we just know something. Or we might experience it as a feeling about something. We just feel this is right; it's not like a personal feeling, but is a deeper sense of feeling. Or we experience inspiration or intuition through our bodies, we 'sense' something.

Potential also appears in dreams and images. All the spheres on the Tree of Life have multiple functions, and one of the functions of sphere 9, the past, is as the sphere of astral energy. Astral energy is the invisible energy out of which things that are immaterial, that are not physically manifest yet, form themselves. So if we wake up and remember a dream, the dream might be something to do with what has happened to us in the past, it might be a processing of things that happened to us today, or we might have a dream that is something to do with what's going on at that moment - for instance, a digestive process will create images in our unconscious and we will dream that. Some dreams have another quality to them that is to do with our potential, the invisible aspects of our movement through life. And it is astral energy that forms the building blocks, the substance that the potential energy uses to manifest itself. Often we don't understand images because what we try to do is process them with our brains. It is often important for us to just stay with images that we don't understand, and not try to work them out.

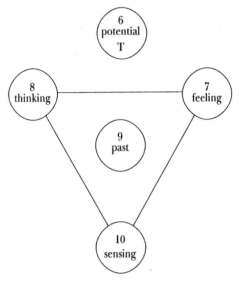

Diagram 8: The Self and the Tree of Life

The amoeba of awareness moves around and has different focuses on the Tree of Life. One of the 'arms' or pseudopodia of the amoeba can reach up around the central sphere, as it were. This yellow sphere is numbered 6 and called, in Kabbalah, 'beauty' (diagram 8.) This sphere corresponds to the Psychosynthesis 'I' at the centre of the egg diagram. It also corresponds to the heart at the centre of the human body, and the sun at the centre of our solar system. If I asked you to imagine the sun then connect it to your heart, which corresponds to the yellow sphere at the centre of the Tree of Life, this is where you would tune in. It is possible, through meditation and other techniques, to pull in all the 'arms' of the amoeba of awareness and focus totally around this central sphere. In Psychosynthesis this experience is sometimes described with the words: 'I am I, a centre of pure self consciousness.' Nothing else: no thoughts, no feelings, no sensations. 'I have thoughts and I am more than my thoughts. I have feelings, and I am more than my feelings. I have a body and I am more than my body. I am I, a centre of pure self consciousness.'

When we move into that central place, when we connect to our heart energy, to the central aspect of our being, there is also a push, an energy, a 'will', a 'transpersonal purpose', or 'spiritual thrust' - you can call it all sorts of names - something that pushes us back into life. It is as if, when we enter into the energy of the heart, something says: hey well, fine, we made this connection, very good, now do something with it. Activate it, make it more manifest on the planet. From a Kabbalistic viewpoint, people use the Tree of Life to meditate, and will focus on this spiritual centre, but always with the idea of being able to bring the energy back to earth.

The Kabbalistic system, as well as being a way of the heart, is also a way of everyday life. The Kabbalah focuses on manifesting soul energy into everyday life. The danger for many 'spiritual seekers' is that they like it on the sun so much they never want to leave there. They become so involved being the sun, being a light source, that they forget the shadows they cast. In terms of the solar system, in terms of our heart energy, if we stay just there, there aren't any shadows. Absolutely, and that's a wonderful place to experience. But often it is the shadows, the dark places, which reveal to us more things about how we are going to manifest. If everybody existed in a place of no shadow, there'd be no need for relationship, for contact, for service. We need places with shadows to remind us of our mortality and our totality.

PSYCHOSYNTHESIS AND THE TREE OF LIFE

The Kabbalah is a guide to self-awareness, personal and spiritual growth inspired and developed through the work of Western Esotericists and psychologists. It is the perfect model or map of consciousness for it is able, through its simplicity and clarity, to act as a central synthesising agent for any and all other systems, maps and models. In its modern forms, it is a progressive development from the Jewish Kabbalah, which is the mystical branch of Judaism.

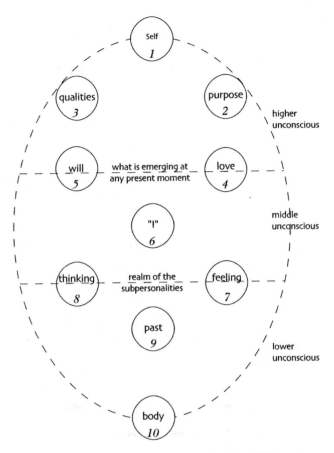

Diagram 9: Psychosynthesis and the Tree of Life

The Jewish Kabbalah, too, has been considerably developed, particularly in the latter part of the 20th Century, but is limited by its convergence with a specific set of religious beliefs. The non-Jewish Kabbalah, on the other hand, is placed beyond all belief systems, yet at the same time, includes them. It is remarkably unique in this way.

The Tree of Life is not just an abstract map of the psyche but also, through its system of correspondences, a map of both the structures and energies within the body. Diagram 9 shows an overlay of the Psychosynthesis egg diagram with the Kabbalistic Tree of Life. How well they overlap is striking, although perhaps not so astonishing when we remember Assagioli's interests.

Consider the implications of this for the Psychosynthesis egg diagram, which also corresponds to the Tree of Life! All the correspondences that can be made to the Kabbalistic Tree of Life are valid and relevant for the egg diagram too. For instance, the different spheres on the tree of life relate to the chakras, or energy centres within the body. Through correspondences, you can place these centres onto an egg diagram and increase your understanding of both. Try it and see, it is amazing how alive the egg can suddenly become when you connect with it in this way.

The aim of Psychosynthesis, from a Kabbalistic perspective, is to bring a client into relationship (spheres 4 to 10 inclusive) whilst holding connection to underlying spiritual principles (spheres 1, 2 and 3.) The practitioner aims to bring a client into existential reality through inclusion. How far this process goes depends upon the type of therapy being practised and the individual practitioners aims and abilities. For instance, Jungians would generally work with the energies represented by the whole Tree of Life excluding the top triangle; traditional psychoanalysts focus their work particularly on spheres 7,8,and 9; humanistic therapies on spheres 6 to 10; and so on. Psychosynthesis aims to include the whole Tree of Life as represented in simplified form by the egg diagram. Diagram 10 develops the connections that the three categories of principles, relationship and techniques make as they relate to the Tree of Life and the egg diagram. This three-fold understanding of the therapeutic and healing process - principles, relationship, and techniques - corresponds exactly with the three triangles on the Tree of Life.

EXERCISE: THE SACRED TREE

Here's a beautiful Kabbalistic meditation that is also pure Psychosynthesis. It starts off through creating sacred space, and then uses will and imagination to connect with the energies of the Tree of Life

Sacred space is any place you make holy (whatever holy means to you.) To imagine a circle around yourself and state your intent to use this circle to separate what is inside your sphere from what is outside your sphere, is a simple and effective way of creating sacred space. In this exercise, you will create this personal sacred space and then honour spirit within and without.

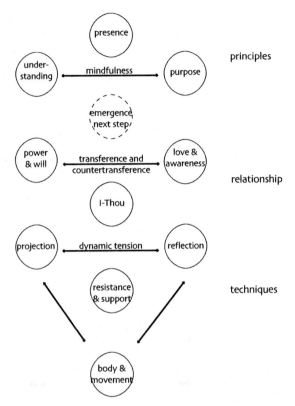

Diagram 10: Principles, Relationship, Techniques

The exercise is most effectively practised (at least in the beginning) in an actual physical space, but if you cannot do that for some reason, you can always do it as a visualisation.

Create a circle a round yourself. You might like to imagine you are drawing a shining white circle of light with an extended finger held out before you. You might want to reach up and below you and imagine not just a circle, but that you are enclosed in a sphere of white light. You might prefer the sphere to be night-blue, and twinkling with stars. Find your own way of defining this protective, psychic barrier around yourself...

However you choose to do this, the important point is to define that nothing can penetrate this barrier unless you choose to let it in... when you feel satisfied that your sacred circle is strong enough, continue the remainder of this exercise within the circle.

Standing at the centre of your circle, make three prostrations (in whatever way is appropriate to you; I like to lie right down on my belly sometimes, and sometimes I just bow down a little.)

At the first prostration, connect with the earth energies beneath you... stay on the ground for as long as feels right, then stand up again... On the second prostration, honour the guardians or spirits of the place you are in (wherever that is)... On the third prostration, whilst doing it, find some way to honour the Self (or deity) within your body...

Stand at the centre of your circle, and imagine a strong cord coming from the middle of your body and going right down into the centre of the earth. It roots you firmly to your spot... Imagine there is a hook or anchor on the end of the cord, and feel it attach to the earth very firmly...

Look round the place where you are... Imagine, sense and feel the presence of the guardians and angels of this place. Welcome their presence now...

Close your eyes, and expand your awareness to the immediate environment and nearby countryside... Silently ask the good spirits of this countryside to be present for you and your work, and to assist you in your life's work...

Return to full awareness of your physical body, be very conscious of having brought yourself right back into your body...

Turn your attention into your heart, and be aware of the energy in your heart... Breathe into your heart centre now, feeling energy building up... Let your heart centre open as much as is appropriate for you right now (in other words, don't push or force anything, just go at a pace and as far as suits you...)

Draw energy from the universe into your heart... Only if and when you feel ready, you can also channel some energy from your heart to wherever you wish...

This first part of the exercise can be used on its own as a way of creating sacred space, and before other rituals or visualisations. The remainder of the exercise involves a visualisation of the energies represented by the egg and the tree.

Imagine a bright white light hovering over your head...
- draw this white light down into your heart...
- as the white light reaches your heart it glows like a bright yellow sun in the centre of your chest...
- imagine this yellow light fills up all the space around you, pervading all directions with bright yellow light...

Imagine white light above your head again:
- visualise it flowing down into your yellow heart...
- then feel this light flow down into your lower body, your genital area, your legs, then into and around your feet...
- imagine a bright purple energy pervading all of your lower body, connecting you to the ground beneath you... feel the presence of your feet on the floor, supported by the earth.

Keep the sense of the white light flowing down from above your head, down through your glowing yellow heart, down into a purple light where you are in contact with the ground:
- imagine you are surrounded by a dark but bright blue aura...
- visualise this blue light surrounding and protecting you...
- affirm that this blue light brings you fully into manifestation, so that all that you are is here right now.

Again feel the presence of the white light above your head, down through your glowing yellow heart, down to the purple light in your lower body and where you contact the ground;
- be aware of the blue aura surrounding you...
- ask yourself: how can I manifest my connection to spirit?...
- ask yourself: as a soul what is my next step here on earth?...
- ask yourself: what practical steps can I take in my life, now or in the near future, to manifest this energy?

14

WAYS AND RAYS

Typology gives the key to understanding and appreciating why individuals react and behave differently when confronted by the same situation or human contact... The true, deeper understanding is the comprehension of the individual as a unique being, with unique qualities, problems, and possibilities. It is the fruit of empathy, intuition, and love.
(Roberto Assagioli)

There are as many different ways of experiencing the world as there are living creatures. Each of us humans, for instance, lives in a world that, although perhaps in the greater scheme of things is virtually identical to, in the immediate experience of the moment can be very different from any other human's experience. My view of a distant star is incredibly close to yours, from our perspective, but nevertheless is somewhat different. And what we do with that experience of seeing a star, how we interpret it, feel about it and so on, may be, from our human perspective, massively different. There's so much awareness, it sometimes feels like there's too much awareness! So what is the source of all this awareness?

A simple yet powerful exercise is to allow yourself to sink into the flow of consciousness and then ask yourself: what is the source of all this awareness? Of course, the answer is beyond words, but what is interesting is how easily we can slip beyond the witness position and have an experience of this source of awareness. In one sense, we can become aware of its eternal presence, always behind whatever we are experiencing. So, what is this source of awareness? The Hermetic Tradition offers an answer that leads us to a deeper understanding of Psychosynthesis.

Simply put, the idea is that there are seven dimensions. The first two dimensions exist before and behind our material world and are likened to a point and a circle. This point and circle represent the source of all awareness. For some reason beyond human understanding, this source of awareness, in wanting to know itself better, created a reflection of itself, thus giving rise to further dimensions. Kabbalists say not to worry about what all this exactly means because, as we are a created reflection of this 'source' we can best understand what it is through understanding ourselves.

Beyond the first two dimensions lies the world of three dimensions,where we humans live. Everything we experience, however infinitely small or infinitely large, has three dimensions. Without any past or future, however, without time or motion in other words, no substance could either know anything of itself or of the world around it. The fourth dimension is therefore that of time. From the original two dimensions, a three-dimensional something has been created that, through moving in the fourth dimension of time, can know itself. This knowledge of itself is the fifth dimension, that of pure self-consciousness and of will.

Now it can know itself, this self-consciousness uses its will to create vehicles for its journey of self-discovery, both to experience the world outside and to express itself in that world. These vehicles, in the human being, are called thinking, feeling and sensing. They create the substance of the sixth dimension.

That original source of awareness, through a process of unfolding self-awareness has progressed thus far in getting to know itself; it is now different from all other being(s), and through its difference can get to know itself more thoroughly. All the different ways in which each individual being relates to the world is the seventh dimension. This is sometimes described as the seat of ego, and also understood as the depository of all the past events in a life that colour its existence. This is true both on individual and collective levels. Many esoteric systems of knowledge describe a 'Law of Seven' or similar. Theosophy, which strongly influenced Assagioli, particularly in his middle years, describes there being Seven Rays that are the basis for all manifestation. Often metaphors and analogies are drawn from the physical world to support this theory. Light, for instance, is composed of seven parts, the colours of a rainbow, and music (in its Western form, anyway) can be understood through octaves where there are seven notes and an eighth which brings us back to the first again.

Through how we humans, individually and collectively, experience the seven dimensions, we can understand more of the source of all awareness, for we are created in its image. Psychosynthesis theory, following the Kabbalah, suggests that because everything of which we are aware exists in the created world of duality, then each of the seven dimensions must have a dual nature, a bright side and a shadow. An understanding of these light and dark sides can help us to understand the seven dimensions in terms of human experience.

SEVEN LIGHTS, SEVEN SHADOWS

In the first dimension, that of unity, the uniqueness of each individual is emphasized. The shadow of this is loneliness and isolation, going through an experience but not in relation to anything or anyone else. Aloneness is experienced in a negative way, as separate, cut off, and isolated, yet the ensuing existential crisis may paradoxically lead to an experience of uniqueness.

The second dimension is that of duality, emphasizing the possibilities of experience: for anything to be experienced, duality has to exist. The shadow of this is separation and division. The individual experiences being separate, misunderstood, and unloved. Duality is experienced in a negative way, as separating, divisive, isolating, yet being in this experience is a necesary precursor to an experience of at-one-ness.

The third dimension is that of form and dynamic balance, thus emphasizing the possibilities of synthesis. The shadow is confusion and stuckness, a feeling of being trapped and an inability to move forward. The third point for a synthesis between the polarities cannot be found. As we progress through the different dimensions, it becomes harder to see the way through any situation. The world is experienced in a negative light: people feel like giving up, and even committing suicide. As with the previous two dimensions, however, if we do not cut off from the experience, but rather see it as an experience of the world of concrete and manifest duality, the possibility opens up of finding a new synthesis.

The fourth dimension is that of motion and time, emphasizing the existence of movement in space and introducing the idea of past and future. A sense of individual identity is born which in turn engenders purpose, self-worth and true value. The shadow side of this is feeling trapped in time. Everything seems to hinder and frustrate because the world moves too fast, or alternatively because things don't happen fast enough. A person experiences impatience, or may think they are missing many opportunities. However time is experienced, it can easily become a major distraction, and a source of much suffering.

The pure experience of the fifth dimension is to be simply oneself, being and doing whatever one is doing with the consciousness of pure self-awareness. The fifth dimension is that of self-knowledge and self-worth, not because of anything that is thought, felt or sensed, and not because of anything that is done, but simply because we exist as self-aware beings. The shadow of this is self negation. Whereas on the positive side the experience is of being truly awake, on the shadow side the experience is of being asleep. Like a ship just keeping afloat in a tempestuous sea of experiences, we feel devoid of self-worth and value. There is no captain and no one is at the helm. In fact, coming to a pure experience of the fifth dimension is sometimes likened to becoming the helmsman of a life ship. To experience this dimension is to be in touch with the deeper meaning and purpose of life and feel innate worthiness simply through being who one is.

When feeling lost, worthless, or asleep, we can recall the fifth dimension and accept our experience as part of life. Even at times of becoming caught up, the inner connection is not lost. There is no need to deny anything; there is the potential to include all experiences as part of the journey of the soul. Upon awakening, we start to find meaning and purpose in life, for ourselves individually, for human beings collectively, and for the whole of existence. To be fully awake is to enter this dimension and truly say: I am I, and that in itself is enough. I have thoughts, feelings, sensations, I have experiences in the world and can choose to express myself, but at heart, in essence, I am simply who I am, a being with an inherent, individual identity.

The sixth dimension is that of the vehicles for experience and expression in the world. Other beings, whether animal, plant, extraterrestrial or other-dimensional, may have other methods of experience and expression, but humans have three: sensations (body), emotions (feelings) and thoughts (mind). Along with intuition, which is the connection with soul, they are used for everything that is experienced and expressed by a human being.

The shadow of this is when, instead of these vehicles being a joyous and interactive connection to the world, they become a prison. We become so connected to thoughts, to emotions or to sensations, or some combination thereof, that we forget who we really are. This is not to say that the shadow is a bad thing, quite the contrary. It is through getting caught up, becoming totally identified with what we are doing, through attachment to the world without holding back, that it is possible to come to a true experience and expression of oneself. A problem only arises when, through forgetfulness, instead of having the ability to pull back, as it were, and observe what is happening from a clearer space, we become imprisoned and forgets our wider perspective. This is, according to esoteric doctrines, a necessary experience for the growth of both individual and collective soul.

The seventh dimension is that of the different ways each manifesting soul relates to the world. There are seven rays and whilst everyone has these seven rays within, each individual soul is on the path of a predominate ray which then affects its every experience. The seventh dimension involves a soul's intent in incarnation, using the appropriate ray energy for its particular purpose. The shadow is to become so disconnected from spiritual origins that we may change, for instance: power into aggression and tyranny; love into possession and hate; action into apathy and sloth; beauty into ugliness and discord; knowledge into dogma and prejudice; devotion into blind allegiance; ritual into bureaucracy and control.

THE SEVEN WAYS

The Seven Ways model is a Psychosynthesis typology developed by Assagioli. He based it on the theosophical version of the original Hermetic conception of Seven Rays, and cleverly changed the seven 'rays' into seven 'ways' (which in English is especially elegant.) He called his work 'The Seven Ways to Transpersonal Realisation' and this was to be his next Psychosynthesis book.

Some Psychosynthesis practitioners have questioned the inclusion in Psychosynthesis of a system derived from Theosophy. Whilst this is understandable considering the 'quirkiness' of many theosophical writings, the power of the system as adapted by Assagioli, means it transcends its origins. Just because someone may 'borrow', 'adapt' or in any other way use a model from one system doesn't mean they have to take the whole system lock, stock and barrel. I might use some of Jung's concepts in my version of Psychosynthesis but that doesn't mean I have to adopt the whole of Jung's work.

Psychosynthesis did not all come from Freud or a reaction to Freud and then somehow mysteriously 'happen' in Assagioli's head. He worked on it, and read and studied widely. Psychosynthesis has roots in many traditions as we have already seen, some more 'kosher' than others. Psychosynthesis is a brilliant attempt at a synthesis of both Western and Eastern knowledge and practice; of pragmatic and mystical approaches to the human psyche; and as an easily adaptable system that is useful in many different fields. Psychosynthesis is not an esoteric school or a religion either, but that doesn't mean we cannot recognise and include ideas from esoteric sources. Assagioli makes the point that the confusion of science is in it being restricted to the quantitative. The practical brilliance of the seven ways typology is just that it is not quantitative but effectively *qualitative*.

The seven ways to transpersonal realisation are within us all, are not sharply divided and, in fact, frequently overlap. By their very nature, we can come to experience them in others or ourselves through an intuitive rather than intellectual process. Each of the ways is associated with a particular soul ray that emanates from the source of all awareness. In other words, each individual soul is 'charged with' or 'informed by' the energy of one or more of these rays. Each of us has one or more of these rays manifesting through different aspects of our being. Although in essence we are connected to all seven of the ways, some of them become foreground in our particular stage of evolution.

Name of Way	Number	Alternative Name
WILL	1	Power
LOVE	2	Wisdom
ACTIVITY	3	Action
BEAUTY	4	Harmony
KNOWLEDGE	5	Science
DEVOTION	6	Idealism
RITUAL	7	Organization

Most people have two primary influences, one for the Soul and one for the personality. Then, within the personality, one way will be found to particularly influence the mind, another the feelings, and a third the body and senses. When looking for the influence of these ways within yourself or anyone else, it is important not to be dogmatic. The divisions between the ways are not clear-cut, and it is often difficult to tease out the difference between the influences various ways have on different parts of the person.

The 'height' of the way is how it manifests in its 'pure' form; the 'depth' of the way is, to a greater or lesser degree, how it manifests through the personality. The task, once a way's influence has been identified, whether in its 'height' or 'depth', is to elevate it. This means to use techniques to create dynamic balance between the various components involved in the manifestation of that way. This might take the form of personality work, meditation and visualisation; always, however, it will involve a deep-rooted connection with Soul energy through self-identification exercises.

• The Way of Will

Sometimes called 'the heroic way', this is the way of leaders, for 'good' or 'bad'. People on this way are wilful, one-pointed, quick to action, prompt, decisive, competitive, and have the power of physical endurance. They tend to judge emotions as negative. If distorted they are self-centred and isolated, assertive in a judgmental way, and sometimes even violently psychopathic.

Key:	Action and Adventure
Types:	Leader, Adventurer, Warrior, Advocate, Athlete, Builder
Examples:	Mahatma Gandhi, Nelson Mandela, Bill Gates
Task:	To develop skilful, good, and strong will, to temper their Will with Love, to become more understanding and co-operative, to build as well as to destroy, to align their personal will with their true Purpose.
Objective:	'I choose to act; to express my free will.'

• The Way of Love

Love permeates all things, and the Way of Love is particularly difficult to separate from the other ways, yet it is a very specific path. People on this way tend to be 'servers' to humanity, whether through medicine and healing, or in more indirect ways. It is the path of inclusiveness, of seeing the 'divine' in everything.

Co-operation, brotherhood, and group consciousness are all important concepts to these people. Their purpose in life is to love and to ultimately transform individual love into Universal Love. The person on the Way of Love will want to include as much as possible, and will realise him- or herself through relationships. They tend to be soft, sometimes to the point of inertia. They tend to hold the impression made by the last person who 'sat on them'. They are sometimes without boundaries.

Key	Romance and Relationships
Types	Actor, Lover, Parent, Healer, Counsellor, Teacher, Gardener
Examples:	Dalai Lama, Roberto Assagioli, Casanova
Task	Enlarging and refining their overall positive attitude, cultivating love in its pure form, to nurture, heal, forgive, develop intimacy, learn to use will more, to be courageous, have direction, be able to say 'no'.
Objective:	'I desire to love; to help others express their highest potential.'

• The Way of Action

For people of this type, there is no need for any ultimate goal, the going is sufficient in itself. They can be passionate and dispassionate at the same time. They can act on behalf of others with absolutely no self-interest. They are pragmatic and skilful, and deal with the element of earth very successfully. On the negative side they tend to be unconscious of deeper and higher feelings, so often are insensitive and manipulative and devious. They are very efficient and effective at getting a job done, but can get caught up in their activity and lose touch with its purpose.

Key	Activity and Intelligence
Types:	Writer, Entrepreneur, Financier, Media networker
Examples:	Florence Nightingale, Albert Schweitzer, George Soros
Task	To be still, to slow down, to allow 'being' as well as 'doing', to develop the higher, intuitive mind, need to cultivate love, connect with feelings, develop aesthetic appreciation.
Objective:	'I wish to know; to create from my resources.'

• The Way of Beauty

They are creative and intuitive people, and often have a deep understanding of both themselves and others. They see the divine in all forms; they can see true beauty in all manifestation. Ecstasy and agony are both familiar to these artistic types. On the negative side they find it difficult to make choices, and are easily spaced out (both in pleasant and unpleasant ways). Often they are adversely affected by other people's negative energies. They can be dreamy and impractical.

Key	Beauty and Artistic Expression
Types:	Artist, Musician, Dramatist, Mediator, Designer, Naturalist
Examples:	Beethoven, William Blake, Princess Diana
Task	To cultivate persistence, and the will, particularly in self-assertion, to synthesize polarities, resolve conflict, and develop sensitivity to beauty to connect with creative impulses and manifest them in as pure a form as possible.
Objective:	'I wish to live in harmony; to express my artistic abilities.'

• The Way of Science

Using the mind, in both its abstract and concrete modes, with strong intuition and imagination, these types love exploring, and are often filled with waves of curiosity. Bright and clear of mind, they can be tireless in the pursuit of knowledge. They tend, however, to be very out of touch with their emotional life, and are often stuck in mental identification. They can be excessively analytical, and opinionated, even sometimes arrogant about their beliefs. They can also be insensitive to others.

Key	Scientific Investigation
Types:	Scientist, Researcher, Engineer, Inventor, Mechanic
Examples:	Stephen Hawkins, Einstein, Mengeles
Task	To get in touch with feelings, develop and appreciate their emotions, need to balance head and heart. can also learn to use the mind to go beyond itself, to

develop the soul of technology in service to humanity and the planet.

Objective: 'I wish to discover nature's mysteries; to invent new technologies.'

• The Way of Devotion

This is the way of mysticism, of devotion to a 'god', 'guru', ideal or cause. The devotion of this type is intense, and they are often completely dedicated to their work. They have a great urge for unity, and union with their desired transcendent goal. On the negative side they often lack joy in their lives, and are overly serious. Often they don't see alternatives, and want to convert others to their 'one true' way. They include those who become harsh fanatics and 'fundamentalists'.

Key	Passion Plays
Types:	Mystic, Guru, Crusader, Martyr, Idealist, Fanatic
Examples:	Mother Theresa, Bob Marley, Osama Bin Laden
Task	To enlarge themselves both mentally and emotionally, refine their sense of devotion. To develop high ideals and refine spirituality.
Objective:	'I aspire to uphold my ideal and to transcend the ordinary.'

• The Way of Ritual

This is the way of magic, of organising matter in such a way as to change consciousness, both on the inner and outer planes. People of this type tend to be organisers, making order out of chaos. They are in touch with Purpose and how to achieve their intention. They are disciplined at their chosen creative tasks. Although not as inspired as the Beauty type they will usually get a lot more done, giving tremendous attention to detail. On the negative side they are often controlled by routines and their endless organisation can be boring both to themselves and others. They can also be rigid and, if given the opportunity, bureaucratic.

Key	Organization and Magic
Types	Conductor, Organizer, Magician, Dancer, Priest, Architect, Manager
Examples:	Isadora Duncan, David Blaine, Peter Sutcliffe (Yorkshire Ripper)
Task	To develop Ritual, to put matter into rhythm, to give order to things that help people appreciate rhythms/cycles of Nature, need to 'build a bridge' between Soul and Self.
Objective:	'I wish to bring order out of chaos, and to live spontaneously.'

Exercise: The Ways Within

There are tasks associated with all the ways to transpersonal realisation. You will probably recognise some of yourself in all these types, but your task is to find which of these ways are those with which you particularly connect on the personality and on the Soul level. Once you have worked on this for yourself, it becomes a useful typological tool when interacting with others.

For the personality Way, it is useful to ask yourself: from which Way do I live my everyday life? To find your Soul Ray ask yourself: which Way do I experience during peak experiences?

When you have elucidated this, then ask yourself these following questions for both the personality Way and soul Ray:

• What needs to be refined?
• What needs to be elevated?

The previous sections on the individual ways should help you answer these last two questions.

Once you have found your ways it is a useful exercise to then apply your knowledge of this system to other people; what ways do your parents, lovers, friends, colleagues, etc., operate from? What do they need to elevate and refine?

It is worth noting that whatever way each of us follows we are all 'pilgrims' with the same goal, notwithstanding the difference of method. Through the diversity of the Seven Rays we make an approach to the essential divinity in us all, individually and collectively.

15

BEFORE BIRTH, BEYOND DEATH

Deep in each of us there is an inner pull toward some higher form of life, an underlying but insistent urge that prompts us – like the flower which innately turns toward the sun – to look toward something greater than ourselves...This secret force has been called man's divine discontent, the hound of heaven, the evolutionary urge... it is the story of man's life on earth, for it covers his progression from the earliest forms of consciousness to whatever worlds of realization may lie ahead. (Roberto Assagioli)

Everything that happens to us, from when we incarnate and are born to when we die, has meaning. Through exploring the journey of individuation within the developmental cycles of the human psyche, we come to understand that the journey of life and the journey of the soul are one and the same. Our life journey is a process of cycles within cycles, punctuated with significant times of transition and change. We are not just a personality, something else runs through our lives, a deeper presence or knowing that brings meaning to the journey of life.

Start by considering the whole of life, from birth to death, as one cycle (diagram 11.) Perhaps something happens between

death and life, no one knows for sure, so we leave a little gap in the diagram to show this. Within this whole cycle of life, we go through various other cycles or stages of development. These can be classified in various ways; we will consider the seven human ages, based on developmental theories. These are: baby/infant, toddler, child, adolescent, young adult, mature adult and elder. We go through

Diagram 11

transitions that take us from one of these life stages to another. For instance, when a baby turns over and starts crawling, she or he enters toddler stage; when a child reaches puberty, he or she enters adolescence. Each passage and each stage have their own signs, symptoms and peculiarities.

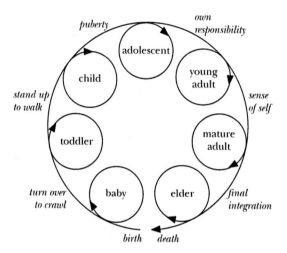

Diagram 12: The Seven Stages of Human Development

Of course, within each of these cycles, there are smaller cycles of transition and change. For instance, one of your cycles includes your interest in reading a book like this, for you would not be reading it if this was not the case. Now here you are today, at this particular time, involved in reading this chapter: cycles within cycles.

Another cycle you may be involved in as an adult is that of being a partner to someone. Another cycle within a cycle might involve living on your own. You may have children and are involved in the cycle of parenthood, guiding other beings through their cycles of development. Within the cycle of parenthood you might have a difficult adolescent living with you at this moment. And so on ...

This model for life helps us to recognize how feelings, emotions, events, reactions, thoughts, and many other responses to any situation, instant or on-going, are patterns that repeat themselves through many life cycles, and usually originate in earlier cycles. The model of cycles within cycles with its patterns of behaviour that are constantly being repeated, also paradoxically reminds us of the basic, universal truth, that everything changes.

The whole life of each person is unique, beginning with incarnation (or conception), or from the time of the first cells dividing in the embryo, a journey of differentiation. We all experience times in our lives when the focus is on integration, and there are times when we seem to be dis-integrating. In whatever way we experience all these different aspects of life, we are continuously affected by what has happened to us in our individual and collective past. Not victims to the past, however, we have sewn seeds that give us clues to our deeper soul purpose. We also experience this deeper sense of purpose, or at least get a glimmer of it, at times of special awakenings, and at times of crisis. Sometimes we experience ourselves as heroic and sometimes as quite something other than that, but for those willing to work with the soul's journey, life offers the ultimate challenge of knowing oneself.

The turning points in our lives could just as easily be called growing points, whether we experience them as growing up or growing down! We grow through both experiences of joy and times of pain. It is said that a breakdown can always be reframed as a breakthrough. To learn to face suffering with acceptance, not passively, but where it allows us, somewhat paradoxically, to make better choices for ourselves, is our aim. Turning points are times when the will is activated, and through learning the lessons held within these times, we bring greater perspective and proportion into our lives. Perhaps all our experiences of change are part of a larger evolutionary pattern.

To summarise, our development is affected by: all the events that happen to us in our lives (the effect of the past, represented in the Psychosynthesis egg by the lower unconscious); the potential we manifest each time we take the next step on our journey (the middle unconscious); the pull we feel within ourselves to know ourselves better as spiritual beings manifesting on this physical plane (the effect of the superconscious upon us); and all this development is directed by the I or self who is in direct contact with the author of it all (the Self.) In other words, we are developing body, feelings and mind as vehicles for expression and experience, for the incarnation and manifestation of the Self.

AT ONE AND SEPARATE

The process of birth involves a separation (from the womb) and a bonding (with mother). Most people continue to unconsciously and compulsively repeat patterns set up at this crucial time in an attempt to both meet basic needs and to manifest the Self. The primal events in our own experience of birth and our early relationship with mother affects our subsequent life, particularly in repeating cycles of behaviour. The underlying issue can be found in the experience of oneness and separateness. This primary polarity is key to understanding ourselves because it describes two opposite experiences that coexist at the same time. We can recognise that we are both separate and at-one at the same time, our primary experience depending upon which pole we focus our attention. Looking at the processes of birth, bonding (oneness) and separation from mother, each of us, as an individual, learned to be in the world, and negotiated our eventual separation from mother.

Our psychological birth or separation from mother is the time of primary importance, and involves a process that occupies much of our early infancy (from birth to three years old, sometimes called the oral phase.) This time inevitably includes an experience of optimal failure by the mother that sets the stage for the development of personality. During our subsequent life, the pattern of experience set up at this time is experienced through the polarity of trust and mistrust. It is an important part of our development for us to have a good, strong ego because it acts as a container for our growth and a vehicle for the experience and expression of our spiritual energies.

When we can recognise polarities within us, the opportunity opens for us to move to a third position from where we can observe the polarities and choose how the needs of both may be satisfied.

BIRTH AND THE PSYCHOSYNTHESIS EGG

The Psychosynthesis egg diagram is much more versatile than at first appears. Assagioli's creation of the egg diagram is one of his finest achievements, being a workable simplification of the Kabbalistic Tree of Life. What is presented, through the diagram, is a way of understanding the human condition in many different ways. If you start exploring the diagram with the spirit of inquiry, it becomes alive with possibility, and offers both mystery and revelation. For instance, the egg diagram can be used to describe the birth process from a Psychosynthetic viewpoint.

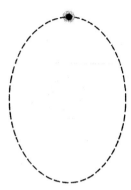

Diagram 13: The Universal Self (the Star) chooses to incarnate, shown on the 'egg diagram' as part in and part out of existence, ready to become an individual but in no way really separate from itself or its source.

Diagram 13

Diagram 14: The individualised spark of self separates itself and enters the egg. An embryo is created, having an embryonic 'self'.

Diagram 14

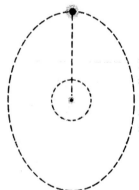

Diagram 15: The foetus develops, and starts to individuate. It identifies with the contents of its awareness and has an experience of being 'self' but not separate.

Diagram 15

Diagram 16: The time of birth. Differentiation occurs, duality (between upper and lower unconscious) is formed, and there is the first physical sense of self and other. The seed or potential for 'height' and 'depth' are now fully present.

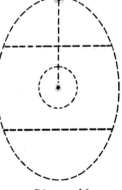

Diagram 16

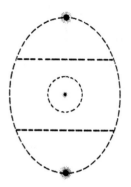

Diagram 17: The presence of the polarities of height and depth causes the Self to be drawn down into incarnation. The original Self is now incarnated, 'divided for the sake of love and for the chance of union.' From the perspective of the individual, this separation is experienced as rejection and abandonment and/or opportunity.

Diagram 17

Diagram 18: After spending five or six months in a state of union with mother, the first response to the realisation of self as separate is fear that heralds the birth of the ego. From the outset, ego is a survival response, intent upon protection and control. It is, of course, the best response the infant has available and is appropriate to the circumstances.

In its earliest months a newborn child is a living extension of its mother (or whomever or whatever plays the mother role for the baby.) The mother and child live in a constant physical and energetic interchange. For the little one the early months are lived in a world where there is no distinction between what is inside and what is outside, they are one and the same. This baby also lives in the illusion that it has created its world. The mother meanwhile (at least ideally) feels empathy, doesn't expect anything in return for her constant attention, and is basically dedicated to the survival and well-being of the baby. Many mothers report this unconditional love phase of the early relationship. Of course this feeling, coming from the depths of her procreative archetypes, will trigger the woman's own issues about oneness and separateness, so this period can bring great difficulties for her personally, and within her relationships.

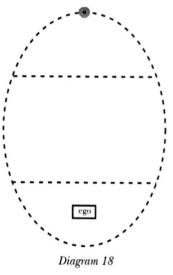

Diagram 18

Then, around six months (or earlier in some theories) this changes. The baby experiences a failure on the part of the mother who is starting to noticeably withdraw and assert her separateness. She no longer attends to the baby's every need so the baby experiences the feeling of abandonment. This is inevitable and part of our human development. How present or absent the mother is, and how well she copes with this phase (both within herself and within the relationship) has a profound effect on the child's development. Our basic connection with the archetypes of oneness and separateness is programmed. One result is that we internalise the image of mother, and split her into two parts, the good mother and the bad mother. Whether incarnated as a male or female , our relationship with the feminine archetype is set.

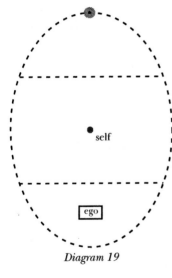

Diagram 19: Each transition and crisis the developing child (and adult) experiences is an opportunity to re-centre at the core, our 'self' or 'I', or to remain in continuing reaction to the past, controlled by ego. This is not to suggest anything negative about ego; rather the issue is whether ego acts as an unkind master or as a trusted friend. The Psychosynthesis egg diagram shows us how we need both, the ego forming a 'bridge' between the self and the earth and body (the periphery of the egg.) Ego depends upon the (past) contents of consciousness. The self is unique and exists without content.

Diagram 19

Moving to 'I' or self as centre of one's being rather than being centred on the ego is a life time work in progress. It is best viewed with the spirit of inquiry, not as a task to be completed at the end of which we will apparently be 'okay.' Psychosynthesis asserts that we are already okay as we are in the process of development. Developmental stages are the work of bringing connection to the Self. This is the Great Work of the alchemists, sometimes described as turning the lead of ego into the gold of the self.

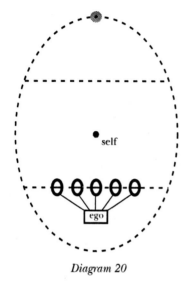

Diagram 20

Diagram 20: Subpersonalities sit half in and half out of the middle and lower unconscious 9as shown in diagram 20). They are formed as responses and reactions to experiences during our life journey (particularly early life.) Set up as survival mechanisms – 'outposts' of the ego, as it were – they make forays into the 'dangerous' (to ego) territory of the middle unconscious, but are always held in position by their experiences from the past.

A subpersonality breaks free sometimes, as for instance in the case of a mystic subpersonality, but it is still rooted in the past. Sometimes a subpersonality takes over the centre, creating a false sense of self based on the content of experience (rather than the source of all experience.) It is, of course, always partial.

The differentiated newborn and, in a sense, the individual throughout the rest of life, is on a journey towards individuation and, eventually, re-union. How this life is lived is dependent upon what was experienced during the earlier developmental stages and how these experiences are dealt with during the subsequent stages of development. By way of example, we could briefly consider mid life and approaching death.

MID LIFE

As we go through our different developmental stages, we walk a path between ego and self, becoming fixed in some places, avoiding others, having peak experiences that 'take us up to the self', sometimes being 'drawn down into the depths.' Both experiences are of equal importance and the true unattached self may be found in either.

In adult life we are particularly prone to existential and mid-life crisis. We all experience such crises throughout our lives, often in cyclical patterns. Mid-life crisis, so-called, can occur any time from 30 to 60, and may indeed be an on-going

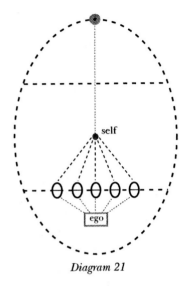

Diagram 21

theme throughout all these years. Certainly, we all have 'crises of existence' - times when we find life too difficult, meaningless, empty, or we lose track of ourselves and any sense of purpose.

Unlike any of our experiences which are determined by the past, however, for instance our fear of abandonment because mother left us in the pram, and so on, existential crisis is more about the present and future (the middle and higher unconscious in the egg diagram.) What we embark upon then is markedly different as we are concerning ourselves more with what comes after ego, the emergence and 'growth' of soul. Of course, the past is still very relevant, because what we experience in our existential crises mirrors energies from the past, unresolved 'stuff' brought up once again for us to face.

Existential crises can be seen as happening in three stages. Firstly, there is a separation from what has been in one's life before, the comfortable or at least familiar patterns of daily life. Finally, after the crisis, there is a return to the old life, but renewed by the experience. The stage in the middle - sometimes called 'liminality' - is what concerns us most. The 'limen' is the doorway, so to be in liminality means simply to be in the doorway - that is, neither where you were before, nor where you are going afterwards. To be in the midst of things - a similar concept to the phrase 'to be in limbo' (although that might suggest nothing before or after!)

An important aspect of the journey of life is to have companionship, whether this is close loved ones or fellow travellers we hardly know. It is important to be able to recognise others on the journey and let them recognise you too. In other words, our journey is enhanced through compassion and heart energy. Our wounding is unique to us, and mirrors or corresponds to the wounding of the world and the universe. We often read today about the wounded planet. If our individual wounds bring us closer to soul energy, then perhaps our collective and planetary wounds can do the same.

The journey of life can be seen as one of cycles within cycles, each cycle in life having within it smaller cycles, each of these having within them even smaller cycles. Issues from one cycle reverberate through and affect issues throughout all the other cycles. The whole process starts happening when we leave the undifferentiated unity characteristic of the secure, safe womb. Psychosynthesis theory suggests we come into incarnation so we can learn lessons useful to our soul's journey. This is the purpose for our being here. Within this over-riding life purpose we take many smaller steps towards this unfoldment, and each small step is vitally important. We cannot take each step with an awareness of the bigger picture, but we can hold this as an underlying intent. Our birth memories, and memories and experiences from the early stages of our life, act as models for the rest of our lives, enabling a shift from a victim position towards a holistic vision where each cycle contains the pattern of the whole.

The Elder and Beyond

The last two turns of the wheel on the journey of life are the one from mature adult to elder, and from elder into death. Of course, not everyone (either developmentally or literally!) reaches the status of 'elder', but with certainty everyone reaches death. On reflection, it seems that one of the major features of a life that qualifies someone for the status of 'elder' is not what age they reach (although they may well deserve the title then just for having reached a certain age!) but how well they have integrated the lessons of life. This is not to say anyone is better or worse than another, just that we all live unique and idiosyncratic lives, developing more in some areas and less in others. Perhaps the truest sign of integration - and the wisdom that comes with it - is recognising that we are just right as we are, wherever and however we have developed through life. Certainly the wisest old people I have met exhibit great acceptance of themselves and others.

Consider this: there are approximately six billion people on the planet today; about 50-100 million die each year, which is equivalent to about 1 million people dying each week, 200,000 each day, 1,000 each hour, or somewhere around 20 people die each minute. Sit quietly with a clock in front of you and watch one minute pass, and reflect on the twenty or so people who die during this minute. Death is always with us, maybe death is waiting just behind your left shoulder, waiting to tap you, and when it does and you look round, you are facing your death. It is important in the Psychosynthesis journey to find ways to acknowledge the presence of death and start to build relationship with it.

There are many different ways of approaching death, for instance where death is treated as an enemy to fight, or is faced with resignation, or denied, or considered as a noble sacrifice, and so on. Death can be accepted, seen as a deep sleep, a blessing, return to nature, the end of life's tasks. Death can be thought of as simply transitional, a passage before an inevitable rebirth. Death may be seen as an executioner, the grim reaper who comes and cruelly takes life away. There is no right or wrong way to face death, though Psychosynthesis strongly suggests an attitude of acceptance where possible, following the formula that acceptance is a necessary prelude to successful transitions. Death can also be met through embracing its reality, treating it as something that has been lived with as a presence through life, and that is always treated as a friend.

Of course, this is a lot harder to understand or accept when someone dies prematurely, especially as an infant or child. Those who survive into old age do not necessarily become 'elders' in a developmental sense. Issues from earlier stages that have not been integrated may arrest the development of an individual acting out unintegrated physical, emotional and mental identifications. At least someone who lives to old age has had a chance with their life's tasks, unlike someone who dies younger. A major aspect of dealing with such deaths is to see our lives not only as individual but as part of a larger, collective unfolding of evolution. An individual spark of consciousness may be extinguished but the light of the Self is everlasting.

FOREPLAY FOR TWO EGGS

If we consider the relationship between two people, it is fun to consider some of the different possibilities of meeting by using the egg diagram to represent the contact. There are four basic possibilities.

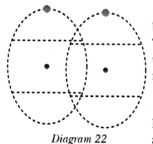

Diagram 22

(Diagram 22) Two people meeting, but their contact is only superficial. They make contact in their middle unconscious area, but there is little or no height or depth to this meeting.

(Diagram 23) Two people meet and have a strong instinctive feeling for one another. They might, for example, be very passionate in their relating. All their lower unconscious material is charged through the contact. Perhaps however on the more mundane level of the middle unconscious there is little in common between them, and the relationship is unlikely to last. There is no meeting on a superconscious level.

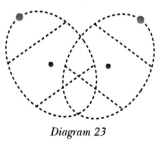

Diagram 23

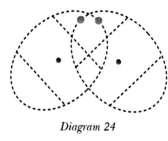

Diagram 24

(Diagram 24) Two people meet and recognise the divine spark in one another. They might, for example, form a platonic relationship, having a deep sense of each other's essential self. There is little common contact on the mundane level, however, and no fire from below to stoke the furnace of their relationship.

(Diagram 25) Two people meet and contact one another deeply on all levels, finding relationship between their superconscious, middle unconscious and lower unconscious levels. They can relate easily, understanding the nuances and subtleties expressed on all the levels. This is an ideal, not an expectation, a potential for the meeting of souls, described by Buber as the 'I-Thou' relationship.

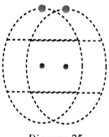

Diagram 25

These four ways of relating is a vast oversimplification, but offers some insight into the types of relationships we build. You might like to explore other ways of putting two egg diagrams together and what the contact might suggest.

THE FOOL'S JOURNEY

Ego develops as a container for all our energies, to protect and support us through our lives. We should not denigrate our relationship with ego. Ego is not a good master but is an excellent friend. When we become totally identified with ego (a stage we all go through, and which people do not necessarily pass beyond) we live by our learned and adapted behaviour patterns based on a split between oneself and the other, predicated upon the mechanisms of what was once a useful container but has now become a limiting prison. We have built ego to protect us and now our unfulfilled needs control us. This is sometimes called the adapted personality. It does not have to be a permanent condition.

To add to our understanding in a more unusual way, it is interesting to learn that tarot cards, rather than being just a system of divination, also offer interesting insights into the journey of life and our developmental stages. Tarot cards can be used as a potent guide to self-development and the realisation of creative potential, combining pictures with words to form symbols that represents natural energies. The tarot is a way of framing, articulating and evoking these energies into conscious recognition.

Each tarot card represents a facet of who you are. The first two cards in a tarot deck are the Fool and the Magus. On the surface the Fool is stupid, often depicted as blindly stepping over a cliff. Similarly the Magus is wise, conjuring the world into existence through magical arts. On a deeper level, however, we find the Fool is not as first appears; letting go into the world, surrendering to a larger wisdom, he or she lives life to the full. The Fool that persists in folly becomes wise. And the Magus is not so wise when fixated with ideas and techniques and missing the natural flow of energy, trying to make things happen that will happen anyway in their own good time. We have to discover how to trust our inner processes both when we feel 'wise' and when we feel 'foolish'. Accepting ourselves as we are, we recognize where we are in life and can creatively and joyously divine our future.

The only certainty in our lives is that everything changes. The tarot is a sophisticated tool, not for showing us what will be, but for reflecting on what is and revealing the possibilities of what might be. Using the tarot involves a process of self-transformation as we are offered the opportunity to discover more of who we are. We can then make informed and life-affirming decisions about who we want to become and where we wish to go. When we use the tarot for divination we find our lives are not predetermined by outside forces, but that we really can make choices.

Two primary polarities we consider in Psychosynthesis are differentiation (which corresponds to identification) and integration (which corresponds to disidentification.) Life is a search for and discovery of self, experienced through a constant polarity between moving forwards into life and/or backwards towards the womb. At all stages we become attached to our experiences and it is necessary for us to engage with these experiences and learn to differentiate. We forget; so, conversely, we are offered the opportunity to remember. To *re-member* is to put ourselves back together through an act of disidentification that enables a move towards union with consciousness and choice.

The major arcana (or trumps) from a pack of tarot cards, if designed well, can be used as a model for the journey from differentiation to integration. Indeed, the first card, the Fool is sometimes referred to as beginning the fool's journey. This journey is primarily a metaphor for the journey of life as a whole. The divine spirit (the fool) is imprisoned in a physical body, ignorant of its divinity. The journey of life is to become more differentiated, chiefly through identifying with objects or things that are encountered on this journey. Sometimes we are blindly moving on, sometimes very consciously, but our journey is always affected by what has already happened.

Moments of crisis force an awakening in the journey, or sometimes we have moments of spontaneous awakening. We realise at these times of awakening that we are on a journey back home and may learn to hold an awareness of self as both separate and together at the same time. The fool's journey is an adventure, a quest for determination and courage as old as humanity itself. The challenge of knowing oneself is the challenge of life, and the tarot is a potent asset for getting to know oneself. The following table shows correspondences between the stages of life and aspects of that journey as depicted in the tarot.

• *Stage 1: Separation*

0. FOOL: First emergence: the new-born baby, purity, innocence, from unity, unconscious of separation (spirit is divine but comes into physical form and looses knowledge of divine connection.)

1. MAGUS: Emergence of individual ego, the dawning of self awareness, (the inner companion or angel who guides life.)

2. PRIESTESS: Spiritual influence, intuition, stillness, inner influences, fire, wand.

3. EMPRESS: Female, feelings, reception, mother, water, cup.

4. EMPEROR: Male, thought, projection, father, air, sword.

5. HIEROPHANT (PRIEST): Material influences, sensation, action, earth, disk.

6. LOVERS: relating to others, from family to choosing partner(s), onset of responsibility for actions (interacting with others.)

7. CHARIOT: relating to self, construction of safe 'vehicle' or persona (interacting with world.)

8. STRENGTH (LUST): relating outwards, fearless confrontation with forces of life, extraversion.

9. HERMIT: relating inwards, self-examination, narrowing path started by chariot, commencing of journey back to spiritual home, introversion.

• *Stage 2: turning points, awakenings, transitions*

10. FORTUNE: Transition, awakening, sensing turn of the wheel, crisis (such as midlife), entering chapel perilous, the midpoint in developmental progress, attention turned inwards, start of descent from peak of midlife.

• *Stage 3: liminality, entering the darkness, confronting ego with depths of own psyche, establishing links with inner self, introspection.*

11. JUSTICE (ADJUSTMENT): adjustment to new life, encounters with dualism, balance to be created between conscious and unconscious or leads to stagnation.

12. HANGED MAN: reversal of values in second half of life, initiation, sacrifice of old values.

13. DEATH: ego transcendence, emergence of self-awareness, peak experience, transformation, move to maturation.

14. ART (TEMPERANCE): balancing through inclusion, true alchemy begins, process of bringing conscious and unconscious together, alchemical (influx of spiritual energy.)

15. DEVIL: realising immanence, it is all here already, the battle to stay on course, between submitting or absorbing and transmuting into higher form.

16. TOWER: the material reorientation that follows spiritual reorientation, crumbling of old world view, blocks removed, light irradiates personality (shattering of earthly delusion.)

17. STAR: actualisation, becoming your own star, a guide in the darkness.

18. MOON: the dark night of the soul, test of Gnosis and of faith (that is built on experience.)

19. SUN: reconciliation, the dawning of new day (golden dawn), marriage of alchemical brother and sister.

• *Stage 4: fulfilment and return*

20. JUDGMENT (AEON): the rebirth of the integrated self, awakening, deeper reflection.

21. WORLD (UNIVERSE): wholeness, fulfilment of the mature psyche, union (rather than unity), completes cycle back to fool.

EXERCISE: THE WALL

The following exercise, whilst not directly about birth, involves connecting with some of the energies of that time, and your subsequent experiences and responses to this. *Only undertake it if you have the time and support appropriate to its power.*

Start with physical exercises to loosen and warm up your body. When you are ready, stand in a comfortable and relaxed position with as much space as possible around yourself.

Imagine there is a wall surrounding you. Explore its surface (do this physically, starting with your hands)... What is the wall made of? glass, stone, what?...

Feel the wall with your back... feel it with your hips... and feel it with any other parts of your body that seems right to you... Is your wall really firm, or is it yielding? Does it feel alive or dead?

Does the wall around you make you feel secure and comfortable, or does it make you feel restricted or trapped?

Press against the wall, gently or with force, quickly or in a sustained manner, whatever way feels right to you ... Is it resistant or flexible? Exaggerate how it feels by pushing against it ...

Be sensitive to how you feel about the size, shape and resistance of your wall, its height and thickness ... stay in relationship with how you feel about your wall...

Now let the feeling of the wall remind you of some space you have been in before ... let the images, thoughts and feelings associated with this space emerge, do not judge or censor them, but only go as far with these feelings and images as appropriate to you at this moment ... Respond accordingly to these memories letting your body move as it wishes...

Come back to yourself, walk around a little, shake off any unwanted energies and, when you are ready...

Consider:
- Did you learn these responses as a child? Do these learned responses work?
- Did you get what you needed? What did you do about that?
- Were you allowed to do this when you were a child?
- How did those around you respond when you acted like this?
- What else did you do?

16

THE PROCESS OF WILLING

For spiritual realization, the will is required for controlling other psychological functions... while the centre of consciousness reaches up to and is one-pointedly fixed in the spiritual or transpersonal Self. The right use of the Will's steady effort is to stand in Spiritual Being.
(Roberto Assagioli)

The will is not a static entity but a natural process, the spark of life that energises the choices we make on our life journey. The process of willing is a deep expression of both the moving and the maintaining functions of soul. Empowerment comes through our ability to surrender to this inner power.

To understand the will we have to move away from the idea of the will as a thing and reframe it as a process - the act or process of willing. Also, we can only really understood the will in terms of our personal and human existence, for as Assagioli said, there is no such thing as will, only willers (and added, there is no such thing as love, only lovers.) The problem with trying to describe the process of willing is that everything we say about it, although it might be true in some cases, it is not true in all cases. Therefore all descriptions of the process of willing are partial. The best descriptions are usually found in poetry, paradox, Zen koans, mystical riddles, aphorisms, and the like. The famous Zen koan: What is the sound of one hand clapping? expresses the process of willing precisely.

There was once a student of Psychosynthesis who really wanted to understand what the will was, so he worked hard on his course, went to all the seminars and workshops that he possibly could, made all the notes, did all the exercises, and he still could not get it. He tried putting everything together and it still didn't sink in. Eventually he got totally cheesed off with this state of affairs and decided to leave Psychosynthesis and forget the will altogether. He went to live in the country in a little house with a smallholding, and seemed to himself and others content with digging his garden. Then one day as he was preparing a vegetable patch, his fork caused a stone to fly up and hit an iron post. Clang! it went. At that moment, the student finally understood the will and exclaimed, 'Aha! Now I realise. There isn't much in this will after all.'

This story demonstrates how through completely letting go of trying to understand, the understanding came. At the moment the student 'knew', he was enlightened. The person who has a moment of truth, and yet as soon as he utters a word has moved away from it, is the subject of many stories of enlightenment. The words in this story: 'there isn't much in this will after all' are about the nearest to truth that we can probably reach with words.

Beyond words is the Word, the divine utterance that heralds the moment of creation. But is this Word that can create a universe different from words that cannot describe the will? Is there a Word that can describe the process of willing? There is an esoteric belief that at the beginning of each new age of humankind a Magus (not necessarily a man) appears and utters a Word for the forthcoming period. This Word describes the current of the divine will for that age. The belief is that if we attune ourselves to that Word then our acts of will succeed; if we are somehow off-course, then however hard we try, we will not make things happen.

Is this the same Word that was spoken by God in the Christian Bible, and if so what is that Word? Perhaps it is the creative utterance itself, the first cry of a newborn baby, the shout of joy of someone released from imprisonment after many years. Perhaps it is an exclamation we can only really describe with a symbol - !

We may find a clue to this Word if we look at the first letter of the alphabet. The letter 'A' is graphically like an eye looking downwards, a symbol used by freemasons to represent the eye of the creator that oversees all our processes (of willing and loving.) The first letter in the Hebrew alphabet, aleph, means ox. The ox is the Egyptian goddess Ta-urt, the mother of cycles of time. So the Word we are looking for can come from a female source as much as a male source. Perhaps, just as it transcends gender, it also transcends all attempts at analysis.

What is the Word of the will? Even though we may utter a sound as pure and untainted as that of the first cry of a newborn baby (and each of us have done that at least once!), to reach the Word we have to delve deeper, earlier, to the source of that utterance. When we can be in the awareness of the source of the utterance of that sound, and maintain relationship with everything else in our consciousness, then we are a complete and pure expression of the process of willing. Of course, no one is that perfect. The truth is that we have moments of this pure willing; we come in and out of its presence. We cannot force it or make it happen. Sometimes such a strategy appears to work, but more often than not it fails because we are pushing our energy in the opposite direction to, or at cross purposes with, the flow of the divine willing, at odds with the Word in some way. It is paradoxical but true that we have to be flowing with will before we can use will.

We need to quieten ourselves so in silence we have the space to become more attuned to the process of willing. When this happens the world glows. Here words become inadequate, we have to move to imagery or poetry to try and describe what we are talking about. Once I stop trying to describe what I am talking about then the words may just flow, and in tune with the process of willing. If I could fix this into a description, then it would be an imperfect description of the process of willing.

The process of willing is just to be. Everything comes to you. This is what Laotse is trying to describe in the *Tao Te Ching* when he says that non-action is more powerful than action. The willer in a state of becoming is a perfect embodiment of the process. She is holding the tension; simply being with what is, being an integral part of what is emerging, what is *be-coming*.

WILLING WITHIN THE PROCESS

Entering the forest, he does not disturb a blade of grass; entering the water, he does not cause a ripple. (R.H. Blyth)

Assagioli's model of the act of will has a distinctly linear appearance. He may well not have intended this, but it is implicit. The cultural mind-set into which he was born inevitably informed the map he created. As described in Chapter 6, the 'act of will' starts with purpose and passes through six stages until the will is executed. Nowhere in *The Act of Will* does he say this isn't a linear process, and in fact, he asserts: 'the act of will consists of six sequential phases or stages. These six stages are like the links in a chain; therefore the chain itself - that is the act of willing - is only as strong as its weakest link.' So the performance of an act of will is going to be more or less successful and effective according to how successfully and effectively each of the stages is carried out.

The act of will does not have to be linear, and it's possible to loop around in this apparently linear map. After making a choice, for instance, you might need to go back to deliberate, then you might do some planning, then you might need to reconnect to your purpose, and so on. In fact, you usually only succeed either through your spontaneous ability to jump from one stage to another, or through the process of trying to align yourself with a linear model.

Assagioli's original will model is theoretically brilliant in its simplicity, and it describes a way of making the will work. For instance, if I were a physically able teenager I could train in an athletic sport, and by working very hard and keeping myself to a particular training schedule, preferably with a coach to ensure I'd stick to it. I could turn myself into a great athlete and win races or jump the highest, excel in whatever my sport. This programme would be very much in line with Assagioli's model. Speaking of the will, Assagioli asserts: 'Its training and use constitute the foundation of all endeavours ... applying all the necessary means for its realisation and in persisting in the task in the face of all obstacles and difficulties.'

An athlete might put in an inordinate amount of daily effort, but that still wouldn't be what makes them the best athlete. That would be something else, something that originates from the source of the process of willing. This something cannot be attained through a programme of exercise. Assagioli agrees with this, saying: 'the true function of the will is not to act against the personality drives to force the accomplishment of one's purposes.' He immediately retracts somewhat, however, by then adding: 'The will has a directive and regulatory function,' which returns us to a rigidified description of what is essentially a fluid process.

THE WILLING CIRCLE

Start with the three basic shapes of a point, a circle and a line. A point has no direction, takes up no space, and is non-dimensional. This point could be seen as the source of the will, because when something happens, the happening comes out of nowhere. It did not exist then it did. My desire for a bar of chocolate didn't exist, and then my desire did. Next we have a circle that represents the process of willing happening, like the ripples around a stone dropped in still water. Finally, the straight line represents an alignment. It 'squares the circle', and the process of willing that originated from the original desire (the point) now happens. In other words, if my willing is successful, the chocolate bar now exists in my world!

When the process of willing is conceived of as a circle, we can understand the process more through discovering what the circle contains. Whilst words cannot convey an understanding of the process of willing, they can suggest areas where we might wish to look if we want to uncover more about the process. Firstly, as already said, we have the point at the centre of the circle which is the source of the energy for the process of willing. In other words, it is the place out of which the willing happens. We can define this point as both spiritual and also as something material, our own human existence.

I want to go outside and sit in the sunshine. Assuming the conditions are there (I am in the right place at the right time) then what is going to make it happen is me. The source of the energy that moves me into the sun comes from the point inside me where my willing potential resides. So long as it remains potential, the act does not happen. As soon as the potential is realised the act is taking place.

Of course, I have to consider the outside conditions (in this instance, is it sunny or not?) as I co-create my world experience. I only exist through my relationship with this external world. I have to trust in the space being available. If my mind is too cluttered, I am not going to be able to discriminate as to whether the space is there or not. I might not even have the (internal) space to realise I want to go out in the sunshine, I might be too busy with other things. Or I may not be able to make the space to do it, I think I have to do the washing up, or must go and write those letters, or oh well I'll do it in a while when I'm ready, I don't want to do it yet. We become caught up, caught in or caught out one way or another.

To make the space, we have to trust that what emerges as foreground (or into our field of awareness) does so at the right time and in the right space. We can try to force something to emerge or we can watch what emerges and go with it. This involves trusting that what emerges is appropriate for us because it is emerging out of this point at the centre of ourselves. Trusting in that way, we can see that events happen in their rightful time. To everything there is a season; as the wheel turns, the right thing for you emerges at the right time.

If I want to watch a sunset, I have to consult an almanac to find out what time the sunset is, or I have to observe the sun in the sky and predict the time and direction in which it is going to set. I have to decide where I'm going to be to watch it. I have to create all the right conditions, but if the timing isn't right then I will miss it. I can only make the sunset happen when the sunset happens. That's a different aspect of trust, moving onto a deeper level that connects with soul, both the soul of oneself and the soul of the world. In reality, that's an artificial division, for soul is not divided, only our sometimes partial impression of it.

At this level, we can comprehend the depth of meaning in the Sufi phrase: trust in god and tie up your camel. We trust in god that there will be a sunset. We tie up a camel by preparing the conditions as much as we can to have our wish fulfilled. We have to be facing in the right direction, we cannot have a brick wall between the sunset and us, we have to be there at the right time, and so on. Space and time are vitally important factors in the process of willing which involves co-operating with the flow of universal forces.

A CHOICE EVENT

Diagram 26 is a two-dimensional representation of a multi-faceted, constantly changing process. Imagine both the trust/space circle and the soul/timing circle as constantly turning and continually changing direction. At any moment they may happen to move in the same direction and at the same pace. Perhaps much of the time they move in different directions and at different speeds. Only when the choice and the event meet, do the soul, trust, space and timing become aligned, which is why they are placed in the central circle. When the soul, trust, space and timing are aligned, then the choice and event happen simultaneously. In other words, when these conditions are attained, whatever the choice is, whatever we wish, happens.

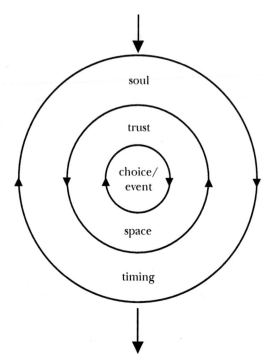

Diagram 26: The Process of Willing

If I'm trusting, I have the space, and the time is right, whatever I choose happens. My role here is as a witness of this, not to force the issue. I do not have to try and make the sunset happen before its time, but witness the inner and outer conditions, so that when the alignment happens, it - my choice and the event - happens. It is a paradox, in accordance with many spiritual teachings, that the less I do the more happens.

We can increase our understanding of this model of willing through studying the juxtaposition of concepts within the diagram. Space and timing, for instance, immediately suggest the space-time continuum, the place (it isn't really a place) within which everything happens. You have to be in the right space at the right time for your choice to happen. Indeed, if it really is your choice, something in line with your purpose for being part of the space-time continuum, you are inevitably in the right space at the right time. An important factor in willing, then, is not to try and be in the right place at the right time, but to be in touch with your purpose. This can be found in many ways, from complex procedures involving ritual or years of therapy, to simply pursuing a dictate such as Joseph Campbell's famous: follow your bliss.

At the top of the two circles, we find the concepts soul and trust. Trusting in soul carries the same meaning as flowing. An old Chinese story tells that Confucius and a friend of his were looking up at a very high waterfall above a deep gorge. All of a sudden they saw someone leap into the water. They were sure he must have been a suicide, for no one could hope to survive the fall with such a great flow of water. To their amazement, the man appeared in the water at the bank beside them and came clambering out. They rushed up to him and exclaimed: 'We thought you were a goner! How did you do it?'

The man was calm in his reply: 'I just go with the flow, and allow the water to take me, I am flowing with the current.' The supreme surrender implied in this story is clearly intended to impress the hearer with the importance of flowing. Yet we can also understand a deeper meaning in the story through attending to what is omitted. If what the diver said expressed the whole truth, when he jumped in he would go this way and that way with the current and never be able to leave the water (unless the water happened to beach him). What is omitted from his response is the key to understanding the secret or silent aspect of going with the flow - the act of trusting in soul. This is what leads to him reaching the bank, climbing out of the water and offering an important insight to Confucius and his friend. Through trusting in soul, what we are choosing will happen. To do this we have to accept that our lives are perfect as they are. This is my life, now. I'm not going anywhere; I'm not going to be somebody different in the future. I might be, but right now, when I live my life in this moment, then what I'm choosing happens.

THE SILENT MEANING

I am not angry when I speak gentle words. I do not beat the donkey and call myself beloved of gods. Truly, I strive to carry the load without noticing the burden, to be on this hot earth a cool jug of water, to stand in the wind like sturdy sycamore branches, a place where birds sit, where cattle gather, where sap rises, wherein earth and sky are home. (Normandi Ellis)

Assagioli chose to call his book *The Act of Will* to emphasise that will only exists through a verb, motion. He could have called it The Act of Willing to emphasise this more, but we do not usually describe doing willing so it would have sounded strange. Yet we do use the phrase 'being willing (to do something)' and this approximates more closely to the nature of the process of willing. Willing is an expression of both the moving and the maintaining functions of the soul brought together in fine balance. We may find we are 'being willing' without having to trans-personalise or categorise the process. It just is - or more correctly, we just are.

The will only exists, as far as we are able to comprehend and experience it, through the process of willing. In other words, it only exists through its manifestation; when the willing is happening and when there is a willer to witness or be involved in it. Power (the Will) only exists in relationship with the willer (whether its a shared or a hierarchical relationship.) We have the choice to make our willing part of a process of *power with* - that is we are tuned into the universal flow of willing - or *power over* - when we exert this power to the detriment or at odds with the flow of willing.

In esoteric teachings, the four powers of the sphinx are described as to know, to will, to dare and to keep silent. The first three of these powers clearly relate to the process of willing. Traditionally the fourth power - silence - has been described in terms of containment. To make our willing successful we are advised not to prematurely share it with others, to keep close to our hearts our most important willing processes. There is another deeper meaning to this fourth power of the sphinx, however, which we can now understand in the light of the process of willing. To keep silent means to go with the flow of the willing process, to follow the path of least resistance, to be uniquely oneself in osmotic relationship with the unfoldment of life. We do not achieve this silence through rigorous exercises that attempt to make us other than what we are. Indeed we can only achieve this silence when we accept who we are in our entirety. That has to include both our spiritual potential and all the atavistic aspects of our nature that make us fully human. We can then circle the square: we began with the word and we end with silence.

EXERCISE: THE WAND OF THE WILL

In the Western esoteric tradition, the wand is often used as the supreme symbol of the will. This exercise uses the wand to good effect and, through archetypal connections, empowers this use.

Relax and centre yourself...Imagine you are in a meadow, holding a magical wand. Visualise the kind of wand you would most like to have, its shape, size, colour – is it plain or encrusted with jewels, etc... Take time building up the strongest sense possible of your wand as if it really physically exists.

Taking your time, walk up your mountain until you reach the top... Holding your wand in the air, visualise a beam of light from the sun striking the wand and energising it in a powerful way. Perhaps the wand will change form, or shape, size or kind, or perhaps it will simply become brighter and more powerful...
When you are ready, thank the spiritual forces that connect you to the Divine then bring your wand back to the meadow. Realise you can use your wand to make acts of will that further your personal and spiritual development, even in your everyday life. Your wand, representing your will, through being energised by spiritual energy, is now stronger and more powerful.

Consider something you want to change in your world. Holding your wand before you, create a spell for this event to happen. In this context, to create such a spell simply means to imagine the situation or object you wish to change before you and, as you point your wand at it, visualise it changing in accordance with your will. As you visualise this change, hold your intetion as clearly and strongly as possible, but don't force anything. Use your power wisely, remembering that power is most effective when applied through Love.

17

BODY, SEX AND SELF

The actual nature and mechanism of the psychophysical interaction have been and are the subject of lively discussion. Contrasting conceptions and theories have been advanced, but psychosynthesis, with its essentially pragmatic orientation, takes no stand in regard to them. It takes for granted the reality of this interaction and utilizes its ways of functioning for therapeutic purposes. (Roberto Assagioli)

The importance of attending to our own body and paying attention to the body language of others cannot be stressed enough. When you bring more awareness into the physical realm, to the physical body, whether through touching or non-touching depending upon the circumstances and the relationship involved, you increase both the other person's and your own potential for taking a new, grounded stand in your lives.

It is easy to understand how the body expresses a person's personality and history. For example, someone with depression may hold his or her head down, or someone with unexpressed anger may have a clenched jaw. If these postures, or holdings, become chronic then it is as if the body sticks in these distorted positions, creating protective armour. Body armouring, as this process was called by Wilhelm Reich, is what we create as a physical and psychic barrier against experiencing the pain of our wounds. This includes the patterns of holding or tension that originally served to protect a child against the pain of not having needs taken care of in a loving or timely manner, but also includes muscular holding patterns formed when older. It is important to distinguish armour from boundaries, which are energetically alive rather than blocked, and extend outwards both to keep people at an appropriate distance and to contain Self.

Character can be defined as a combination of body armouring plus the repetitive emotional and mental patterns set up in childhood. We all 'have character', that is, we are all armoured to a greater or lesser extent. We can loosen it through bringing more awareness into feelings and through releasing blocks associated with memories. The body's rigidity keeps us stuck in the past, so when we release tension it aligns us with gravity, we can take a new stand in life more in harmony with self and others. Considering all this, it is not surprising that Assagioli said that the full name for Psychosynthesis is BioPsychosynthesis and we only call it Psychosynthesis for convenience. BioPsychosynthesis works with the life force as experienced primarily through sexuality, which is not anything specifically to do with sex, more about how we relate energetically with others.

It is not an exaggeration to say that everything we experience happens in our bodies. Our bodies as like temples in which we perform our life tasks. As Jung said in *The Visions Seminars*: 'When the great swing has taken an individual into the world of symbolic mysteries, nothing comes of it ... unless it has been associated with the earth, unless it has happened when that individual was in the body... And so individuation can only take place if you first return to your body, to your earth, only then does it become true.'

THE THREE BODY WEIGHTS

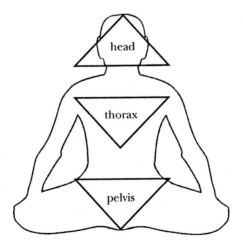

Diagram 27: The Three Body Weights

The three main body weights, as often used by actors and dancers in their work, are the head, the first weight, which sits upon the thorax, the second body weight, which sits upon the third, the pelvis (see diagram 27). We can easily move our focus of attention between these different body weights. Notice where in your body your breath is going to right now - it will almost definitely be focused on either your chest or your belly. Don't try and change anything about your breathing just now, simply notice where your breath is going, is it into your chest, your belly or somewhere else?

Now put your attention on your first body weight, your head. See if you can breath just into your head - imagine it, tune-in to it happening. Don't lose your head! Don't let it topple off your chest below! Look around you and notice what the functions of your head are: you see things through your eyes, hear through your ears, smell through your nose, taste with your mouth. The only one of the five senses not particularly involved with the head is touch - and of course, we all know how nice it can be to have our scalps massaged, our faces touched tenderly, or how painful to be slapped in the mouth!

Your head and neck are also concerned with the input and output of air, with vibrating air to create speech, and of course your head acts as a container for your brain. I know that in our modern Western culture we usually believe that we do our thinking in our brains, but we can 'think' in any area of our body. Consider your brain as the organ involved with processing your sensory inputs, storing information, and processing the thinking and feeling that might happen elsewhere, not just within the confines of its own structure.

Now put a hand on your chest and consciously choose to breathe into that area of your body - the thorax, the second body weight. Feel your lungs fill with air as you breathe in, expanding your chest, then empty of air as you exhale, letting the chest relax. Don't breathe too deeply - this isn't a re-birthing session! As you breathe into your chest let your attention move from your head into your chest. Let your attention become more heart-centred.

This second body weight, the thorax, is positioned between the other two - the head balances on top of it, and it in turn balances on top of the pelvic weight. The thorax is involved with centralised attention and balance. Amongst other things, it contains your heart and your lungs. They are both involved with circulation - one of blood, the other of air. We could call these the functions of vital energy exchange. If one or the other of these is restricted we suffer, and if either is cut off we can die. The body of a headless chicken will still run around, but you don't see many heartless humans running around - or maybe you do! People usually appear to be heartless when they are fragmented in a way that causes them to live too much in their head or too much in their pelvis!

Stand up, with your feet a comfortable distance apart, and feel the floor beneath you, supporting you. If you are in a situation where you cannot stand up, simply imagine standing up and continue anyway. Perhaps the most important healing for any of us is learning what choices are available to us and how we can make the most life-enhancing choice each time we have the opportunity. Put a hand on your belly, and feel it being pushed out as you breathe in, using your hand to move your breath lower now, not in your chest anymore, but deeper into your abdomen. Let your knees flex and bend, allowing a bounce to enter your legs. Really feel the weight of your body supported by the floor beneath you. Your head weight rests upon your thoracic weight, which then in turn rests upon your pelvic weight. Tune into your pelvis now. Let your hips sway from side to side a little, and forwards and backwards, too. Make gentle circular motions with your hips. Don't force anything; this isn't a Tantric sex exercise! Let your hips move as they want to, as you continue breathing deep into your body. Imagine you can breathe right into your pelvis. Feel your breath go as deep as is comfortable for you.

Get a sense of the three weights in your body - the biggest pelvic weight supported by the floor; the middle weight (thorax) supported by the pelvis, and the head supported by the thorax. Move your body a little and as you do so get a sense of aligning the three weights. If you imagine a cord that comes out of the top of your head and pulls you up slightly, and another cord that comes out from your perineum - between your legs - and down into the earth, with a weight on it, pulling you down slightly, it helps to align the three weights. Try it.

Once you get a sense of these three weights, one resting on the other, you start to notice various things. For a start you can see how comedians do funny walks. You might like to try some for yourself - simply allow different body weights, or combinations of weights, to lead as you walk. Then try holding back one of the body weights as you walk and notice the different effects, not only on how you walk, but how you feel in yourself.

More importantly, you can start to realise where you lead from, and where you hold back. Some people, for instance, lead with their heads - we all know this 'heady' type - rushing around, being interested, knowing everything, or wanting to. There are those who lead with their chests - sometimes all sweetness and light, sometimes proud and overbearing. Some people lead with combinations of weights - for instance, leading with the head and pelvis forward, and contracting the chest back, protecting the heart. It's a sign of how we meet the world - and how we withdraw or retreat from the world and contact, too. In other words, it's about both what we hold back and what we push forward. If you lead with your head, for instance, then what are you holding back? What are you protecting?

I am not saying one way of being is better than another. We have all learned the ways we lead and hold back from our life experiences. Most of us probably learned much of this in our earliest years, and then have reinforced the behaviour as we have projected onto the world how we expect it to be. At the same time, the world has reinforced our patterns by being like that.

I often find that when I'm out walking, or after I've done some good strong exercise, my mind seems clearer - I can think better. At these times I am 'thinking on my feet' or doing 'pelvic thinking'. Pelvic thinking isn't just about being obsessed with sex, anymore than heart thinking is just about being all lovey-dovey, or head thinking is all about being solving puzzles. When our energies are flowing and our three body weights are aligned, we think more clearly. We don't have to locate our thinking in our head, heart, pelvis, or anywhere else, it just happens where and when it happens.

We do have a choice to focus on our bodies and work at aligning our body weights, observing how we react differently to different events in our lives. This way we start learning to respond rather than react, responding to our contact, whether painful or joyful, with the world, the environment, people, all the beings around us. We observe other people, too, and notice how we interact with different types. This way we can enter into an experience of life where our life energy is flowing more freely.

THE PSYCHOSYNTHESIS SERPENT

Many mystical traditions tell of a special power within our bodies, called the dragon power, the snake, kundalini, shakti or shekhinah. It is a power closely linked to our sexual energy and is sometimes described as a snake coiled at the base of spine that uncoils and stretches up through the body as the energy is activated. It is also described as a dragon power that resides at the base of the clitoris or penis, which similarly rises up through the body. It is considered dangerous to raise this power prematurely, but it is important that you start to build a relationship with it.

When this energy is activated it brings an inner excitement, a joyous thrilling sensation throughout the body. This is a true mystical experience, of connectedness with universal energy. It is not a substitute or 'dangerous short cut' but an experience, available to everyone that allows them to experience themselves as living centres of energy, free to express themselves in their own, individual and unique way.

In case there is any confusion, let me stress again this energy is the 'life force' itself and whilst closely allied to sex, it may be engaged and a relationship built with it, without the necessity of any particular or specific sexual activity. Indeed, some mystics have used the absence of sexual activity as a pathway to contacting with this energy.

The two best-known snakes are the serpent of knowledge (from the Garden of Eden story) and the serpent power or kundalini which resides at the base of the spine. The Western mystery tradition includes a third serpent which is coiled around the egg of life. Imagine the Psychosynthesis egg diagram with a serpent coiled around it, its tail at the bottom of the egg, its head reaching the heights. The serpent in this 'egg girt with a serpent' (as it is called in esoteric literature) is an ideal metaphor for our Psychosynthesis work. Interestingly, the image has a correspondence to the rosy cross as the egg can only crack and release its potential new life when the serpent is activated.

As we come to the ground or the earth and invoke the serpent energy within our bodies, then the awakened serpent makes the connection for us between the different realms of the unconscious, expanding our field of awareness, our knowledge. A bridge is created between the areas of the unconscious and our conscious intent. Divine and human will are aligned. The work of

Roberto Assagioli is intended to guide us towards this wisdom and understanding, and as Piero Ferrucci so succinctly puts it in the title of his book, Psychosynthesis leads us towards *what we may be.*

The tree of life, the egg of being and a serpent supply us with the essential components of alchemy, one of Assagioli's life long interests that is also central to the Mystery Traditions. Whilst not true of all Jungians, the tendency in the Jungian approach is to psychologise our view of alchemy. The notion is that alchemists were really talking about the inner world, our intrapsychic manifestations. Turning lead into gold was a metaphor for the process of individuation. Whilst this is true, it misses the fact that many alchemists were talking in guarded terms not just intra-psychically but also about physical and sexual alchemy. They weren't just working with transforming psyche inside, they wanted to do this through the sexual gnosis. Central to this 'Great Work' is the inclusion of what in Psychosynthesis we term the lower unconscious, as is made very clear in Assagioli's written work, as for instance when he states: 'we have first to penetrate courageously into the pit of our lower unconscious in order to discover the dark forces that ensnare and menace us...' You already know about the importance of grounding, of being in the body, of 'coming to earth.' But what about the importance of working with the snake energy from a Psychosynthesis perspective? What of the serpent of desire, another aspect of the serpent energy both from a kundalini viewpoint and its role in the Garden of Eden story?

Assagioli had what some people might describe now as a rather old-fashioned attitude towards sexuality. The core of what he wished to express, however, is that we need not suppress or repress any aspect of our energy. Instead we can learn to regulate and appropriately express ourselves, including through sexuality. This may be summarised by his statement: 'No drive, emotion or desire needs to be repressed or should be condemned on its own account; it is the skilful regulation of its use and manifestation that is needed.' The Psychosynthesis approach to transforming sexuality is simply putting it into perspective. Rather than sexuality 'having us' we can learn to have it. We have sexuality so that we can use it rather than sexuality having us (so it can 'use' us!) Of course, as always, disidentification should not be used as a means of avoidance - to 'have sexuality' you must be coming from a genuinely disidentified place or you cannot choose to let go and surrender to it when that is appropriate. Through such surrender we are constantly turning our old 'leaden' nature into a new 'golden' embodiment of our deeper truth, that we are always becoming Self.

A VISION OF SEXUALITY

Body and psyche come together in sexuality, and the issues that people experience around their sexuality relate directly to the development of the individual. Many people try through sex to meet unfulfilled needs for intimacy, touch, tenderness, and belonging, to feel better about themselves and how they relate to the world. Some people use sex to assert power and to act out in ways that are abusive both to themselves and others. The work of Psychosynthesis, in this area, focuses on awareness and choice around sexuality, experiencing how soul is present in both the dark and light sides of sexuality, and the contrasexual complex (anima and animus.) Whilst always keeping the work of the personality in mind, Psychosynthesis considers sex as a spiritual practice, and aims towards the experience of the transpersonal level of sexuality, the yearning for wholeness. This yearning is both the pre-ego desire to return to the womb and the post-ego goal of yoga, the ultimate union with deity.

To understand the sexual component in any relationship, we need to explore the meaning and intention within the relationship. To isolate sexuality is not the most effective way to do this; we can better see sexuality as part of the whole picture. All our negative patterns, for example our resistance to the Self, our identifications, our fears and so on, all are played out in sexual relating. It is very rare for sex to be a pure biological act, for it inevitably involves feelings, emotions, thoughts, fantasies and so on. Sex is often used as a means to a different end than its obvious own end - it can be used to avoid difficulties, to avoid boredom, to try to overcome problems in a relationship, as a form of 'vampirism', to have power over the other person, and so on. The Psychosynthesis attitude to sexuality stresses that most sexual problems fall into one or other of two categories: not operating sexually (too little), and only operating sexually (too much).

Sex has three aspects: the physical and energetic aspect (corresponding to both how we relate to the body and the external world as objects); the intra-personal aspect (corresponding to our relationship with ourselves, and our body as a somatic experience); the inter-personal aspect (corresponding to our relationship with others.) Regarding the physical and energetic aspect of sex, how present and in contact we are with another person is very dependent upon what has happened during our childhood development (well before adolescence.) For instance, a child who has learned to restrict the normal expression of energy (to protect herself in some way) splits off or creates her own separate world. This may then be repeated through being cut-off or going into observer role during sexual experiences. How we breathe directly relates to our emotional state and level of excitement. Splitting off often leads to inhibited breathing (possibly leading to many different psychosexual issues arising.)

If containment and boundary issues around sexuality become disturbed, one common energetic result is that sexual arousal is equated with inevitable sexual activity. The experience of sexuality and the act of sex are linked. This can lead to acting out through inappropriate sexual behaviour. Yet clearly sexual arousal need not inevitably lead to sexual activity, and sensuality may involve not just the genitals and secondary sexual areas but the whole body. It is the experience of sexual energy without splitting off or acting out, without thinking and fantasy interrupting the energetic flow. It has to include all the pain, remorse, disappointment, longing, and other shadowy emotions and feelings to be truly whole.

THE CONTRASEXUAL COMPLEX

A complex is a totality of many parts (or subpersonalities) in relation with each other. A complex can be positive or negative, and more or less in or out of consciousness, Freud saw complexes as mostly negative whereas Assagioli (like Jung) saw them as either positive or negative, depending on how they are working. The 'contrasexual complex', what is more usually referred to as 'anima' and 'animus', is a particular type of complex (or set of subpersonalities working more or less together.) It is formed within each of us through three different sets of influences:

1. Personal history: formative experiences with significant people of opposite sex, particularly their responses to our sexuality (these

affect and then are coloured by our introjects and fantasies.)

2. Definitions from culture: sex, race, class, nationality, and current morals. This includes stereotypes of what our sexual behaviour 'should' be like, and dominant cultural patterns (what boy thinks of boys and girls and vice versa, etc.)

3. Deep imagery, often experienced through meaningful dreams, and visions. (This includes archetypes, connection to and messages from The Self.)

The more work we do on this in ourselves, the more able we are to recognise the appearance and behaviour of the contrasexual complex in others.

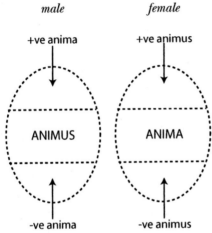

Diagram 28: Animus and Anima

The contrasexual complex appears differently in males and females. In males the 'animus' is the conscious part of sexuality and sexual relating. The 'anima' is then the unconscious (or shadow) part, and can be split into two parts; the 'positive anima' which feeds images and experiences of potential, light, trust and so forth; and the 'negative anima' which attempts to control through repressed feelings, memories and instincts, and feeds images and experiences of darkness, limitation, or fear. The same situation applies for women but the 'energies' are reversed (as shown in diagram 28.)

Regarding sexuality, Assagioli speaks of the need to move from repression (which has a theological and moralistic foundation) to liberation. He clearly states this should not be used to justify the uncontrolled gratification of all drives and impulses, of following every whim. This brings different complications, conflicts and misery; excess is followed by exhaustion (or disgust.) He states that it may also bring out inner conflicts between ethical and spiritual principles. In other words, neither extreme of total repression or total liberation can give satisfactory results. Compromise will not work, so the only way forward is to take the third synthesis position, where we can choose where to place ourselves between these two poles and adjust our position accordingly.

Assagioli says this is the best way to work with sexuality, to work with its transmutation. He suggests an objective attitude, that the sex drive should be seen as neither good nor bad in itself. We have to be aware and include all its levels: the sensual aspect; physical pleasure; emotion; union with another person; the creative impulse, including both the birth of a new creation or procreation (the birth of a new being.)

Transmutation can take place on two planes. The vertical plane is the work of, for instance, mystics engaged with 'the mystical marriage', love for god, and so on. The goal is to unite personality and spiritual self, leading to the birth of a new creature - a new, regenerated person (the lead has been turned to gold.) The work of the horizontal plane includes, for instance, the substitution of other pleasures, for example food or nature, using the sexual impulse to foster artistic and intellectual activities, for 'platonic love' and for compassion for others.

In *The Act of Will* Assagioli writes that a major problem with sexuality is attachment that leads to excesses, and above all the exploitation of sexuality promoted for commercial purposes, which leads to such excesses. Another major problem is the disassociation of sexuality from the rest of the psyche which may engender alienation, conflict and discord. When we include the Self in our considerations of sexuality it can lead us to ask: what is the Self doing this for in my life? Anima and animus are then revealed as the links between ourselves and Self, enabling us to bring in different ways of seeing, relating and being. As Jung said so succinctly, the Self uses anima and animus to make us converse with it.

EXERCISE: QUALITIES BEHIND FORM

Please take special care to only do this exercise if you feel completely comfortable in doing so, and in a private, safe and warm space.

Have a favourite blanket or cover or cushion with you to hold, if you wish. Carefully create own space to work in. Tune into your own space with no attention to others. Rest comfortably.

Breathe in your own space and mostly keep your eyes closed. Feel the support of the floor beneath you...

Allow (or create) a rhythm or motion that you can feel in your body - if want to rock or sway allow it to happen. Really be aware of your own self-containment in your own body...

Focussing your attention through your body, notice what places are you drawn to and what areas are you avoiding?

Focus now on your genital area? How do you respond to being asked to do this? How is your relationship to your genitals? Is there anything you want to say to your genitals or they want to say to you? Engage in a dialogue...

What are your most closely guarded secrets about your relationship with your sex and sexuality now?

Now reflect on the following questions concerning your relationship with your body right now:

How are your emotional patterns reflected in your sexuality?
How is your self-image reflected in your body and sexual areas?
What attitudes and beliefs do you have about sexuality?
What is the meaning within your sexuality?
What aspects of union are present or absent?
What are the Qualities present behind the form?

Sexuality as we experience it is a mix of messages from body and psyche, including physical issues and psychological and emotional factors. When we explore the deeper meaning in sexuality and how we experience it, there is no ideal. The aim is to move towards freedom of expression within a healthy container, to bring the Self (as the 'true self') within ego (as the container we have built to experience the energies of 'true self'.)

18

AWAKENING WITHIN THE DREAM

Lift your centre of consciousness upward to the inner worlds, the soul. Through the sphere of feeling and imagination we penetrate to the world of thought and even higher – to spiritual levels. Our propelling energy is that of aspiration directed by the great unrealized potency of the will.
(Roberto Assagioli)

Whilst Psychosynthesis practitioners may work with dreams in the more usual ways, including dream recall and interpretation, they also may include the cultural relevance of the dreaming, the investigation of lucid dreaming, and dreaming as a spiritual practice. As well as exploring the dreams we have whilst asleep, Psychosynthesis also focuses on how to awaken ourselves within 'the dream of everyday life'. Rather than awakening from a dream, we can learn to awaken *within* the dream so we are awake to the beauty and meaning within our lives. To wake up from a dream suggests a movement from 'being asleep and dreaming' to 'being awake.' To awaken within suggests something quite different, where we can be fully ourselves, here and now, whether we are physically awake or asleep.

Assagioli's attitude to dreams is found in *Psychosynthesis*: '... although dreams do give access to the unconscious of the subject ... [they] often only give access to one part of it - only one part of the unconscious is able or cares to express itself through dreams.' After stating that there are many types of dreams, differing in quality and meaning, Assagioli continues: ' in our practice [we] point out dream interpretation is only one of the techniques and not the chief one.' Jung, who worked extensively with dream interpretation, wrote: 'I share all your prejudices against dream interpretation as the quintessence of uncertainty and arbitrariness. On the other hand, I know that if we meditate on a dream sufficiently long and thoroughly, if we carry it round and turn it over and over, something almost always comes of it.' Assagioli seems to be suggesting something just like this, and not just interpretation but also other dream practices. He only gives one direct clue in his books, however, to what he is referring.

Assagioli asserts that there are two major limitations to dream analysis. One is the potential for passive dependence on the uncontrolled appearance of dreams. Clearly Jung would not have agreed with this as he relished 'the uncontrolled appearance' of dreams. This is a good example of the different emphasis between the two men, which Assagioli would have ascribed to their differing 'rays'. Assagioli emphasized the importance of the will more than Jung, who, following the more 'feminine' track, worked more with what emerges spontaneously.

The other limitation to dream analysis, according to Assagioli, is the impossibility of fully understanding 'the forgotten language' of dreams. Jung agreed: '... it is obvious we lack the sense and ingenuity to read the enigmatic message from the nocturnal realm of the psyche.' Jung proposes, as a way forward a systematic study of dreams, to which, of course, he devoted much of his life. Assagioli, on the other hand, proposes 'symbol projection' as a better alternative. By this, Assagioli means the visualization of specific items to induce fuller imagery. It involves being aware or awake whilst at the same time being in 'dream state', that is a state where the unconscious can speak to us in its language. Thus the proposal to practitioners, at the outset of most Psychosynthesis meditation and visualization techniques, that they relax and centres themselves, and follow their breath into a still, undisturbed space.

Jung wrote: 'In sleep, fantasy takes the form of dreams. But in waking life, too, we continue to dream beneath the threshold of consciousness, especially when under the influence of repressed or other unconscious complexes.' Of course, as Jung was well aware, we live our lives under these influences, continuously in a socializing and restricting trance produced by such complexes and repressed material. Jung's methods of working included his own version of symbol projection, which he termed active imagination. More than Assagioli, Jung used a wide variety of other techniques, including dance and movement, to explore the edges of the unconscious, the 'borderlands' of consciousness. Jung clearly placed greater importance on dream interpretation than did Assagioli, who through working with imagery had found what he felt was a more readily useful method.

William James, who was greatly admired by Assagioli, wrote: 'Our normal waking consciousness is but one special type of consciousness, while all about it parted by the filmiest of screens there lie potential forms of consciousness entirely different... Apply the requisite stimulus and at a touch they are there in all their completeness.' Perhaps Psychosynthesis offers us our best chance for finding and applying this 'requisite stimulus'. Assagioli certainly felt that, and may well have known the famous quote from Thoreau: 'Our truest life is when we are in dreams awake.' This conveys something similar to the difference between freedom *from* something, which moves us away, somewhere else, and freedom *to*, which moves us towards doing what is right for us in any specific moment. Freedom, one of Assagioli's beloved 'qualities', brings responsibility, and the need to use the will, to not shy away from making choices. Thus the relevance of will as the compliment to imagination, both of which are the key components to personal and spiritual development in the Western mystery traditions. The correct use of will and imagination wakens the higher centers in the human system that bring responsibilities of a deeper nature.

WORKING WITH DREAMS

To work with dreams we obviously have first to be able to remember them. Perhaps Assagioli did not place too central an importance on dreams for that reason. Even when we remember dreams, we often only recall a small part of the content. There are many techniques for trying to improve dream recall such as to not move upon waking, but give oneself time to recall the dream; if you remember a dream to write it down at once; and so on. Psychosynthesis practitioners can use many of these techniques as seem fit, then always record any recalled dreams in their ongoing journal. Generally it is considered better to try to not judge or interpret the dream whilst it is being written, but to try to include feelings from and about the dream whilst writing. A well-used adage in Psychosynthesis is that 'understanding comes later.'

Only later does the practitioner work with the dream, and explore its content and meaning, looking for both everyday and deeper correspondences to the dream imagery. Psychosynthesis borrows techniques as needed to complement or enhance more traditional interpretive techniques, procedures from

Gestalt Therapy, or Jungian techniques of amplification. Using associations to find the archetypal level in dreams, particularly through mythical connections, is particularly useful to the process of Psychosynthesis. Like Jung, Assagioli liked to work with personal, cultural and archetypal associations.

Homer's *Odyssey*, which Assagioli knew well, contains a myth which is appropriate to the Psychosynthesis approach to dreaming. Phaecia, an island where Odysseus is shipwrecked. is described as being at the edge of the world (that is, in the liminal space between waking and dreaming.) The myth tells us that in Phaecia the gardens are highly praised. We can interpret the gardens as the territory of the unconscious, and the place accessed through imagination and dreams. According to the Odyssey, the men in Phaecia are known as valiant seamen. They represent the masculine, animus aspects of us exploring the depths of the unconscious. The women are skilled weavers, representing the feminine, anima weaving the web of both everyday life and dreams. The 'men' and the 'women' in the tale bring both their will and imagination to their tasks.

A garden can be used as a symbolic starting place in a Psychosynthesis visualisation equally as well as can the more often used meadow. A garden, as in Phaecea, represents the edge of consciousness. This is the place, in Psychosynthesis terms, where the amoeba (or field) of awareness meets the middle unconscious. Like all boundaries, shown with dotted lines in Assagioli's egg diagram, this one is 'semi-permeable', allowing exchange of information through its constantly flowing and changing edges.

Practitioners undertaking such a visualization are asked, after the usual induction techniques of closing the eyes and focusing inside, to picture themselves in a garden. They are told to look around at what they see, and pay attention to the other senses, noticing what they can taste, smell, and hear. They are told to be aware of their feet on the ground. This is to make sure they stay grounded whilst they use their imagination to 'sail into' the realms of the unconscious. It also creates a base from which the will can operate.

The visualization can then follow many different directions, as discussed elsewhere. In a free visualization the person is asked to allow, follow and engage in whatever images and senses emerges from their unconscious. Whatever happens in the 'dream' is encouraged to unfold freely through the use of a few well-chosen supportive interventions. Then after a while the 'dreamer' is gently led back to consciousness in the room, where the telling of the dream or imagery, its interpretation and other dream work can begin.

Whilst Psychosynthesis borrows dream work methods as appropriate, it also has some of its own particular approaches that can be applied to dream work. For instance, a Gestalt therapist may ask a dreamer to play, enact or describe themselves as the different items in a dream, not only play the obvious central character. The dreamer might, for instance, be asked to speak as an animal that appears in their imagery. 'I am a dog; I have shaggy fur and am always running round on the spot. My life is ruled by my obsession with food...' Simply talking as a dream character often reveals interesting and useful insights into the workings of that dreamer's psyche. A Psychosynthesis practitioner will use the same approach, but take it a step further by exploring which part of the psyche was following these instructions and playing a part. This might be accomplished through a timely asking of suitable questions: who is it that is playing this animal? How do you know? Who experiences all this? This is intended to accomplish an awakening, however brief, of the 'I' experience, central to the work of Psychosynthesis.

We may use amplification techniques for working with a dream. Amplification involves working with a small image or sense from a dream to bring out its richness and depth. This can include items that are beyond the personal realms, or just of the middle unconscious. For the personal level of symbology and to explore the immediate realms of the middle unconscious, a practitioner may use free association around dream images and check what thoughts and feelings this brings us, both for the client and for him- or her-self, being aware of possible projective and reactive identifications. Working with social and cultural imagery is more complex for it involves finding items that are common as signs or signals to us all - a red light meaning 'stop', for instance. This involves delving deeper into the lower unconscious where such signals are lodged, which will then inevitably involve analysis of any other more shadowy unconscious material that is evoked. It is important however to allow for something being only what it obviously is: a book in a dream, for instance, might simply be something to read (and not, for example, a mysterious edible missile that wants to devour the dreamer!)

The archetypal level of imagery transcends the individual psyche but is experienced in each individual in a variety of idiosyncratic ways. However idiosyncratic an individual may be, there are common archetypal figures that tend to appear, including the fool, the wise person, the mother, and the lover. Assagioli loved to include what he termed 'the wise old man' archetype (that modern Psychosynthesis practitioners have renamed 'the wise old person'.) Archetypal imagery also includes events such as birth, marriage and death.

Archetypal figures have to be distinguished from subpersonalities that may have similar characteristics. Indeed, Psychosynthesis stresses that at their heart subpersonalities have the same archetypal qualities. But when these archetypal figures appear in dreams they bring us messages from the higher unconscious. These messages can include important insights, precognition, telepathy, prophecy, and forward-relating imagery. Jung felt that time-wise we live somewhere 'behind' all our dreams. Subpersonalities are more obviously figures who are caught up in the past, either the more recent past (where the dream may be playing out and perhaps re-configuring recent events,) or the more distant past of repressed psychic material and complexes. In Psychosynthesis it is important to work with both directions. The depth work is to enable a subpersonality to descend into its true inner quality and express it. The height work is to learn to co-operate with archetypes to help clarify issues for subpersonalities.

To amplify images on an archetypal level we have to be familiar with myths, folklore and fairy tales to provide a base for understanding such imagery. Assagioli discovered that whilst it is important to have a wide spectrum of such knowledge, to focus on a few central mythical events, such as found in Dante, for instance, allows close investigation of all archetypes. He realized that any and all archetypes can be recognized in each and every story. He was also aware of the usefulness of the Tree of Life, as we discussed in an earlier chapter, and utilized his 'hidden' knowledge of the deeper model behind the simplified egg diagram to help understand the different levels of dreams.

Psychosynthesis also suggests dream and imagery work as spiritual practice. For instance, if we are going to awaken ourselves to the fact that in our everyday life we are also living within a dream, central to 'dream work' in the Psychosynthesis sense, we have to find ways to 'check out reality' and see if we are dreaming or not. The famous 'pinch me to see if I am dreaming' is not so silly: if you check yourself out that way, if the pinch doesn't hurt, you know you are in a dream. This opens up the possibility of becoming lucid - that is, awakening within a dream. In our so-called 'waking' life we can perform many such 'reality checks' throughout the day, thus reminding ourselves that we are in a dream: thus, we may awaken within 'this dream' too. This is the famous 'waking state' in many of the mystery schools of both the East and West. Such reality checks include asking: 'Am I dreaming?' and 'Who is dreaming?' then to do something to check if it is so or not. If you try to fly for instance, you know whether you are awake in this dream or not! Whilst requiring great will and imagination, a simple and effective practice is constantly trying to recall and remind ourselves that whatever we are doing, we are in a dream. This echoes the words of Chuang-Tzu, the Taoist: 'Only when they are awake do they begin to know they dreamed. Then comes the great awakening, when we find out that life itself is a great dream.'

DAYDREAMING

In Psychosynthesis, we tend to give as much (perhaps sometimes more) importance to daydreams as we do to 'night dreaming.' As daydreams arise from the unconscious they can connect us to our deepest sense of values, and are not just meaningless fancy and illusion. For instance, consider how you may feel angry and hurt when reading about the plight of African people at the mercy of war and disease. We can try putting it out of our minds, but in today's world we turn the page and there's another report of catastrophe, horror, genocide, death camps, bombs, ethnic cleansing, hate-mongering and so on. We have to live with it, but what does living with it mean? We can send donations to starving refugees but does that only assuage a conscience and not solve a problem? We can numb ourselves, and pretend, and sometimes we have to do that. We can try to find a mystical solution, or use 'the therapist's excuse', that, if we work on ourselves, as we are all connected, we will be causing a change to all human life. Perhaps that is true, but all those people in a war are still there, trampling children underfoot as they run scared, frustrated by their helplessness.

Like helpless children, we sit in our comfort, yet we too could easily be crumpled in the rush for survival. Imagine, just a few decades ago, a Yugoslav counsellor, sitting in cafés, living a fairly relaxed life, and helping her clients. Suddenly this woman, a Muslim, is a gender-race-colour mismatch to the oppressor, and is thrust unwittingly and unwillingly into a war that includes her multiple rapes, beating, and murder. Who would rape your partner if you happened to be in the wrong place at the wrong time? Who would use a machete to literally slice you into pieces?

Being conscious of all this does not change the plight of the people I've been describing, but consciousness *can* change things. I know that often the simple recognition of a pattern can change the behaviour of one of my clients. Much psychotherapy is predicated on the idea that it is necessary to make conscious what has been hidden or unexpressed. In expressing our pitiful helplessness in the face of these horrors, we allow these feelings to come into the light of day. We can now see what effect this has. Maybe we will send some money, maybe we'll form an action group, and maybe we'll do nothing. Perhaps just bringing this into consciousness is enough. Perhaps we can collectively own our power. The people in East Germany did it and the Berlin Wall came down. In the face of great adversity, people do make changes simply by standing up and being counted.

We could shout with rage and anger, or describe our intense sadness in the hope it might affect a change in the oppressors' hearts. When we listen, however, our inner voice is simply saying: 'wake up!' All that has happened previously is a bad dream from which we have awoken. The grain mountains in Europe will be feeding hungry Africans, the Serbs will befriend the Muslim Bosnians, we all work to fulfill others' needs and our own, only when not at the harmful expense of other people.

This may sound rather like a utopian fantasy, but a principle of Assagioli's life, something for which he always strived, was freedom. Coming from that place, Assagioli believed that anything is possible, and founded Psychosynthesis with one of its implicit aims to aid other people to move towards freedom. Psychosynthesis, therefore, is not only useful in the therapeutic realm, but can be applied in every arena of life. If we don't allow ourselves the freedom to create possibilities - even if they don't manifest - then we don't allow ourselves the freedom to be fully human. That would limit all free thought and open hearted feeling everywhere. It would censor and repress our dreams, even the wildest ones. Psychosynthesis honours the importance of daydreams as much as, maybe more than, sleeping dreams. The daydreams of people like Martin Luther King and John Lennon are known and felt worldwide by many people, and we all have such dreams. We need to express them and keep expressing them whilst also encouraging others to express their dreams, too.

EXERCISE: DREAMING TRUE

Reflect on your dreams and dreaming. What part do dreams play in your life? How important or not is it for you to have and remember dreams?

Now remember (or imagine) what the most exciting and fulfilling dream for you is (or would be.) Write this dream down.

Visualize a scene from this dream as if you are having it now. Build up as much detail as possible, as if you are in the dream right now.

Now, within this visualized dream image, find and look at your hands and study them awhile. Then look ahead of you at the scene before you, then look back to your hands. Alternate your attention between the dream image before you and the image of your hands. Keep returning to look at your hands each time the dream image fades or you feel drawn away from it. Continue this for as long as feels comfortable.

Consider what this dream image has to tell you or show you now.

Before going to sleep for the next few nights, remember this dream image as vividly as possible, and say to yourself: I am awake within this dream.

19

THE PASSIONATE WITNESS

The Presence of the Soul abides with me. I walk with God night and day...
I see divinity on every hand in every form. (Roberto Assagioli)

In Chapter 17, I introduced the three body weights, but there is a more mysterious 'fourth body weight' as well. Firstly, let's briefly recap on the three physical weights. The largest weight is the pelvis, the functions of which involve digestion, physically and psychically and energetically, and assimilating what the body needs, excreting the rest. On top of that sits the middle body weight, the thorax whose function involves feeling things, physically and psychically and energetically. It contains the lungs and the heart, both involved with energy exchange. The third body weight is that of the head, the smallest of the three, sitting on top of the other two. The head contains the brain and eyes, ears, nose and mouth. It senses and processes information, physically psychically and energetically. The three body weights sit on top of one another, the thoracic weight on the pelvis weight and the head weight on the thorax. If you imagine them as three weighty globes, the largest sphere is the pelvis, with the middle-sized chest sphere on top of it, then the smaller head sphere atop the other two. The body is aligned when the three weights are balanced one on top of the other.

Now imagine a fourth body weight, a 'weightless weight' that has two modes. The first of these is its transcendent 'spiritual' mode, which we can visualise as a sphere balanced atop of the other three body weights. The second is its immanent, 'earthy' mode, which is the planet earth, which although it is composed mostly of heavy matter, is weightless to our perceptions. When we experience this weightless weight, in both its transcendent and immanent phases, we ensoul our world and we embody soul energy. We become less fragmented through making a connection between the individual soul and that of the planet itself.

Who witnesses all this, who is it that experiences the three body weights, and then imagines a fourth body weight?

This part of us is aptly called the passionate witness. This witness is not concerend with escaping from life or disembodying itself. It is possible to witness in a disconnected way, but the passionate witness combines the witness with the willingness to feel the totality of oneself, whatever is being experienced. To live the life of a passionate witness is to be engaged in life and at the same time centred in the core of our being, thus removing the fundamental fragmentation that separates our spiritual nature from our earthly nature.

To be a passionate witness is to touch into the source of awareness, to sometimes experience the central core of your identity, to be able to tune-in to your sensing processes, and at the same time to just be in the world, experiencing what you are experiencing in the fullest way possible. We all lose out when we try to side step the everyday world, the limited, the mundane, instead of allowing our wholeness of being to ensoul the everyday world. To incarnate is to be here now, living life with awareness, including the awareness that sometimes we are not aware!

REALMS OF SHADOW

Psychosynthesis takes an inclusive approach to the realms of shadow. The Psychosynthesis egg diagram shows the human psyche split into three distinct areas, drawn in such a way that the dividing lines appear to convey the notion of levels. Assagioli emphasised the diagram was not supposed to suggest this, that all areas of the unconscious have equal importance. The 'lower unconscious' representing instincts and repressed psychic material is generally thought of as the shadow, but the egg diagram can help us understand many different aspects of shadow.

The Oxford English Dictionary gives many different meanings to the word 'shadow'. Concerning the shadow of the lower unconscious, the meaning we are particularly interested in is shadow in a psychological sense, the 'regular shadow' comprising material from the individual's past. This is described as 'the dark aspect of personality formed by those fears and unpleasant emotions which, being rejected by the self or persona of which an individual is conscious, exist in the personal unconscious.'

Robert Bly offers a useful and more down to earth definition. He makes the comparison with a bag that we haul round with us throughout our life. This 'shadow bag' is filled with everything we have repressed, everything we don't like about ourselves and push into the background, every memory forgotten, and all our instincts and desires that are 'too hot to handle.' We carry this bag on our shoulders, continuously adding more as we go through life. It is only through conscious psychological work on oneself that an individual can start to remove some items from this bag. To empty it could be described as a lifetime's work, and the chances of ever completely emptying it are extremely slim if not impossible.

The Psychosynthesis view of the shadow emphasises that all the materials that we repress, as described above, are useful to us, are the things in our life that make us who we are, giving us character as individuals on the journey of soul-making.

THE HIGHER UNCONSCIOUS SHADOW

The shadow of the higher unconscious involves a process that in Psychosynthesis is called 'the repression of the sublime.' The idea is that we put our potential into shadow as much as we do with our past traumas. Because we fear being who we really are, expressing our full potential, we divert and repress these energies. For instance, if we are going to be truly ourselves it entails a level of responsibility that we may naturally and understandably fear. Such responsibility can be too much and we shy away from it, or we build a false structure around such beliefs as: I cannot be myself until I've worked through such and such, this amount of 'stuff' needs to be overcome before I can possibly be myself. Yet looking deeper we may be required to ask ourselves if we can handle the responsibility of not being true to soul?

Another fear is of being overwhelmed by the energy we know is locked within our potential. This triggers the basic existential issue, the dread of death, yet in one sense we truly die each day many times over, as we change and grow and become different. Even in a physical sense we have many millions of cells dying within us each day, and it is said that in around seven years from now every single cell in the body will have been replaced. Yet if we can come to experience that there is something which remains, something beyond the contents of the body and personality, we can choose to embrace death gladly each day, and thus live life to the fullest.

It is also possible to fear losing one's individuality, particularly so for the ego for whom surrendering to the universal sounds terrifying. Of course, if it were possible to lose your soul that would be a calamity, but to lose your separateness and false boundaries could be a blessing. It may seem paradoxical with Psychosynthesis constantly stressing the importance of individuality and being oneself, to say you have to lose your individuality. If we resist our inner strength and power, we are not making a real distinction between personal and soul power. Personal power comes and goes, but soul power remains (whether we lose our awareness of it or not.)

Of course, all this is a lot to ask, we are talking a lifetime of commitment to process, not a quick fix therapy. The Psychosynthesis approach says the best course of action is to stop looking for results, just follow the unfolding of life a step at a time, and we will find all the energy we need. Perfection is just being who you are; all the so-called 'good' aspects and 'bad' aspects of ourselves are perfect for each of us at each moment.

Psychosynthesis theory suggests the most insidious fear of all is the fear of success, of being who we really are. Various activities are suggested so an individual or group can work on this: through disidentification, by developing will, and actively working on the expression of Purpose. These activities may allow soul energies to manifest more effectively, instead of being diverted and distracted, but ultimately the trick is to reframe fear as our worthiest opponent, offering us unequalled opportunities for growth.

THE SHADOW OF THE MIDDLE UNCONSCIOUS

The middle unconscious includes aspects of the shadow that currently control us. For instance, many of our behaviour patterns are controlled by unmet needs that have been repressed into the lower unconscious and now exert their powerful and controlling influence. It is these repressed needs that are behind the building of character, the personal history as seen through the body and personality of an individual. Reich's notion of bodyarmour fits here well for just as the body is rigidified and distorted through the creation of physical armouring against emotional as well as physical pain, so the Psychosynthesis egg is said to rigidify and become more or less porous. In this sense, we can understand the dotted outer boundary shown on the Psychosynthesis egg diagram to be the body itself.

The Self can be put at both top and bottom of the egg, and for that matter anywhere else on the edge of the egg. The implications of this are apparent: that all the areas of the egg are the work of the Self. In other words, the shadow is a creation of the Self, and the difficulties and problems we experience in life are in fact opportunities. At the very least they offer an individual the chance to work on the issue to build strength, grow and even become more effective and integrated in life.

So all three realms or areas of the Psychosynthesis egg are equally of spirit and of shadow. The inclusive Psychosynthesis model is different from dualistic models of the realms of spirit and shadow, taking a 'both/and' rather than an 'either/or' stance. It does this precisely by including both spirit and shadow into a larger container (a 'synthesis') that by definition is more than the sum of its contents.

The following list highlights some of the different aspects of shadow as they manifest through different projective, introjective, retroflective and confluent devices, firstly seen as 'negative' (created by ego to defend itself) then seen as 'positive' (the underlying intent of the spirit in creating such devices in the first place.)

Negative

Projection	Spirit – e.g. joining a cult Shadow – e.g. nationalism, making foreigners into negative
Introjection	Spirit – e.g. devotion (to illusion) Shadow – e.g. believe its own fault, feel bad to belong to negative world
Retroflection	Spirit – e.g. narcissism Shadow – e.g. self-harm
Confluence	Spirit – e.g. 'merger' Shadow – e.g. negative cults avidly joined

Positive

Projection   Spirit – e.g. healing energy work
Shadow – e.g. banishing ritual

Introjection   Spirit – e.g. nature, sacred space
Shadow – e.g. healing through merging with demons

Retroflection   Spirit – e.g. positive affirmations
Shadow – e.g. keep it to oneself

Confluence   Spirit – e.g. communion/ community
Shadow – e.g. owning one's own and the collective shadow, inclusion

THE BALANCING AND SYNTHESIS OF OPPOSITES

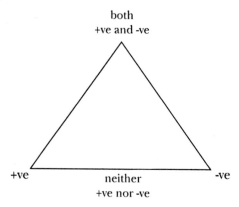

Diagram 29: The Higher Resolving Factor

As the primary polarity is that between spirit and shadow, a central concept in Psychosynthesis theory is the balancing and synthesis of opposites. Psychosynthesis intends for an individual to feel able to willingly enter the realms of both spirit and shadow where he or she can access true values and feelings, insights and meaningful connections. From the realm of spirit we may gain knowledge and understanding of our potential for future growth.

From the realm of shadow we can release energies - blocked or suppressed - from the past. As well as heights and depths we can experience something that remains constant throughout, an 'inclusive self' that doesn't dualise or polarise but adds purpose to our experience.

As Assagioli asserted, we can only know the 'absolute', the Oneness from which everything arises, through what it is *not*. From the moment that anything exists, duality is created. In cosmic terms we could see the first duality as being between the unmanifest and the manifest, which is of course also true for each of us individually. Another way to understand this is that the process of manifestation is based upon the fundamental polarity of spirit and shadow. Some Kabbalists maintain that we who think we are so fully rooted in matter have never actually reached the fullness of physical incarnation. We have to step into shadow to fully come to earth, which is our goal in existence. So until then, living in this 'cosmic illusion', the primary polarity of spirit and shadow metamorphoses, as it were, into our self-created polarity between spirit and matter.

All polarity involves a relationship between two elements and is never absolute but by definition must always remain relative. Something that is positive in relation to one 'pole' may well be negative in relation to another, and so on. Even with spirit and matter we can already see this in action; for instance, spirit can be seen as not grounded at all (in relation to matter) or integral to everything that is manifest.

In day to day human life, we find many dualities which are familiar to us all: pleasure-pain, excitement-depression; confidence-fear; attraction-repulsion; love-hate, and so on. The life of a typical human being is based on emotional reactions to things, to events and to persons all of which are tied up in such polarities. This engenders another polarity, that between mind and feelings (or intellectual and emotional responses to events.) Then in the mental sphere there are two more basic polarities, the one between the analytical activity of the concrete mind and the synthesising operation of the abstract or intuitive intelligence; the other between the inductive process (from the particular to the general) and the deductive process (from the general to the particular). No wonder we sometimes feel like we don't know whether we are coming or going!

There are also many interpersonal polarities of vital

importance to an understanding of the operation of the human psyche. The fundamental interpersonal polarity is that between male and female; then others exist between adults and young people, the various relationships between individuals and the different social groups to which they belong, including within families. Even more polarities exist amongst every type of grouping, for instance, between families and families, classes and classes, nations and nations, between the family and the state classes and nations; between an individual state and a union of states, and so on. On an even larger human scale we find, even in our increasingly global culture, a kind of polarity between the northern and southern hemispheres and continents, and again between Western and Eastern peoples and ideas.

Whichever kind or level of polarity we are concerned with, it confronts us with the problem of finding dynamic balance, that is, a balance through inclusion rather than exclusion. This means to create balance through the creation or discovery of a principle higher than both of the opposing poles. This is a typical Psychosynthesis approach and can often be brought about by consciously and wisely directing the poles so that the result is harmonious and constructive. This may lead to a synthesis where a higher element or principle transforms, sublimates and reabsorbs the two existing poles.

If we consider the balancing of feelings, the first task is to prevent the drives and the emotions from overwhelming and submerging the reason and the will. Assagioli says that the best way to achieve this is to learn how to disidentify oneself from them at will, in order to be free at any time to maintain the 'I', the centre of consciousness, to observe and evaluate them, and to wisely regulate them as needed. To fully embrace the passionate witness, however, we also need to be willing and able to enter into the dynamic of the polarity, as it exists, even if this means risking overwhelming and losing ourselves. If we consider the polarity of pleasure-pain, for instance, ss long as we remain slaves of this duality, always actively seeking pleasure and fearfully fleeing from pain, we shall not find lasting peace or permanent satisfaction. On the other hand, a forced inhibition, an artificial impassivity, certainly does not constitute a satisfactory solution. We rather need to recognise that, in Assagioli's words, 'in accepting pleasure without craving for it and attachment to it, and in accepting pain, when unavoidable, without fearing it and rebelling against it, one can learn much from both pleasure and pain, and 'distil the essence' which they contain.' The solution of the so-called 'middle way' does not work as it leaves us at the same level, in a state of compromise, trying to create a blending of the two poles and ending up in an in-between state with neither operating effectively or fully. The Psychosynthesis way is achieved at a different level through the fusion of the poles into a higher synthesis.

What Assagioli calls 'the process of spiritual Psychosynthesis' is indeed that of finding and living from the passionate witness. Through working in this way, a fundamental polarity between the human personality and the spiritual Self can also be resolved into a unity. At times, we have to face and enter into intense crises and conflicts, whilst at other times our growth may be more gradual and harmonious. In either case, though, an understanding of the process of synthesis enables us to achieve growth more easily and rapidly. The essential requirement of a passionate witness is to learn to not identify oneself with either of the two poles, whatever they are, but to control, transmute, and direct their energies from a higher centre of awareness and power, whilst consciously and willingly entering into their interplay, bringing the witness part of ourselves with us. Then, paradoxically, even when lost we are everywhere to be found.

THE IMMANENCE OF SOUL

As you have already seen, Psychosynthesis is not primarily concerned with transcendence, with 'going some place else' to avoid the realities of living. Quite the opposite in fact, for Psychosynthesis encourages us to engage with the world, with the unfolding moment, to live in the present. We may have an eye to the future, and an awareness of how the past has affected us, but it is in 'everyday soul' that we can find ourselves and live an engaged (and engaging) life. One of the greatest, and best-known, esoteric maxims is: 'as above, so below'. This statement asserts the essential identity between the Creator and the Creation. We could say 'god' made man in his own image and 'goddess' made woman in her own image. This is not really acceptable, however, because it implies a dualism that denies our experience when we connect with our inner world. It would be truer to say 'goddess-god' made 'woman-man' in its own image, then split this creation into two so that, through this division, the creation may experience love and realise its true essential identity with the Deity.

Self-knowledge has to be a direct experience, not simply a matter of faith. Of course, faith is wonderful in itself, but to add an experience of the Self brings it alive in a new way. From this experience we may then have a living faith, based on our direct, experienced understanding, which is very different from a 'blind faith' based upon what someone else has told us to be the truth. For some people such faith alone might be enough to sustain them and help them develop and grow closer to an understanding of their own inner nature, but if we are to truly know ourselves as one with the Divine, we must experience this directly.

Let's say, as a working hypothesis, that there is for each of us, as individual souls, a particular purpose for being here. We have special lessons to learn, and until we truly experience and understand our lessons, we continue spiralling through an endless cycle of experiences (and incarnations perhaps), with these lessons being presented to us in numerous different ways. Once a particular lesson is learned, we can then move on to the next lesson. Each step in this unfolding process brings us nearer to the realisation of our purpose or 'true will', the reason why we are here. For one person the purpose might be to express love in some lofty, abstract sense, for another to express love in caring for sick or handicapped people. Perhaps for someone else it may be to stand against a particular injustice so more truth can be made manifest, for another it might simply be to act as a catalyst for someone else's progress. Someone else might design elegant and functional buildings. No individual's purpose is better or worse than another's. The key is to find our own purpose or true will and then to do it. When we achieve this we have truly aligned ourselves, as souls, with the universal Spirit.

All men and all women have both 'female' and 'male' inside them. A soul that manifests as a man usually manifests a deeper soul connection to the 'feminine' and vice versa. From the Mother-Father Deity right through to the most earthly manifest 'maleness' or 'femaleness', this polarity appears basic to existence. If we apply the maxim 'as above, so below' to our development, within this polarisation we can see that an important aspect of the work for a woman is to elevate the 'inner male' and to refine the 'outer female'. Correspondingly, for a man the work is to elevate the 'inner female' and refine the 'outer male'. This work ensures balance and the subsequent alignment with the soul. It also, of course, aids the work of the soul in its journey towards alignment and integration with the Deity.

We are all divine, not in some abstract sense, but in our everyday lives. Whatever we do, we are never disconnected from our essential nature. The myths of gods and goddesses often show us that even divine beings may stray from their purpose and misdirect their energies. We humans are no different! To realise and, more importantly, to manifest our essential divinity, we have to work at it. This is a life-long process and extreme caution is advised when we meet those who would tell us of their 'great initiations', 'spiritual attainment', 'understanding of the true Mysteries' and so forth. Part of our spiritual development, in finding our own true nature, is for us to re-own our power from all the 'masters', 'secret chiefs', gurus, shamans and the like. Everyone met on the path is at least an equal, and always possibly just the person we need to teach us a particular lesson.

As well as being surrounded by this endless multiplicity of other 'divine beings' masquerading as humans, all other entities in all the universes, whether imagined or 'real', are truly aspects of the Divine. We can always be on the look out, therefore, for messages, teachings, understanding, not only from other humans or from some direct spiritual inspiration, but also from archangels, angels, demons, animals, plants and rocks! If this sounds fantastic, consider what it means to view the world this way. Whatever we may believe (consciously), our unconscious carries endless possibilities. If we can connect to this realm of the unconscious, we can liberate energies that can enrich our understanding of ourselves and all our potential. We may then realise that everything in our lives is a manifestation from the unconscious. From this viewpoint it is no less strange or fantastic to talk to an archangel than it is to dream of a goldfish.

It is also important with self-development work to remember the sacredness of all life. Everything has its 'angel', its 'divine breath', from each individual cell through to the planet earth and the whole universe. Everything is interconnected, nothing in our universe is separate (however temporarily separate it may sometimes appear). To be truly divine in ourselves, we cannot deny the divinity of any other being, for to do so would deny our own divinity. We have a collective responsibility to the totality of life. Every time we do anything that is thoughtless, uncaring or 'off-mark' in some way, we lessen the total amount of connection and consciousness on our planet. Conversely, every time we do something with care, whenever we act from our true selves, we add to the pool of positive consciousness on our planet. We are all individually responsible, and each act we take does make a difference. When we live our lives from this true Divine perspective, we are working for the collective responsibility, and participate in the work of planetary healing.

RECOGNISING INTUITION

Intuition is very different from 'psychic intrusion', and comes when contact is made between Soul and personality, between 'divinity' and 'humanity'. To be able to fully and clearly receive intuitions, however, we need to work on the personality so intuitions are received in a harmonious way, with as little distortion as possible. Basically, the receptacle has to be suitable or the messages received will be unclear.

There are three basic ways we receive intuitions:
• 'I know but I don't know why' - a kind of common sense that comes through your thoughts, feelings or body. We often distrust these intuitions as being 'fantasy' or imagination, which of course sometimes they are. On the other hand, though, we can learn to separate those we can trust from those that are fantasies through using our discriminative faculties. If you still yourself and look at your thoughts and feelings about a situation, sometimes it becomes easier to tell if this 'knowing' is genuine intuition or something you have created in your imagination without a connection to a deeper level of knowledge.
• 'I have a sense it is right' - this 'sense' comes from the superconscious, and is to do with rightness and choice. For it to manifest, you have to look at the most holistic, largest vision you hold. Without a connection to this 'larger picture' it is too easy to have all kinds of 'senses' about situations or people that are way off mark. If you hold your connection to your deeper or innermost self, then you can trust that your intuitions are in line with 'the highest good'.
• 'It came to me in a flash'. These intuitions include major insights, glimpses of an intuitive plan at the highest level, and can manifest

directly or through great music, works of art or even in the most unexpected and strange ways; for example, when synchronistic events occur or strange connections are made between you and someone or something else. The nature of this kind of intuitive insight leaves little doubt about the veracity of its message, for a true 'flash' enters your consciousness with enough light to make itself felt in an unambiguous way. If there is any ambiguity then you have to question where the intuition came from and whether it is truly guidance from the Soul.

When we investigate brain functions, and look at the different modes of thought of which we are capable, we can see a primary split between abstract and concrete functions. There are no sharp divisions between these two, rather a more gradual division where one merges into the other, but they can, for convenience, be viewed separately. The apparent difference between the right and left brain functions is well known, although some research suggests this is far too simplistic a model of brain functioning. Whether it is a good description or not in terms of the actual physical organ we call a brain, it is a useful division to help us understand the abstract and concrete thinking modes that we all experience.

The left brain (connecting to the right side of the body) is concerned with rational and linear modes of operation. From the left brain you think, order, make lists and organise your life and actions. It is from here that concrete thinking takes place. The right brain (connecting to the left side of the body), is concerned with non-rational, intuitive, non-linear modes of operation. From the right brain you feel, intuit, make crazy connections, and generally live in a non-ordered, more fluid way. Both sides are of equal importance and both are equally necessary for the full and healthy functioning of the individual. Problems only arise when one assumes an unhealthy dominance over the other, or there is a critical identification with one or other of the ways of operating.

Concrete functions (left brain, thinking and sensing) involve physical matters, they help us to understand our actual, physical existence, our functioning here on the planet earth, in this dense earthy energy. Abstract functions (right brain, intuiting and feeling) involve making connections in a non-linear, non-verbal way, helping to increase our awareness and process our expression of who we are at our depest levels.

We are all moving towards greater awareness. Anything

abstract, or non-manifest, can come to life through a number of forms. It can emerge through your thoughts, feelings or body, perhaps as a 'sense' or 'feeling' or 'flash' or knowledge and understanding. Patterns are trying to emerge, and the more we are open to their emergence, without trying to force them into a particular form, the better they are able to emerge. If a triangle is emerging you will receive its wisdom more easily, and more clearly, if you can create a triangular receptor in your being with which to receive it. Fitting squares into round holes is a far more difficult, and daunting proposition. In other words, the more we do to connect with our deeper, innermost nature, and the more we create a well functioning personality, the better able we are to receive or channel the inner wisdom and unfoldment of purpose which is inevitably trying to emerge into consciousness.

Everything you think is a belief, a mental construct. What time of day is it? What day of the week? Answers to all such questions involve a belief, a mental construct. about the meaning of time and space, being here as opposed to there, being now as opposed to then. To be alive on this beautiful planet in this vast universe is also a construct; indeed, everything is a construct. Being in a galaxy, on a planet, in a house, in this room, all these ideas are constructs. The kind of person you believe you are - this is a construct, different from the simple perception of being. The world you live in, this is a construct, too. Remember that constructs are not 'real' in any concrete sense and can be changed.

All your beliefs or 'world views' you probably learned as a child, from parents, the church, schoolteachers and so on. You might not consciously believe them anymore, but unless you work on them they are still there as unconscious constructs and will affect your life, and can at least potentially, and in most cases most definitely hold you back from expressing who you truly are. If a construct is a useful map then its fine, it can help you find out where you are and connect you to where you wish to go. On the other hand, a construct can affect and colour the territory of your life in a way that it is no longer supporting or enhancing to you. The choice is yours.

EXERCISE: HOW DO YOU KNOW?

Start by reading this story very carefully.

Realising that he didn't know who he was, a man ran through the streets, looking for someone who might recognise him.

He rushed into a shop and demanded of the shopkeeper:

- Did you see me come into your shop?

- Yes, I did.

- Good. Now, have you ever seen me before?

- No.

- Then how do you know it is me?

Reflect now on the following question: how do you know you are you? (N.B. *Not* how do you know who you are?)

Spend at least 15 minutes reflecting on this question.

Focus now for a few minutes on one or two of the main answers you discovered to this question...

Carefully focus your attention on the question once more: how do you know you are you?

Without thinking about it, or interpreting what comes in any way, allow a symbol to emerge in your consciousness that answers the question...

Now once more carefully focus your attention on the question: how do you know you are you?

What are left with now? Trust what comes whether nothing, words, silence, pictures, etc.

Now one last time, carefully focus your attention on the question: how do you know you are you?

Use your physical form to express this, move into dance or movement that expresses not who you are but how you know you are you!

20

COMING OF AGE

By deepening our consciousness of essential divinity – of the Immortal God within – our power to radiate it is increased, and our ability to shed light in our surroundings, transform our environment, and live with spiritual creativity is intensified. (Roberto Assagioli)

During the last two thousand years of human evolution we have developed individual consciousness into a fine art form, and now define our identity in terms of separateness rather than togetherness. The last vestige of collective identity, albeit a distorted one, passed away with the failure and demise of communism. Equally we can no longer rely on strong arm 'everyone out for themselves' tactics, the approach of the last century fascist movements that have also had their day. In the new world order, each of us is a potential victim of the enemy in our midst, outwardly identified as the terrorist threat, inwardly yet more elusive.

We are learning to behave like responsible adults, each with a separate individual identity (me) whilst also in touch with the collective energies of life of which we are a part (we). Our consciousness moves from 'me' to 'we', not through returning to an imagined golden age, or through somehow re-merging with the collective oceanic oneness of bliss out of which we emerged. The golden age of the past (that never really existed anyway) is gone. Our direction now is forward, as we each take our individual part within the collective, both individual and connected at the same time, like stars in the heaven, each star with its own particular path, or separate identity, yet each also part of the one heaven.

To successfully transit this shift in consciousness, we are learning how to release our essential divinity, not to become stronger or more powerful or 'holier than thou', but rather to honour the essential divinity of all living things. We are finding new ways that blend an understanding of collective consciousness from the East with the individualised consciousness of the West. We find that we are all divine beings, not in some abstract sense but in each moment, each event in our lives.

Our primary concern as incarnated divine beings is with healing the pain we experience through our fragmentation and disconnection. When we are fragmented it is as if an unbalanced part of the personality 'takes over' our awareness and it seems to become all that we are. Everyone has such experiences of fragmentation on a daily basis. Imagine you have just struck your thumb with a hammer, it is throbbing, and the pain is so intense it has 'taken over' your awareness. You cannot think of anything else; you rush around, cursing, alternately sucking your thumb, shaking it, frantically trying to change your awareness (that is, stop the pain.)

When you are 'taken over' by the pain from a physical mishap, like the hammer example, the pain is soon reduced to a manageable level. Some physical pains are more chronic; if, for example, you suffered from appendicitis, you would not be able to just make the pain go away, you would need assistance from others, and even then there would be no guarantee of success. We have to recognize those situations where we can do our own healing, those where we can call on others and have a good chance of success, and those where we need to contemplate some things cannot be healed. If you work with people as a guide or therapist, these conditions apply in assessing a client.

The same is true with emotional or mental pain. It can be very sudden and intense, such as the shocking news that a loved one has died (we feel intense sorrow), that someone has committed a gross act of abuse against us (we feel intense anger), the forthcoming important meeting (we feel intense fear), and so on. Just as if you hit your thumb with a hammer and the intense sensation involved took over, you can be just as easily taken over by the intense emotional or mental reactions to events in your life. In fact, these mental or emotional reactions can be more painful at their outset and much harder to shift.

People also feel fragmented when they feel a lack of spiritual connection in their lives. The classic 'mid life crisis' is a good example. Everything has been going fine when suddenly the individual starts to ask: what am I here for? What's the purpose of my life? Is everything I've done so far meaningless, shallow, and disconnected from any deeper or meaningful significance? What is my responsibility in life? There are many ways that spiritual pain can affect us, and it can be equally as difficult to shift as mental, emotional or physical pain. You might be cured from a serious, life-threatening disease but it does not ensure you won't still feel angry. You might discharge your anger in appropriate ways, but that would not ensure you find meaning in your life.

To heal something is not just to take the pain away, to make it somehow better. Healing may reduce or even eradicate pain, but primarily healing is about making something or someone 'whole'. To bring wholeness to something or someone, to heal them, is to complement fragmentation with harmony, and pain with wisdom, not to replace or somehow overcome the fragmentation and pain. To experience successful healing simply means to become less fragmented than you were before the healing.

To heal the system you are working on, whether for instance your own body and psyche, or someone or something else, is to move it towards de-fragmentation, that is, to bring together the component parts of the system in an including rather than an excluding way. When we do this we bring about true healing rather than just that kind of 'healing' which is concerned with fixing pain, disguising discord or in some way treating the symptom rather than the cause. The healing process will be inclusive, holding the vision of the whole person and not just trying to fix a part of them. If it did that it would contribute to the fragmentation rather than work towards the healing. It may help a temporary pain go away in the short term, but in the longer term it will simply create delay to the necessary changes in the system involved.

The value of Psychosynthesis depends upon its relevance in the modern world to political and social issues as well as for individual development and healing. A central principle of Psychosynthesis is respect for oneself and equal respect for others. This respect depends upon the acceptance of oneself and others for being as we are. We may intend change but we do not require it. From this ground of mutual respect a deep relationship can happen, a relationship of equals, rather than relationship built upon hierarchy (someone's better than you and someone's worse), or prejudice (you are the right colour and she is the wrong one). Deep relationships built on a ground of mutual respect are the basis of healing. Indeed, the key to understanding ourselves is through the nature of relationship. The relationship between us and the world, in all its different facets, is what creates restriction and freedom, peace and war, all the different manifestations of harmony and discord we experience in the world.

It is not that we need to become more free, or more harmonious, what we need is to recognise our part in the interaction between polarities and take responsibility for actions that move the balance one way or the other. This is the 'response-ability' for which Psychosynthesis provides a framework. When we stop trying to be better (hierarchy) or believing we are better or worse (prejudice), and accept ourselves and others for what we all are, equally humble and equally powerful human beings, we free up our ability to interrelate, to understand others for their similarities and differences to us.

It does not matter what we believe or what religion we belong or don't belong to, Psychosynthesis remains equally relevant. There are so many different aspects to the changes that are happening to everyone on every level, political, geopolitical, physical, social, climatic, socio-political, social, and so on, and including the esoteric concepts of cyberspace, quantum physics and such like, Psychosynthesis might seem fairly irrelevant and unimportant, but we do know that each little change we make can effect greater changes collectively. Each individual, and each group of individuals, is empowered in this way. Psychosynthesis, because of its inherent openness, which is not weakness but strength, is a suitable container for our collective movement towards increasing awareness and choice, thus enabling the manifestation of the qualities of joy and love for all beings.

The work of Psychosynthesis helps to make us more whole, to heal, to include more of ourselves in the whole picture of life. We need to be whole in ourselves (or at least moving in the direction of wholeness) to be able to combine with another 'whole being' to create a greater inclusion and synthesis. The more of us move towards wholeness in this way, the more of us there are to work together towards the common goal of planetary harmony. Indeed, we do not even have to work together: knowing and understanding this togetherness exists in itself releases vast potential.

FINDING A SOUL

An understanding of how the Self operates within the world as well as within the individual psyche helps us contact creative potential and improve the quality of relationship. Everyone is in a constantly changing relationship with themselves, other people and the world itself. Recognizing and accepting this brings meaning and value to life. It brings about the realization of responsibility on individual and social levels. It adds a dynamic sense of self to the present moment. Individually and collectively, contact is made with the source of awareness itself. This is the source of the dynamic process of relationship that guides awareness and sharpens intent. The gates open that allow us to access the bridge to transpersonal realms.

The Self is a name for the something out of which everything originates. An individual can only know the Self through what originates from it: through 'knowing thyself'. The notion of 'knowing thyself' has been the focus of most religions, mystical and magical practices throughout the history of humankind. 'To know thyself' is not about getting to know a static being, it is about entering into a dynamic interplay of forces with ever increasing consciousness.

The collective manifestation of life, ever changing, can be understood through the notion of archetypes, not as static but as dynamic principles. The archetypes are 'behind' or 'before' all human interaction. To love, for instance, is to interact with the archetype of Love. On the other hand, to be vindictive, for instance, is to interact with the archetype of Justice, albeit in a 'distorted' way. Because they are described as 'distortions', to judge them in a negative way would be a mistake. On the contrary, to interact with them is to take the royal road to 'salvation', to realizing soul as the living agent of the Self and, through truly descending to earth, take up the birthright to immortality. The wounds incurred throughout life are gateways for the passage into the spiritual world. Each wound offers an opportunity of understanding what is the purpose for being here.

In the world of appearance, it is not necessary to dig into what is behind appearance, to find the truth. The appearance of something *is* its archetypal structure, and is the clue to understanding its own meaning and value. The idea is similar (and an antecedent) to that of 'the elements of the wise' of the Western Esoteric Tradition. These elements are the commonly known fire, water, air and earth, plus the fifth invisible element, the aethyr. The aethyr is like the soul that is in and permeates everything so thoroughly and at the same time so invisibly that there have been times not only in the ancient world but in more modern times too, when this fifth element has been forgotten.

Indeed, in modern times it is sadly often forgotten that everything is composed of four elements, let alone five! Fire is creativity and intuition; it is the magical body or 'outer aura' that shines in illuminated beings (or any being at times of illumination). Water is receptivity and feeling values; it is the soul or psyche that is imperishable. It is only 'fixed' in the way water is fixed - by being ever present yet constantly moving and changing, like the flow of a river that is always there, yet the same water can never be seen twice. Incarnated, we are like an individual drop of water; individual in the same way a drop of water is individual in the ocean. Air is formative energy and intellectual skill; it is also commonly what is experienced as the astral body, and corresponds to the formative world of the Kabbalah. In a sense, everything that is not the origin of existence or its material manifestation, is this formative world. Earth is physicality and vitality, the backbone and energy of existence.

To the five elements we might add the shadow, the experiences and energies of life which have been repressed into the subconscious from where they attempt to get their needs met through acting out, unconscious behaviour patterns and, when extreme, psychotic and similar episodes. Working with, and counterbalancing the shadow is the heart, which is the place where all memories are carried. In some myths, it is the heart that is weighed at death. It is also the place or function that can be developed in a human to the degree that it can not only exist in the human body, but can assume an independent (and relatively timeless) existence. It is allied to, and in a sense the precursor of the spiritual body that emerges after death.

Many of us have been brought up to believe that somehow, irrespective of what happens, soul remains constant and unchanged. We are led to believe we innately have 'an immortal soul'. From this position, it can appear strange to learn that this may not be the case. For instance, the ancient Egyptians believed that the soul has to be 'caught' or at the very least, 'developed' and cannot just be taken for granted. The Western mystic Ouspensky sums this up well when, describing the teachings of Gurdjieff, he says: 'man as we know him is not a complete being ... nature develops him only up to a certain point and then leaves him, either to develop further, by his own efforts and devices, or to live and die such as he was born.'

This notion of having to catch or develop a soul is not peculiar to ancient Egyptian philosophy, and indeed it runs as a theme through many other Eastern and Western ways to spiritual attainment. Even in methods where not-action is stressed, such as Taoism, nothing can be taken for granted. For instance, in the Tao Te Ching, Lao-Tzu says: 'He who attains the Tao is everlasting. Though his body may decay he never perishes.' In other words, it is possible not to attain the Tao and, by implication, perish along with the body. With a few exceptions where it is stressed that there is nothing to attain and, more significantly, there is nothing to be done, everywhere else a division between the person who has and the person who has not attained is clearly found.

It appears as if there are two threads running through most teachings about the meaning of life. On an outer level all that is needed is to have faith in some teacher or teaching, or specific ritual or activity. and that is enough. Embarking on the journey of spiritual discovery, however, involves an inner level where something has to be achieved or the aspirant is lost. In Hinduism, for instance, on an outer level it is said that the soul is innately and indivisibly one with God or the Absolute. For this to be realised in an individual, however, specific practices have to be undertaken. Similarly in Buddhism, it is said that everything in life is an illusion and in a state of suffering because of the desire inherent in duality. The only truth or reality is total emptiness or 'the Void'. To experience this emptiness, however, an individual has to live by certain 'right' actions. Unless this is achieved he or she is bound to an endless wheel of meaningless bondage on the wheel of death and rebirth.

In his book *Lost Christianity*, Jacob Needleman talks about the lost doctrine of the soul in Christianity and the appearance and disappearance of the soul. He says: 'the soul is not a fixed entity ... it is an actual energy, but one that is only at some beginning stage of its development and action.' Whilst every day the individual may experience the appearance of this energy in an embryonic form, it is almost always dispersed and comes to nothing. Needleman goes as far as to say that it was a disaster for Christianity when it adopted the belief that the soul exists in some already finished form.

An essential component in the process of catching and developing soul is to find an inner state of total and undiluted silence. But to do this is not easy and involves effort, persistence, sacrifice and even suffering. It is this very effort and suffering that enables an individual to catch or develop soul. Gurdjieff says that an individual 'makes a profound mistake in considering himself always one and the same person'. Each person consists of many parts and the soul only appears in life for very short moments. It becomes firm and permanent only after a very lengthy period of work. Gurdjieff called this work 'intentional suffering'.

In the everyday state it is all too easy to think about life and conjure up explanations, to react emotionally or physically to cover inner suffering. The ego tries everything to avoid the question 'what are we here for?' Only through persistent effort can the inner quest be held and attention kept focused on the true inner desire to find meaning and purpose in life. The human being and the cosmos of which he or she is part is an attempt to create such conditions. To embark upon the inner quest may not be difficult, but to maintain the work does involve effort and suffering. Perhaps if this is kept in mind, that without this effort and suffering no one is guaranteed to even have a soul, let alone be able to develop a connection to it, more persistent action may be facilitated.

SOURCE AND SELF

This Self is not a disembodied spark of some kind but can be conceived as a whole being, the web of creation seen as the body of, or an expression of, the creator. The Qualities in Psychosynthesis are different archetypes affecting the psyche, which in turn creates 'subpersonalities' to interact with the world. Subpersonalities in this sense are the most material form of the original archetypal energy or Self. It is through their transformation and alignment that the individual can come into relationship with the divine in its purest sense. At the same time, everyone is also in relationship with the divine in its manifest sense through all the different aspects and interactions of their own subpersonalities, and with those of others, which is itself a manifestation of the self.

The Sanskrit word 'om' or 'aum' is composed of three phases, the 'a' when the breath arises, the 'u' where it connects to the emerging life force, and the 'm' sound of completion and continuation. The importance of breathing has been central to most spiritual practices throughout the story of humanity. Many psychotherapists recognize, more or less consciously, the relevance of how a client breathes. In relationship, the therapist and client conspire, that is 'breathe together.' This is a conspiracy of sound rather than silence, where 'talking about' is encouraged rather than taboo. Yet in this breathing together, a radical threat is made to the society of the individuals involved. That they may come to be more themselves in some way is threatening to the status quo. A good therapist keeps in mind the place of the individual within the society. Who is to decide what is best for the society is a difficult question. Who decides what is best for the client is not so difficult (in theory if not always in practice!)

After the beginning of the breath, the 'a' sound passes through the throat and changes to 'u'. The sound in the throat may start as silence but it inevitably moves to an utterance, a cry: from the first cry of birth (and creation), through all the expressions of suffering and joy that humans may utter. A therapist encouraging clients to make sounds, when appropriate, and to notice when and how they feel blocked in this area of the body, enables the cry to be felt, opening the throat to process.

Next is the 'm' sound as the breath reaches the closed lips. This is the eternal 'hum', the 'am' and 'ma' (mama), the first spoken word. The breath creatively forces the mouth open and rises to the nose. Expelled it creates the 'gn' sound which is the vibration of life, similar to the 'gn' of gnosis, the knowledge of existence and the source of self-reflective possibilities. The four elements of fire, water, air and earth also correspond to force (A), activity (U) pattern (M), and form (N). The force (energy or intent) and activity come together to create the pattern (the blueprint or balance) and the form (or being) of the world. Breath is the source (or force) of life; the pattern comes from mother; these two create within each individual and within society as a whole all activity or doing and all form or being.

A wish to overcome whatever obstacles block our aspirations, whatever stops us reaching our goal, is natural. This is done through rising above the problem either in a positive sense, by realizing letting go can often liberate the intent, or in a negative sense of avoidance and denial. To rise above something is the way of transcendence. As well as rising above the problem, it is possible to become immersed in it, investigating and working within its field of influence, watching for the outcome to emerge, allowing the process of soul to unfold. This is the positive side of immanence. The negative side is to be so immersed in the material to forget who one is and one's inherent divinity.

Sin, in its original conception, did not mean to disobey some law that however useful and meaningful is of necessity partial and transitory. Sin was seen as the making of a mistake. To divert from one's individual path was a sin, primarily because it meant the person had mistaken their way and needed to find some way to get back on track. This was the meaning of repentance, when applied to sin. Secondarily, it was a sin because, if off track, a person almost inevitably interferes with other people on their paths. A vehicle off course is very dangerous and can cause damage to others and their property. This required atonement to match the repentance. You give to God what belongs to God and to Caesar what belongs to Caesar, as was clearly stated by Jesus.

Sex, sensuality, good food, intoxicants, art and beauty, the colours in nature, and so on, are to be appreciated by the adult as his or her tastes become more refined. Society's repression leads to the abuse of these pleasures, which perhaps is necessary for the growth of society but does not always serve the individual. Food itself doesn't create bulimia or anorexia, nor is drinking alcohol a sure road to alcoholism. Sex can be enjoyed for the energy it brings without fear of judgment or blame. These pleasures become distorted when the human is out of touch with the instinctual within, not tame, but also not reactive. The ability to enjoy the good life, with all its hedonistic tendencies, is one of the qualities of the Self to be appreciated, not scorned or judged. When the Self is in touch with herself in that way, she knows when to stop. This is part of the true animal nature within that makes the connection between the individual and the collective self.

Attention and intention are closely allied states. Doing something without attention or intention decreases energy within the individual (or collective). Being with attention or intention, on the other hand, without doing anything with it, increases energy levels. Being with intention is allied to what in shamanism is called dreaming; doing with attention to what is termed stalking. The more the individual contacts silence, the more the state of being is maintained, the stronger is our ability to shamanically dream and stalk our purpose in life.

One of the most striking and persistent questions of human life is where do we come from? Is there existence before birth? To accept that there is a place of origination is enough, however. When speculation ceases, each one of us is left with our own experience. This is to be able to experience unity through diversity. It is the fact that everyone is different, and has a myriad of emotional responses and reactions to others. This is one of the greatest opportunities facing us. As with the revelation of most opportunity, difficult and dark times have to be negotiated. Humanity now stands on the threshold of adult life, and it is time to recognize the Self walks with us and within us. Everyone and everything is a manifestation of the Self and all the different aspects of personalities, subpersonalities, shadow, ego, repression, denial, insight, intuition, all the dark and light qualities that make up existence are the plays of the divine within an individual, family, society and globally.

There are mysterious aspects to life. There is always more in life - more than 'this', whatever 'this' is being experienced. To learn to respect and enjoy what is unknown is to take the opportunities this offers, instead of making what is unknown into a shadow to be feared and repressed. What is known, the state of the planet, for instance, or the atrocities fostered through ethnic intolerance, has a large enough shadow content. To respect and allow the unknown is to become a better practitioner of the art of life.

The fears and hopes of any individual human are the fears and hopes of all humanity. Each person has tendencies and predilections, and these are all equally aspects of the collective. What is needed is to recognize and accept collective heritage, as the product of the one source of everything, whatever that source is described as, and however diverse it may be in its manifestations. Whether it is named God, Allah, Atum, the big bang or a universal accident, everything known originates here. Instead of arguing over what to name it, or who has a better understanding of what it is, it is timely to grasp its presence and find ways to co-operate with the process of unfolding life. That has value and can be enough meaning in itself.

Our self-reflective capabilities are the link to divinity. Everyone and everything is divine. The difference is we know it, are aware of our predicament, of being alive in this wonderful, mysterious and terrible universe. This awareness brings responsibility and it is time for us to take this responsibility collectively. It is our collective responsibility to be willing to listen to our hearts and follow through the new, clearer connections that are made; and through learning good listening skills, being willing to listen to others and hear their position. To listen to the divinity within self or another requires a particular skill - that of stillness, quietness, and the ability to turn off the inner dialogue to hear the silence within. Being open to another means being open to oneself. Within oneself awaits the other.

MINDFULNESS

'The therapist acts without doing anything and teaches without saying anything; things arise and she lets them come, things disappear and she lets them go.' So said Lao-tzu originally about a leader, but the statement is equally relevant for a therapist or guide. Behind all words we may find the mystery of silence, and inner knowing. This mystery is our source of understanding. Using words can give rise to and/or kill meaning, can describe experience or separate us from experience. Entering the mystery means letting go of desire to be right or to be in control, to give way to openness and receptivity. A good guide works without judgment - a welcoming presence meeting the client with acceptance, inclusion, trust - not as a technique but as a wordless principle. The essential component of this position is mindfulness, which can be defined as a state of alert but relaxed attention that does not restrain, add to or interfere with what comes into awareness.

Mindfulness is deep reflection, bare attention that is receptive and enhances awareness of what is. At its simplest, it is what is at any moment. Buddhists might add that mindfulness includes a commitment not to interfere with processes of life but to celebrate their spontaneous organic intelligence. Then mindfulness promotes respect for subtle almost imperceptible movements of mind, body and feelings, and the Self behind this, nourishing these movements rather than correcting or conquering them. It is letting go of ambitions to control, solve problems, achieve something, instead choosing to bear witness, be willing to observe, be receptive to and learn from whatever arises, to enter into whatever is happening with a curious, experimental attitude, not knowing what might be discovered, but welcoming, appreciating and savouring whatever it is. A good way to facilitate this is to slow down and let go of automatic reactions that normally tell us what something is or what it means, to not be structured by context of time and space. Then the inner witness is awakened, and we awaken in the client as well as ourselves the spirit of inquiry.

RELATIONSHIP, INTENT AND LEADERSHIP

Psychosynthesis theory says that everyone is in a constantly changing relationship with themselves, other people, and the world itself. If we embrace this viewpoint we may bring meaning and value to life, helping us make decisions about who we are and what we want. It also helps us realise our responsibility both to ourselves and to the world as a whole. It can add a dynamic sense of self to the present moment, a sense of meaning to ourselves and to our future, individually and collectively. The self-identification phrase used in Psychosynthesis ('I am I, a centre of pure self consciousness and of will') can be effectively put into a wider context and re-worded thus: from the source of consciousness itself, a dynamic process of relationship guides our awareness and sharpens our intent. Psychosynthesis co-operates with the process of changing relationship, holding a perspective that helps us move towards wholeness. From this theoretical perspective, what is most important to therapy is the relationship, a real living entity created within the field of the interaction between the client's and the therapist's process.

The main concern in working with people in whatever modality is to foster the release of human potential whilst at the same time acknowledging the limitations imposed by the human shadow, individually and collectively. A good therapist enables others to both break free from, and to include their limitations when appropriate. We live so much in the past, or in our fantasies of the future, the present moment, the 'now' is always unfamiliar. Individually and collectively we have to learn to adapt to the unfamiliar or die out, particularly at this time of rapid change. When we consider our actions in the world and the roles we may play, one of the major questions to arise is whether we as individuals have any importance or influence in the larger global field? If you follow your own life's process, you automatically play the role you must, for even if your role is to be the silent one who feels but cannot speak, you are essential to the world. You may play an unpopular or even a publicly unrecognised role but you are still playing a 'leading' role in the sense that only when all roles are consciously represented, can the world as a whole operate humanely and wisely.

Each role is a leading one because the world we live in is created by the tension and interaction between all its roles. Filling the role of the leader, the follower, the silent one, the wise one or the disturber is essential for the life of the community. Only when all the roles are filled and interact, can the entire world discover its own human and self-governing capacity.

From this perspective, leadership is beginning to take on a new and extended meaning. A leader is anyone at any moment that represents one of the roles in any given situation. Being oneself is a political activity today, as it has always been! Of course, through our subpersonalities, each of us has many roles inside and are too complex to stay identified with one role for too long, flexibility in changing roles is important. The key to good leadership, however, is mostly to just be oneself!

Leadership is often associated with organisations and the business realm. When we look at organisations and businesses from the Psychosynthesis perspective, the almost inevitable starting place is with subpersonalities, the model fits so well. Discussing subpersonalities, Assagioli said: 'The roles of an individual, in whom various psychological traits are not integrated, form what we consider to be subpersonalities.' By substituting 'organisation' or 'business' in the place of individual in the quote, we immediately gain a strong foundation for the exploration of this application of Psychosynthesis.

Just as within an individual, the 'subpersonalities' in an organisation can be called to participate in a non-hierarchical and inclusive committee. Central to Psychosynthesis theory is the notion that we are dominated by everything with which our self becomes identified. Conversely, of course, we can dominate and control everything from which we disidentify ourselves. On our subpersonality committee, the Self is then the chairperson, not a hierarchical boss but more of a mediator (with all qualities and functions ascribed to 'personal self' in Psychosynthesis.)

Assagioli describes Psychosynthesis as being essentially about '...the genuine living experience of interpersonal and inter-individual communications, relationships, interplay; by cooperation between individuals, and among groups - and even by a *blending* (italics his), through intuition, empathy, understanding and identification.' From the source of consciousness itself, a dynamic process of relationship guides our awareness and sharpens our intent.

EXERCISE: THE FOURTH ATTENTION

Some forms of shamanism say there are four different ways of using our attention.

The first attention is when we put our attention on something. 'I see - whatever, I touch - whoever, I smell - whatever,' and so on.

The second attention is being aware of the totality of oneself. 'I am me, everything I do, and everything I am is me. I am I, a centre of pure self-awareness.'

The third attention is becoming aware that there is a source to all this attention. 'Not what am I doing or who am I being, but where does this attention arise?'

Before moving on to the fourth attention, let's experiment with the first three kinds of attention. Where is your attention right now? Have you chosen to be consciously paying attention to what you are reading here, or has your attention just strayed to where it is, unconsciously? Right now, as you focus on your attention, it is conscious, but for all of us most of the time our attention is not conscious.

Focus your attention now on top left corner of this book and hold your attention there for a little while. It would be impossible for you to hold your attention there (or anywhere else) for all the time without becoming disconnected, sapped of your energy, and passionless. This is the experience of the first attention, where we are attending to something and our attention either becomes fixed on that something or it doesn't.

Become aware now that at this moment you, yourself, are a totality. There is nothing missing. You are all that you are right now. Let this awareness come instantaneously. Don't focus on anything in particular; simply give your attention to the fullness of yourself. Don't focus on your head, your thorax, your pelvis, don't focus on the light above your head, or the earth beneath your feet, don't focus on your breath or anything at all. Just let your attention rest on the undivided presence of yourself.

This is the second attention where we are not doing anything, not being anything, not focused on any thing in particular, simply aware of the undivided presence of oneself. Again become aware that, at this very moment, you are a totality. There is nothing missing. You are aware of this or you are not. You do not have to strive for anything, do any particular exercises, you just realize, by putting your attention here, that you are always here, now. You can't become more enlightened or spiritual than this, and you can't become less so, you are simply you, all you have been, are, and ever will be. This second attention is called self-remembering.

Deliberately choose to put your attention on your breathing. Notice how your inclination is that once you put your awareness on your breathing (or anything else,) you lose contact with the second attention? You are no longer remembering that larger awareness. Notice how this happens, but don't strain to hold both attentions, just focus on what is happening right now in your awareness.

Now consider: who is doing this focusing? Is it someone trying hard to get it right? Someone who thinks they do not understand? Who is focusing? Is it the wise therapist who knows all this already? Someone who craves for a relationship and hopes this will make it happen? Is it someone happy? If you focus on what is happening right now in your consciousness, who is doing the focusing?

What are you focusing for? Because you have been told to do so? Do you desire to be more alert, more present, to learn how to become self-actualised? Be aware of your motive to focus? Now, if you look closely: from where, right now, is your attention emerging?

Not where is it going, but from where is it arising?

Where? Now where? Allow yourself to experience the source of your attention. Be aware of the pure consciousness in which everything arises, including all this witnessing of consciousness.

Who or what is this presence, this totality of being that emerges through your consciousness? Who comes alive inside you? Don't look for an answer, but instead look inside your looking. This is the third attention - awareness of the source of consciousness.

So what about the fourth attention? Remember yourself,

that you are a passionate witness: to sometimes touch into the source of awareness, to sometimes experience the central core of your identity, to be able to tune-in to your sensing processes, and at the same time to just be in the world, experiencing what you are experiencing in the fullest way possible. The fourth attention is to not side step the everyday world, the limited, the mundane, but allow your wholeness of being to ensoul the everyday world.

Psychosynthesis sessions, courses and training

Psychosynthesis may be started from various points and angles at the same time, and the different methods and activities can be wisely alternated ... according to circumstances and inner conditions. (Roberto Assagioli)

Sometimes it is said that Psychosynthesis is 'a psychology that includes the transpersonal or spiritual'. For me it is more than that; if I had to describe it in this way I'd rather say it is 'a method of spiritual realization that includes psychology'. Many people use Psychosynthesis for counselling or personal therapy and find it very effective. Others use it for enhancing their creative work and do not feel the need to include the spiritual realms, and for them this is most effective. Psychosynthesis is a unique method, however, in that it centres on the Self around which all else is said to cluster or revolve. When we centre on the Self in this way we are making a commitment to spiritual unfoldment as well as to psychological development. Instead of being 'a personality that includes the self' we become 'the Self which has a personality'.

It is very exciting to live within the vision and by the principles of Psychosynthesis, and how we do this creates our own version of Psychosynthesis. If we want to share it with others, we have to honour our personal vision of what it is and equally honour their 'version' of it too. We also have to remember that we are all teachers, and Psychosynthesis is best understood and applied when it is a shared experience. Remember, too, that you already know the best Psychosynthesis guide there is, and he or she is that same guide that knows you best, too - your own inner wisdom and understanding.

So where do you go from here? There are several tracks you could follow, including individual study and investigation, individual Psychosynthesis therapy, attending seminars and courses aimed at personal and spiritual growth from a Psychosynthesis perspective, a full time training as a Psychosynthesis guide at a training centre, or a distance education programme. Each of these options is now discussed in detail. The following, therefore, are suggestions of what you can do to increase your understanding and, most importantly, experience of Psychosynthesis work. None of these suggestions need to be taken singly and, in fact, are probably best approached in the various combinations and at the appropriate times that suit your own personal evolution.

INDIVIDUAL STUDY, THERAPY AND COUNSELLING

A lot can be gleaned from reading books on Psychosynthesis and related subjects, particularly those books which offer you practical suggestions and exercises, for reading is best accompanied by experiences so that you connect what you read with your own personal process. The bibliography at the end of the book makes some suitable suggestions.

Roberto Assagioli stressed the 'central decisive importance of the human factor, of a living interpersonal relation' between the Psychosynthesis therapist and client. From a Psychosynthesis perspective the most vital factor in your growth is your personal Psychosynthesis sessions. Nothing can replace the experience and growth possible through one-to-one sessions.

There are many different kinds of counselling and psychotherapy, numerous different trainings and certificates and so on - so much so, it can be difficult to know what it all means, who you can trust, if the person is properly qualified and so on. All the evidence shows that of most importance is choosing the right person for you. Of course you want your therapist to be competent and to have done some training but more important is how you feel with them - ask yourself if you feel comfortable telling this person intimate details of your life; do you feel safe with them; do you like the way they act towards you; do you feel respected and heard?

If you are at all concerned about a potential therapist's credentials, do not be afraid to ask them what training they have done; do they have regular supervision of their work; what experience they have had; and what is their code of ethics? It is your right to interview a number of practitioners before making your choice (although you may feel fine about the first person you see, too!); they may charge you for this initial interview - some do, some don't. There is a lot of information on the subject available on the web, and your local library should be able to give you more literature on counselling and psychotherapy.

TALKS, PRESENTATIONS, GROUPS AND SEMINARS

Many Psychosynthesis centres and institutes have a 'public programme' that will include various workshops and seminars either on Psychosynthesis directly or on particular aspects and applications. Many individual practitioners of Psychosynthesis also run such groups, either directly on Psychosynthesis or applying Psychosynthesis to other areas of work and interest. The author of this book is available for presentations, workshops and seminars on Psychosynthesis and various related subjects and can be contacted through the address given later in this section.

TRAINING COURSES

As well as one-off introductory weekends, most Psychosynthesis centres and institutes run a 'fundamentals' or 'essentials' of Psychosynthesis course, often a course of several days duration, which introduces participants to the principles and practices of Psychosynthesis. These introductory training courses are very popular and contain enough material for anyone to use Psychosynthesis in their own work and life in an informed and practical way. Beyond this, many centres also have more long-term, in-depth training programmes that often lead to a certificate of qualification for Psychosynthesis counselling and therapy.

In the original afterword to the Elements of Psychosynthesis, I quoted an often repeated statement from Assagioli: 'Psychosynthesis is not a doctrine or a school of psychology... There is no orthodoxy in Psychosynthesis and no one, beginning with myself, should be considered its exclusive representative or leader.' Such a statement is indicative of Assagioli's big heart, his openness and his love of the spirit of inquiry. It leaves the possibilities of what to include and not to include very open to individual training schools and practitioners. There is, however, another side to the coin. In 'Training: a statement by Roberto Assagioli' he makes various points regarding training, some of which I would like to discuss. Primarily, Assagioli states: 'While Psychosynthesis is offered as a synthesis of various therapies and educational approaches, it is well to keep in kind that it possesses its own original and central essence. This is so as not to present a watered down or distorted version, or one overcoloured by the concepts and tendencies of the various contemporary schools. Certain fundamental facts exist...and constitute the sine qua non of psychosynthetic training.' So it is not so simple that one can set up a Psychosynthesis training and include - or exclude - just what one wishes.

Training that veers towards incorporating for instance Jungian or Gestalt therapy concepts and practices are truly, from Assagioli's viewpoint, only valid Psychosynthesis training by also including at their core:

1 disidentification
2 the personal self
3 the will
4 the ideal model
5 synthesis (in its various aspects)
6 the superconscious
7 the transpersonal Self.

In my experience of Psychosynthesis training, it is possible for some or all of these core concepts to be not only downgraded or ignored, but even purposely denigrated. The ideal model, for instance, is often excluded, or referred to in a negative light as if it is some quasi-NLP technique, rather than a resplendent way of activating the will. Even the superconscious can be treated with suspicion, or even as some kind of negative avoidance! So if you hear someone quoting the 'there is no orthodoxy in Psychosynthesis' quote, it may well be worth remembering that despite this, there are core principles that have to be included to make a training truly Psychosynthesis.

In the same training statement, Assagioli says that Psychosynthesis functions in five main fields: the therapeutic; personal integration and actualization; educational; interpersonal; and social. So often these days Psychosynthesis is seen as a counselling or psychotherapy training and little enough emphasis is placed on its other applications. Indeed, Assagioli saying that: 'the field of self actualization and integration being the heart of Psychosynthesis' clearly places Psychosynthesis primarily as a self help method for personal and spiritual development. Yet so often trainings require their students to work in one field of Psychosynthesis alone, the therapeutic.

Assagioli also says: 'training in Psychosynthesis has no end. At a certain point hetero training (meaning training guided by someone else) is replaced by self training.' Yet some training centres, whilst giving voice to such a statement, require their graduates to continue a training association with their parent organization, even if under the guise of continuing professional development.

David Platts in his paper 'A basic Psychosynthesis model of counselling and psychotherapy' creates a thorough analysis of the requirements of a good training, running to extensive lists of basic strategy; maps and models; principles and practices; methods and techniques, whilst all the time referring back to and including the seven basic principles required at the core of a Psychosynthesis training. Platts states that all the techniques presented are not unique to Psychosynthesis, and stresses thereby the importance of what is unique and special to Psychosynthesis. This enables students to 'experience the discrete essence of Psychosynthesis, free of the common distortion that Psychosynthesis is so vague, eclectic and inclusive that it can be anything and everything anyone wants it to be.' Indeed, at the other end of the scale, I have a brochure from a Psychosynthesis training running to forty-eight pages that hardly mentions any of these basic core principles.

In his article 'Psychosomatic Medicine and Bio-Psychosynthesis', Assagioli says that the principle aims and tasks of Psychosynthesis are twofold: '1. The elimination of the conflicts and obstacles, conscious and unconscious, that block [the complete and harmonious development of the human personality] and 2. The use of active techniques to stimulate the psychic functions still weak and immature.' Of course, we all move on in our understanding of the self and its manifestations, but I suggest to anyone thinking of undertaking a Psychosynthesis training that they ask the potential training organization how they respond to these two statements that Assagioli described as the principle aims and tasks of the work.

In that same article, Assagioli stresses the importance of body, saying quite categorically that: 'the proper name of Psychosynthesis is bio-Psychosynthesis. In practice it is usually more convenient to employ the word Psychosynthesis but it must be understood at all times that it includes the body, the bios, and that it always stands for Bio-Psychosynthesis.' Yet strangely, or perhaps not so strangely, the body is the area of least concern in some Psychosynthesis training. I have met students in the third year of training, for instance, who when I ask them to stand up and do a simple body stretch are amazed because it is the first time in the whole training they've been invited to leave their seats!

So, what is a Psychosynthesis training? One that adheres to the seven basic principles of Psychosynthesis; that is applicable in the five defined areas named by Assagioli, that includes work with body, and that doesn't pretend to be an end in itself. Despite my criticisms above, I feel the majority of trainers and practitioners of Psychosynthesis attempt to adhere to the basic principles they are taught. The onus therefore, is on training organizations to ensure they include the core values and structures that distinguish a real Psychosynthesis training.

DISTANCE EDUCATION

PS Avalon, of which the author is a director, runs an extensive distance education programme that makes Psychosynthesis for personal and spiritual growth available to many people that otherwise would not be able to undertake training. These courses have had hundreds of students from all parts of the world. Currently students come from areas as diverse as California, India, Mauritius, England and Australia. The courses focus on personal and spiritual development, and aim to make Psychosynthesis understandable and meaningful to our modern life. Students and graduates include people from all walks of life, a wide variety of religious and ethnic backgrounds, and a little over half the students are female. Students undertake the course work, combined with a personal project of their own choosing, at their own pace. Keeping a journal, they send in written material at regular intervals for appraisal and comment. A Diploma in Psychosynthesis is awarded upon successful completion of the full programme.

For full details of distance education and group based courses, or if you want to be in touch with me for any other reason, contact:

Will Parfitt
Box 1865
Glastonbury
Somerset BA6 8YR
England.

From the U.K. please enclose a large (C5) stamped, addressed envelope or from overseas enclose International Reply Coupons.

Alternatively you can find details of distance education and other courses at:

http://www.willparfitt.com

Bibliography and Further Reading

PSYCHOSYNTHESIS BOOKS

ASSAGIOLI, Roberto, *Psychosynthesis* Turnstone 1975
ASSAGIOLI, R., *The Act of Will* Platts Publishing 1999
ASSAGIOLI, R., *Laws and Principles of the New Age* MGNA 1978
EASTCOTT, Michel, *'I' The Story of the Self* Rider 1979
FERRUCCI, Piero, *What We May Be* Turnstone 1982
FIRMAN, John and GILA, Ann, *The Primal Wound* SUNY 1997
FORD, Clyde, *Where Healing Waters Meet* Station Hill 1989
HARDY, Jean *A Psychology With A Soul* Arkana 1987
KING, Vivian, *Soul Play* Ant Hill 1998
PARFITT, Will, *Walking Through Walls* Vega 2002
WHITMORE Diana, *Psychosynthesis Counselling* Sage 1995
WHITMORE D., *Psychosynthesis in Education* Turnstone 1986

Many Psychosynthesis institutes have copies of unpublished articles and papers by Roberto Assagioli and other Psychosynthesis practitioners, some of which may be for sale. Most of the quotes from Assagioli at the beginning of chapters in this book come from such material.

KABBALAH BOOKS

CROWLEY, Vivienne, *A Woman's Kabbalah* HarperCollins 1998
DUQUETTE, Lon Milo, *The Chicken Qabalah* Weiser 2001
FELDMAN, Daniel, *Qabalah* Chariot 2001
HOFFMAN, Edward, *Opening the Inner Gates* Shambhala 1995
KRAMAR, Stanley, *Hidden Faces of the Soul* Publisher 2000
PARFITT, Will, *The Way of the Kabbalah* HarperCollins 2003
PARFITT, W., *The Complete Guide to the Kabbalah* Rider 2001
WIPPLER-GONZALES, Migane, *Kabbalah for the Modern World* Llewellyn 1987

OTHER INTERESTING AND RELATED TITLES

BROWN, B. & KNOFERL G., *Qi Gong* Thorsens 2001
CASTANEDA, Carlos, *The Art of Dreaming* Aquarian 1993
CHODOROW, Jean, *Dance Therapy & Depth Psychology*
Routledge 1991
ELLIS, Normandi, *Awakening Osiris* Phanes 1988
GOODISON, Lucy, *Between Heaven & Earth* Womens Press 1990
GROF, Stanislav, *Beyond The Brain* SUNY 1985
HILLMAN, James, *The Soul's Code* Bantam 1997
HILLMAN, J., *The Force of Character* Random House 1999
KELEMAN, Stanley, *Living Your Dying* Center 1983
JOHANSON G. and KURTZ R., *Grace Unfolding* Bell Tower 1991
JOHNSON, Don, *Bone, Breath and Gesture* North Atlantic, 1995
JOHNSON, D., *Body, Spirit & Democracy* North Atlantic 1994
LEARY, Timothy, *Info-Psychology* Falcon 1987
MASTERS, Robert A., *The Way of the Lover* Xanthyros 1988
MINDELL, Arnold, *The Year 1* Arkana 1989
MOORE, Thomas, *Care of the Soul* HarperCollins 1994
NARBY, Jeremy, *The Cosmic Serpent* Tarcher 1999
NEEDLEMAN, Jacob, *Lost Christianity* Element 1993
NOLL, Richard, *The Jung Cult* Fontana 1996
OLSEN, Andrea, *Body Stories* Station Hill 1991
ROWAN, John, *The Transpersonal* Routledge 1993
ULANOV, Ann and Barry, *Transforming Sexuality* Shambhala 1994
WHYTE, David, *The Heart Aroused* Doubleday 1994
WILSON, Robert Anton, *Prometheus Rising* Falcon 1987
YALOM, Irvin, *Existential Psychotherapy* Basic Books 1980
YALOM, I., *The Gift of Therapy* Piatkus 2001

Indices

3. General Index

Printed in the United Kingdom
by Lightning Source UK Ltd.
101411UKS00001B/379-432